Migration-Trust Networks

MIGRATION-TRUST NETWORKS

Social Cohesion in Mexican US-Bound Emigration

Nadia Y. Flores-Yeffal

Texas A&M University Press   *College Station*

Copyright © 2013 by Nadia Y. Flores-Yeffal
Manufactured in the United States of America
All rights reserved
First edition
This paper meets the requirements of ANSI/NISO Z39.48-1992 (Permanence of Paper).
Binding materials have been chosen for durability.
⊗ ♻

Library of Congress Cataloging-in-Publication Data

Flores-Yeffal, Nadia Y.
    Migration-trust networks : social cohesion in Mexican US-bound emigration / Nadia Yamel Flores-Yeffal.—1st ed.
        p. cm.
    Includes bibliographical references and index.
    ISBN 978-1-60344-826-0 (alk. paper)—ISBN 1-60344-826-8 (alk. paper)—
ISBN 978-1-60344-963-2 (e-book)—ISBN 1-60344-963-9 (e-book) 1. Immigrants—Social
networks—United States. 2. Mexicans—Social networks—United States. 3. United States—
Emigration and immigration—Social aspects. 4. Mexico—Emigration and immigration—
Social aspects. I. Title.
    HV4010.F55 2013
    304.873072—dc23
                                                                            2012029623

This book is dedicated to my beloved husband and children:

Martin, Vanessa, Kevin, Jasmine, Omar, and Yessenia.

Thank you for your patience, love, and support.

I love you.

Contents

Acknowledgments

First I would like to thank all the respondents in Mexico, El Salvador, and the United States who opened their warm homes to me and the members of my team, allowed me to investigate their lives, and who provided their life stories with no hesitation. Also, my most sincere thanks to all of those families who allowed me and my research team to live in their homes and provided me with invaluable information to make this research possible, with food, shelter, and most importantly, with love and bounded solidarity.

During the thirteen years of this study, there were a countless number of individuals who blindly believed in me and who provided me with information, solidarity, and support for this project to become a reality. First of all, I would like to thank my family, especially my husband Martin Cantero, who never hesitated to provide me with his unconditional support and who was deprived of endless days and nights without my company while I did fieldwork and wrote this book. A special thanks to my daughter Vanessa Castaneda, who worked day and night for years as she believed in me without complaining, and took care of all the things I could not, including the children, the house, and the restaurant. I would also like to thank my son, Kevin Castaneda, who was also deprived of my time, but who always understood, as he provided me with cheers and always told me that I was his role model. I also would like to thank my daughter Jasmine Cantero from the bottom of my heart for all the summers she spent taking care of the twins and for all the discipline she demanded from me throughout the years. I would like to also thank my beloved twins, Omar and Yessenia Cantero, who somehow understood me even when they were small. They didn't really prevent me from accomplishing this project, and never questioned why mommy didn't come home after work, but asked me over and over what my book was about.

I would also like to thank my mother, Maria del Carmen Yeffal de Flores, for all the prayers during my travels and for her love and words of encouragement. I say thank you also to my father, who always told me how to think more broadly about the complexities I dealt with while I tried to figure out how to describe what I observed in the data. Thank you also to my brothers, Armando, Karim, and Gabriel Flores Yeffal, who always stood strong and helped me to be strong like them and believe in myself. Thank you to my aunt Emma and my uncle John Eivers, who before dying told me that he believed in me; I know that his spirit followed and protected me through my journeys while collecting the data for this book. Thank you also to Alex, Luis, Rigoberto, Lupita, and all the other members of the Cantero family who provided me with their words of encouragement and support.

A special thanks to Douglas Massey, who opened the doors of his office and his heart and welcomed me and my family to the Mexican Migration Project/LAMP Family (the MMP/LAMP family). I am grateful for his mentorship and his guidance throughout thirteen years and beyond. Also, thanks to all the members of the MMP family, especially Karen Pren, Fernando Riosmena, Maria Aysa-Lastra, and Magaly Sanchez, who stood by my side and always supported and believed in me. I would also like to give a special thanks to all the members of the MMP/LAMP research teams, Jorge Durand, Elisa Muñoz Franco, Adriana Jiménez, Steven Zahniser, Nolan Malone, Mariano Sana, Chiara Capoferro, Sahara Lou Grandé Ferrer, Sergio Alberto Avalos Beleche, Héctor Salvador Monroy Covarruvias, Emma Peña, Veronica Lozano, and Juan Carlos Vargas, and to the El Salvador research team who assisted me to create the survey instrument, collect the data, and process the data to make this project a reality. Also a special thanks to Manuel Garcia y Griego: even though he knew nothing about the topic, he decided to learn together with me, mentoring me on how to think about migrant networks, social solidarity, and altruistic behavior. Thank you to Randall Collins and Lori Rosenkophf, who also believed in the importance of my work and gave me strength to get going. Also, a special thanks to Emilio Parrado and the other anonymous reviewers who reviewed this manuscript several times and provided me with useful comments that considerably improved the quality of this manuscript. Also a special thanks to Paulina Martinez, who gave advice on how to think better about the concepts I wrote about, who helped me for months and months to translate several quotes, carefully edited the entire first version of the manuscript, created and edited all the figures and graphics included in this book, and worked really hard (even after her graduation) redoing all the graphics. Also, I would like to thank Rachel Luna, who helped me to figure out the concepts while writing the final version of the manuscript and who helped me to organize the information more efficiently. I would also like to give a special thanks to Shasta Jones, who helped me to carefully edit the entire final version of the manuscript.

A special thanks to Gilbert Gonzales, who helped me to brainstorm this topic. Also my most sincere thanks to Robert Newcomb, who advised me to apply to the Summer Institute for Demographic Research at University of Pennsylvania in 1997, knowing that there I could find my way to a better future and further discover this project, and who truly believed in me. Also, my most sincere thanks to my colleagues at Texas A&M University, especially to Jane Sell, who helped me clarify the responses to the reviewers' comments. Also a special thanks to Rogelio Saenz, Marco Portales, Zulema Valdez, Bianca Manago, and Ruben Hernandez-Leon, who also reviewed different versions of this book throughout the writing process. I would like to give a special thanks to Mark Fossett, Dudley Poston, Kasuko Suzuky, Nancy Planky-Videla, Esther Quintana, Guadalupe Vidales, Karina Sanchez, and April Plemons for their words of encouragement and support during the writing process. Also, a special thanks to José Villalobos for his collaboration with the "PASALA" column, and to José Cano and Adriana from *La Voz Hispana* in Bryan, Texas, for their support in allowing us to publish the PASALA column, so we can inject crucial information into the Migration-Trust Networks that exist across the Brazos Valley. I would also like to thank the staff of Los Molcajetes Mexican Food restaurant in Bryan, Texas, and all the staff at McDonalds at University Drive in College Station, Texas, for their continuous friendship and for being so patient throught the endless cups of coffee it took to complete the several versions of this manuscript.

I would also like to thank the sources of financial support that helped make the research presented in this book possible. A special thanks to the Mexican Migration Project for providing unconditional financial support for several years to collect data in Mexico and in the United States, and for providing financial support so I could present the findings of this research and receive important feedback in a number of national and international conferences. Also a special thanks to the Mellon Foundation for providing me with the financial support to perform research in two of the communities in Guanajuato, Mexico, and in several destinations in the United States. I would also like to thank the Mexican American Latino Research Center at Texas A&M University and the LAMP for providing the financial support so I could also collect data in El Salvador. In addition, I would like to thank the Glasscock Center for Humanities Research at Texas A&M University for providing a publication support grant, and Texas A&M University Press for providing the financial support to make this publication possible.

Finally, my most sincere thanks to Mary Lenn Dixon, the editor in chief of Texas A&M University Press, for also believing in this project from the very begining and for carefuly guiding me through the review and publishing process. Also, my most sincere thanks to all the staff from Texas A&M University Press for their dedication to refining the final version of this book.

Introduction

About a month before I began writing this book, I was driving my children to school one morning and listening to the Spanish-language radio program "La Preciosa," on 103.1 FM in Bryan and College Station, Texas.[1] The talk-show host, "El Genio Lucas," broadcasted a phone call he received from someone looking for a friend. The gentleman, who affirmed that he was an immigrant from Mexico, said:

> "I am calling to see if you can make an announcement so I can find someone. My name is José, and I am looking for a gentleman called Pancho, who helped me when I arrived to the United States. Both of us lived in a small town in Oklahoma about eight years ago, but I lost contact with him after moving to another state two years ago, and now I cannot reach him because I think he changed his phone number."
>
> El Genio Lucas asked, "And what is his last name?"
>
> "I don't know his last name. I never learned his last name during the three years we lived together. All I know is that he helped me so much when I arrived to the United States, even though it was the first time we had met. He provided me a place to stay, fed me while I was looking for work, bought me clothes, helped me find a job . . . he did so much for me that I won't ever forget. I am very, very thankful for what he did for me, and I wanted to find him again."
>
> El Genio Lucas then asked, "How is it possible that he helped you so much, and you don't even know his last name?"
>
> "All I know is that his name is 'Pancho.' We called him 'Pancho.' I never learned his last name even though we became very good friends with time. I am very thankful for what he did for me and I need to find him again."

He gave his phone number on the air so that "Pancho" could call him back, in case he was listening. El Genio Lucas then hung up and went to commercials. After the break, the radio host returned with the following comment:

"I don't understand how a person doesn't know the last name of someone who helped him so much."

I remember turning up the volume and telling the children to be quiet so I could listen. It was the topic I had researched for the past thirteen years, and here was the perfect example of the social phenomenon I call "Migration-Trust Networks." To El Genio, the gentleman's situation made no sense. Why would someone provide such extensive assistance to a stranger, and why did he never bother to learn the other's surname? "Pancho" is not even a full name; it is usually the nickname for "Francisco" in Spanish. El Genio Lucas was baffled, as I was when I first learned how international migrants exchange favors in the United States. The only thing that made sense was that the gentleman was thankful and wanted to find Pancho, the man who helped him. I knew that the majority of listeners who had immigrated from Mexico and other Latin American countries understood, like me, how and why Pancho helped the gentleman on the phone. After researching the topic for many years, it was exciting to hear this man's story on the radio. Contrary to El Genio, I understood the reason the gentleman was calling, and I knew he was truly thankful. He was not looking for Pancho to return the favor, but to thank him again and again.

In writing this book, I describe why someone like Pancho would assist this new arrival in the way he did, even without knowing him. By doing so, I hope to help readers like El Genio Lucas understand why Pancho's full name was never an issue to the new arrival (nor for Pancho) and, most importantly, why Pancho never expected the favor to be returned. I show why this kind of behavior is normal among international migrants, especially for those who migrate from Mexico to the United States.

In recent decades, social networks have become central among scholars investigating the ways in which international migrants can benefit from having social contacts at their place of destination (see Massey et al. 1987; Massey and Espinosa 1997; Zahniser 1999; Massey and Aysa 2011). In the case of international migration from Mexico to the United States, migrants receive, in most cases, help from previous migrants to arrive at and cross the border (with or without inspection) and settle and find a job at their destination place. This is especially true for first-time migrants. I became fascinated with the topic of social networks and international migration because I am an immigrant. Upon arrival to the United States, I witnessed extensive altruistic behavior among migrants in the immigrant enclave I lived in for more than fifteen years.

When I first arrived in the city of Long Beach, California, I was an un-documented immigrant like most of my neighbors, so my experience was firsthand. I observed and experienced their struggles, their joys, and most importantly, the ways in which migrants helped each other. At that time, I had no idea I would eventually become an academic scholar and study the topic of social networks among migrants.

Because I was born in Mexico City and only lived in major urban areas in Mexico (Hermosillo and Mexicali), I was surprised to see my neighbors helping each other during the years I lived in the immigrant enclave. Most interesting to me was that immigrants who provided help to my neighbors were neither family members nor friends, but rather paisanos, or country-men. Whenever I asked if the person helping them was a family member or friend, people responded, "No, he is from the same town I come from. We are not related to each other, and we are not friends either." The only pre-requisite for giving or receiving help was to be from the same village or from nearby villages back in Mexico, and most of the time they had never spoken with one another until coming to the United States. As time passed, I became more engaged—I could not understand how or why an individual would help someone else in such a way, since they were not friends or family mem-bers. Their assistance included money to pay a smuggler, a place to stay, help finding a job, and even money to buy clothes and transportation for work.

As an urban resident of a border city in Mexico (Mexicali, Baja Cali-fornia), when I migrated to the United States I crossed the border with a tourist visa and later on I overstayed my visa. I was glad I didn't have to use a coyote or smuggler to cross the border in a more dangerous way. In addition, my ex-husband and I only relied on family members when we ar-rived. Our family members allowed us to stay at their homes rent-free and helped us to get settled. I remember that as my ex-husband was trying to find a stable job, at one point both of us went to live in East Los Angeles with his aunt and uncle. His uncle helped him to get a job in a factory. His uncle would take him to work every day while I would stay by myself at the house. Later on we began to have problems with his aunt and uncle's family, as they were not used to having people live with them. We then went back to Long Beach and lived with my aunt and uncle again for a while until my ex-husband found another job on his own. My aunt and uncle were not con-nected with any jobs where my husband could find work. Later on my first daughter was born and it became more difficult to stay at my aunt's house as we needed more space.

At one point we were able to rent an apartment on our own and got to know our neighbors from a rural community in Guanjuato, Mexico. Our neighbors immediately offered to help my ex-husband to find a better job. They also offered him a ride to work every day. The women in the nearby apartments volunteered to watch my daughter free of charge, so I could go to night school to learn English. The women also showed me around and helped me to sign up my daughter in school, told me what to say, where to go to the doctor, and so forth.

We noticed how our neighbors often had new arrivals who were not necessarily their family members living in their modest apartments. We also began offering help to other new arrivals, as at one point our neighbors asked us for help when they needed to accommodate extra people who had just arrived. One of the new arrivals slept on our living room sofa. We provided food for him, helped him to find a job, and gave him rides to work without expecting anything in return. Later on we also let some of the other new arrivals stay in our apartment until they could get going on their own.

After a while, my ex-husband's family began to migrate from Mexicali (an urban border city in Mexico) and we provided them with food and a place to stay, and our neighbors usually helped to find them jobs. His family eventually moved on their own but they were always near our apartment complex. They also began to bring more family members and even friends from Mexicali and helped them in the same way they were once helped when they arrived. All of a sudden the daughter community, which was once composed of only people from two rural communities in Guanajuato, began to grow—it was also joined by my ex-husband's family and friends from Mexicali and so both immigrant flows, from the rural and urban origins, all ended up working in the same jobs and also living next door to each other.

I was legalized under the Immigration Reform and Control Act of 1986 and moved out of the immigrant enclave to continue my education. It was not until I began to explore the topic for my undergraduate honors thesis at the University of California, Irvine, that I began to think more in-depth about pursuing this social phenomenon, which appeared to be extreme altruistic behavior. Through a summer program at the University of Pennsylvania in 1997, I met Douglas Massey, one of the most prominent scholars in the field of international migration, and I mentioned my plan to study the altruistic behavior of my immigrant neighbors. He invited me to partner with the Mexican Migration Project (MMP) so that I could begin my fieldwork in the two rural villages from where my ex-neighbors came, both in the municipality of Abasolo, in Guanajuato, Mexico. That same summer, I began my research adventure, which is now the subject of this manuscript thirteen years later. Throughout the past thirteen years, I did little else but research this topic, as I became more fascinated by my findings.

I was initially discouraged when my honors thesis advisor suggested there was a chance that the solidarity relations and the behavior of my immigrant neighbors had nothing to do with altruism. As a political scientist, he insisted, "No, people rarely do something without getting something in return." I then began to read many books on altruism, game theory, social organization, social support, and the like until I came across the work of Émile Durkheim and his concepts of "mechanical solidarity" and "organic solidarity." I realized I needed to look more closely at the context of the place of origin of the migrants, and take into account whether they migrated from a rural or an urban area.

In my honors thesis, *Reciprocity, Solidarity, and Gender in Mexican Migration to the US: A Case Study*, I argued that the behavior of the migrants from the two rural villages in my study (which was later passed along to my ex-husband and I) resembled the "collective conscience" behavior described by Durkheim in his *mechanical solidarity* concept. I wrote that one explanation for the strong solidarity among international migrants was that the subjects in my case study were from agrarian communities. Therefore, those from agrarian communities behaved differently than those from urban settings in terms of their identity as a community as a whole. This means that immigrants from agrarian communities develop what Durkheim called a "collective conscience," in which they think of themselves as members of a group, and not as individuals.

I then asked, "Under what circumstances did 'collective conscience' work, and under what circumstances did it not?" Soon enough I came across the classic work of Luis Wirth (1938), who noted that there are many factors affecting people's solidarity in urbanized communities, notably the population size, population density, industrial infrastructure, and social heterogeneity of the community. Wirth and others warned that urbanism and industrialization could destroy social relationships and social solidarity values in urban places.

I was in graduate school at the University of Pennsylvania in 2001 when I received a grant from the Mellon Foundation to continue to investigate the solidarity behavior among migrants from two additional communities near Abasolo, one medium-sized town and one working-class neighborhood in a major city. During the next two years, 2002 and 2003, I conducted research at the migrants' origin, as well as the immigrant enclaves at their places of destination all over the United States. In 2005, I finished writing my doctoral dissertation, entitled *The Interrelation between Social Capital, Social Context and Social Networks of Migration from Mexico to the US*. In this dissertation, I continued to explore solidarity relations in urban settings and found that, indeed, if one takes into account the size of the migrants' place of origin, social capital is shared through a very different social network structure. I also found other social dynamics that promoted the expansion of social networks by absorbing migrants from fragile networks. In prior studies, I referred to similar developments as "the clique effect" (see Flores 2005). In this book, I call this new social phenomenon "the Migration-Trust Network effect" (or "the MTN effect") because I argue that although MTNs are formed by a clique-like social network structure, MTNs expand because they are more prone to welcome new members as opposed to cliques, where the membership is usually more exclusive.

Recent research has revealed the strength of migrant social networks. Scholars, including myself, after exploring the concept of social capital in many different ways, are now exploring issues related to the "strength of weak ties" argument of Mark Granovetter. The question was whether this concept could also apply to undocumented immigrants from Mexico, for example, in helping them acquire higher wages (i.e., Mouw 2002, 2003; Amuedo-Dorantes and Mundra 2007; Aguilera and Massey 2003; Flores 2005; Flores-Yeffal and Zhang 2012). Weak ties (in the form of friends and paisanos) for undocumented migrants were, indeed, helping them find opportunities for higher wages. In this book, however, I challenge the argument that friends and paisanos of undocumented migrants are weak ties (i.e., Wilson 1998). Instead, family, friends, and paisanos of undocumented migrants are all part of Migration-Trust Networks. Therefore, they are all either strong ties to begin with, or they are converted or transformed into strong ties once the migrants come in contact with each other in the United States and begin to participate in an MTN. Paisanos or strangers, for example, may be considered weak ties at the beginning, but once they are incorporated into the Migration-Trust Network, they also become strong ties. This is illustrated in the work of Portes and Sensenbrenner (1993) on enforceable trust, and the work of Tilly (2007) on transnational networks of trust among international migrants. In agreement with Tilly, seemingly the most important social force driving these networks of international migration among undocumented immigrants is *trust*. I adopt and apply Tilly's concept of trust networks, and other concepts such as Portes and Sensenbrenner's enforceable trust, in proposing a new concept called Migration-Trust Networks.

In maintaining friendships with my old neighbors from Long Beach and the rural villages I visited in 1997, I repeatedly visited and collected data in Guanajuato, an origin area, and in immigrant enclaves all around the United States in which the immigrants from all four communities have since settled. These friendships have allowed me to conduct longitudinal follow-ups of how social networks have evolved over time. During this period, I have also observed transformations at places of origin through collective remittances sent by migrants in the United States. I have also observed how collective remittances have influenced the expansion of migration at the places of origin as well as at the places of destination.

In 2007, my never-ending curiosity about solidarity behavior among international migrants took me to El Salvador, where I observed Menjívar's work on the existence of fragmented ties among Salvadoran migrants. I sought to understand if there was a difference in the solidarity behavior of Salvadoran and Mexican migrants. However, Menjívar did not take into consideration the size of the migrant's place of origin (Menjívar 2000).

Through grants from the Mexican American Latino Research Center (MALRC) at Texas A&M University and additional support from the Latin American Migration Project (LAMP) housed at Princeton University and Universidad de Guadalajara, I visited four communities of different sizes in El Salvador. Through interviews, I found that Salvadoran networks function similarly to Mexican networks in many ways, although I found slight differences that I attribute to several factors, such as the greater distance between El Salvador and the United States, additional border crossings, higher smuggling costs, a recent war, and more recent political instability. The fieldwork in El Salvador was the culmination of thirteen years of research on the social phenomena of international migration networks.

This book reveals the complexities behind social networks of international migration. Its participants share kindness, trust relationships, altruistic behavior, reciprocal and nonreciprocal relations (or risk-pooling), love for others, and the willingness to help and sacrifice for others in fascinating ways. This powerful phenomenon has the capacity to capture the attention of readers like me for years. This book tells the story of how international migration operates in the transnational context and at micro and macro levels. It demystifies how the migration machine perpetuates itself and creates chain migration effects observable throughout history (MacDonald and MacDonald 1974).

In addition to the benefits of networks, I address arguments highlighting their negative effects on migrants. One perspective argues that the strong unity of social networks can isolate and prevent migrants from assimilating into the host society by depriving them of access to greater social, educational, and economic opportunities at the destination (Nee and Sanders 2001). Whether there are more advantages than disadvantages is a matter of perspective. Network members argue the disadvantages are minimal, whereas outsiders give them greater weight. I argue that when assessing the effectiveness of Migration-Trust Networks, scholars must be conscious of their own associations to the networks.

New theories of international migration claim that social networks are significant drivers of international migration flows. These networks help fuel the process of cumulative causation (Massey et al. 1993, 1998). This book provides an extension to existing social network theories by providing a more detailed description of how social networks of migration function at both micro and macro levels of analysis, with trust relationships as the basis of those networks. In addition, it provides a transnational approach in which the context of the place of origin of the migrant, whether rural or urban, becomes an important variable when analyzing how trust relationships and social cohesiveness develop among network participants. Finally, this book offers the introduction of a new concept that I call Migration-Trust Networks. Here, I introduce a new way of thinking about social networks of international migrants. This concept is relevant when one considers Mexican migration to the United States, in which a great number of network members lack legal documentation (Passel 2005; Passel and Cohn 2010). The level of trust and social support they have to rely on becomes more intimate and of greater strength than if they were participating in a regular network where lacking legal documents is not prevalent. Their dependency on the Migration-Trust Network may be perpetually outside of legalization in the host country, where they risk victimization and deportation. The concept of Migration-Trust Networks encapsulates the new realities of undocumented migration from Latin America and contributes to the academic international migration discourse to advance the study of social networks of migration and of social networks in general.

Notes

1. This radio station is no longer broadcasted locally, but is still broadcasted to several states across the United States. More information about this radio station can be found in the following link: http://www.lapreciosa.com.

Migration-Trust Networks

CHAPTER ONE

Migration-Trust Networks

As described in the opening anecdote of the introduction, a complete stranger helped one migrant named José when he first arrived to the United States. The stranger gave him clothes, food, a place to stay, and help finding a job. Years later, José searched for this stranger, named "Pancho," through a radio announcement, but he could not even provide Pancho's last name. This is only one example that shows how international migrants support each other and do not expect favors in return. Therefore, migration networks go beyond the concept of people having contacts and accessing social capital through those contacts. Instead, such networks function through a series of social obligations based on trust relationships that develop among international migrants and prospective migrants. In this book, I introduce the new concept of Migration-Trust Networks (MTNs) to explain how social networks function in international migration, especially when a considerable number of the members in the migration network lack legal status in the place of destination. I describe the social factors and circumstances that give rise to the trust relationships and social obligations that connect international migrants. As seen in the story of Pancho and José, the expansion and continuation of a Migration-Trust Network relies on the creation of new relationships of trust exchanged between existing members of the network and newcomers, including strangers. Such new relationships only develop as long as the new members meet certain conditions of social cohesion and trust. Social networks of migration can develop, grow, or disintegrate depending on various factors, including the dynamics among individuals at the micro level as well as the broader social processes and transformations taking place in the transnational context at the macro level.

In this book, I analyze data from Guanajuato, Mexico, to present social networks from Mexico as a case study in which one can better understand how the social networks of undocumented migrants are born, develop, operate, and can be maintained. I propose the concept of Migration-Trust

Network, which can be used to describe and understand how the networks for undocumented migrants function.

It is important for me to begin by discussing how and why the international migration flow from Mexico to the United States is unique. Mexico is the only country in the world that shares an extensive border (2,000 miles) with a developed nation but is not yet defined as a developed country itself. Therefore, Mexico's proximity with the United States may allow for the social networks of international migrants to work differently than those for other less developed countries that do not share such a long international border with a developed country.

In addition, no other country in the world has as many undocumented migrants in the United States as Mexico. According to the estimates presented by the Pew Hispanic Center, out of the 11.1 million estimated undocumented immigrants in the United States in 2009, 60 percent (or 6.7 million) were from Mexico (see Passel and Cohn 2010). There are five main reasons why a large number of undocumented Mexican immigrants currently reside in the United States: (1) the unique relations between the two countries through history; (2) their intimacy as international commercial partners; (3) the sudden increase of urban origin migration from Mexico; (4) the lack of legal means offered to Mexican nationals to migrate legally to the United States; and (5) the increased border enforcement strategies through the years, which has created a permanent undocumented population of Mexican nationals trapped in the United States. I explain each of these claims in the next few paragraphs.

Unique history: The two countries have been interconnected for a long time. A large part of the Mexican territory became part of the United States during the nineteenth century. Mexicans were able to cross the border more freely between Mexico and the United States up to 1924, which is when the United States formed the border patrol and began to patrol the US-Mexico border. Therefore, during the time of the Mexican Revolution (1910 to 1917) some Mexicans could freely cross the border to the United States, escaping the violence of the revolution. Later, the Bracero Program brought 5 million braceros to the United States from 1942 to 1964. It was not until 1965 that migration from Mexico and other Latin American countries became restricted due to the Immigration and Control Act of 1965. At this point, the flow of undocumented migrants began to grow, which Massey (1995) called the "new regime." Mexican nationals and their descendents, who had already established an extensive root system in the United States, aided these undocumented migrants. They acted as potential contacts for the initiation of the international migration network flows that evolved at the turn of the twenty-first century.

Trade partners: Mexico and the United States have become very important trade partners since 1994 through NAFTA (the North American Free Trade Agreement). Despite the strong economic integration between the two trade partners, the two countries have not pursued any effort to resolve the issue of the exchange of labor. In other words, there has been no proposal to resolve the issue of labor supply from Mexico to the United States. Also, NAFTA has provoked the displacement of tens of thousands of workers from rural and urban areas in Mexico since its implementation in 1994 (see King 2006; Zepeda, Wise, and Gallagher 2009). Many Mexican growers in rural areas as well as small companies in urban areas in Mexico could not compete with the cheaper prices and better quality of US imports (see Hernandez-León 2008). Therefore, the NAFTA agreement, instead of hindering out-migration from Mexico to the United States, caused more out-migration due to labor displacement in rural and urban areas.

An increase of urban origin migrants: Recent studies indicate that the proportion of migrants originating from urban areas in Mexico has increased, especially over the past couple of decades, whereas most migration flows were previously rural-based (Lozano-Ascencio, Roberts, and Bean 1999; Roberts, Frank, and Lozano-Ascencio 1999; Durand, Massey, and Zenteno 2001; Marcelli and Cornelius 2001). According to Hernandez-León (2008), workers from urban areas who held good and stable jobs, which offered good benefits, lost their jobs due to the adoption of open trade policies in Mexico, such as the General Agreement on Tariffs and Trade (GATT) implemented in 1986 and, more recently, due to the implementation of NAFTA in 1994. Urbanization of the Mexican-US migratory flow has led to increased attention to the relevance of rural and urban contexts for migrants' use of social capital (Roberts, Frank, and Lozano-Ascencio 1999; Flores 2000; Fussell 2004; Fussell and Massey 2004; Hernandez-León 2008; Flores-Yeffal and Aysa-Lastra 2011).

Lack of legal visas: Even though the Mexican and US economies are highly integrated, the United States allows Mexican nationals to obtain a limited number of visas so that they can migrate legally. Despite the strong economic integration between Mexico and the United States, the labor displacement of Mexican nationals due to NAFTA, and Mexico's large population, Mexico must adhere to the same quota as other countries—only

20,000 visas per year. In addition, other types of working related visas are only available to those with professional occupations or extraordinary abilities, while more of the demand for labor in the United States is for unskilled occupations (see Massey, Durand, and Malone 2002).

Permanent settlement: Due to the strict border enforcement between Mexico and the United States as a result of the Immigration and Control Act of 1986 and the terrorist attacks of 9/11, Mexican migrants who once engaged in circulatory migration (i.e., migrated to the United States for short periods of time), are no longer returning to Mexico and instead, they are settling more permanently in the United States. Since 1993, migrants must travel through harsher terrain to circumvent the increased number of border patrol agents and the new surveillance technology implemented by border control (see Massey and Pren 2012). Therefore, undocumented migrants pay higher smuggler prices, but more importantly, they are at a greater risk of losing their lives. The number of deaths at the border has increased since 1993; on average, 400 migrants die every year, adding to approximately 7,600 deaths from 1993 to 2012 (Massey, Durand, and Malone 2002).

Due to the particularities of the history between Mexico and the United States, Mexican nationals have had plenty of opportunities in the past to set roots in the United States, leading to the establishment of future social networks. These networks aided the increase of undocumented migrants in the United States. Despite the geographical proximity, the level of economic integration between the two countries, and the realities of labor demand, the availability of work-related visas has not been addressed. In an effort to reduce the influx, the United States has escalated border enforcement since 1993. The Pew Hispanic Center reports that the number of unauthorized immigrants to the United States declined from 12 million in 2007 to 11.1 million in 2009 (see Passel and Cohn 2010). While net migration from Mexico is currently close to zero (or slightly negative) according to Massey (see Cave 2011; Passel, Cohn, and Gonzalez Barrera 2012), the increased border enforcement forced many migrants to make the decision to stay in the United States permanently.

Such a historic slowdown of the migratory flow, according to Massey, has been a response to a series of different factors on both sides of the border. In Mexico, fertility has declined, there are better educational and economic prospects, and there is extreme violence at the US-Mexico border due to the recent war on drugs led by President Calderon. In the United States, a series of historic anti-immigrant legislations under the administration of

President Obama resulted in massive deportations after the backlash of the 2006 marches. Undocumented immigrants may be relying on MTNs more than ever, feeling trapped in a country where they have to live permanently in the shadows, making them permanently dependent on MTNs.

Given the factors just delineated, Mexico has become an interesting case in which to study how social networks of international migration can function. The social networks of undocumented migrants from Mexico are important and deserve a closer look given that the majority of international migrants have not only migrated with undocumented status, but they have also decided to remain in US territory more permanently, given the uncertainty of circulatory migration. Migrants have responded by creating a type of social network characterized by parameters that are subject to alteration due to future changes in immigration policy.

The Importance of Social Context

A number of scholars have suggested the need for a greater understanding of the context in which individuals interact in order to better understand their attitude toward cooperation (i.e., Bellah et al. 1985; Selznick 1992). In this book, I utilize the size of the migrant's place of origin as a basis for the kind of social structure that develops in the social network. The size of the place denotes its rural or urban status.

As mentioned before, recent research indicates that the proportion of international migrants from urban areas has increased over the past few decades (Roberts, Frank, and Lozano-Ascencio 1999; Lozano-Ascencio, Roberts, and Bean 1999; Marcelli and Cornelius 2001; Durand, Massey, and Zenteno 2001). In his study of migrants from Monterrey, Mexico, to the United States, Hernandez-León (2008) argues that urban-origin cohesive migrant networks developed only among specialized groups and under a set of very particular circumstances, such as with gang members or other residents from urban working-class neighborhoods. Hernandez-León also introduces the role of exogenous ties (those who marry outside the community of origin) in helping to further expand the social network of migration to others outside the origin community. Massey et al. (1987) were able to make an interesting link between internal rural-urban migratory flows in Mexico and the development of social networks of migration. They found that prospective migrants from a city in Jalisco, Mexico, gain access to social capital from contacts they maintained in the rural communities they originally came from. Given the nuances of the new urban-origin international migration flow, more research is needed to understand social network structures that develop from urban origins.

Even though these studies have contributed to the understanding of how social networks operate in the international migration arena, they seldom consider in detail how such networks develop, what specific social dynamics are driving them at both the micro and macro levels, and why and how they tend to expand, extinguish, or self-perpetuate over time. Urban-origin migration from Mexico is a more current phenomena, and scholars are still trying to understand how *context*, such as the characteristics of sending communities (i.e., either rural or urban), help to influence how social networks of migration operate. Beyond that, we must understand if the context of the place of origin affects the initiation of social networks, the social structure that develops, the social dynamics that take place, and the circumstances under which those networks are either extinguished or perpetuated over time.

Solidarity Relations in Rural and Urban Contexts

Relations of Support in Rural Places of Origin

Social behavior may differ for those who live in rural areas compared to those who live in more urban areas because of a number of social dynamics in both types of areas. Classical sociologists began to theorize about how context, or urbanization and industrialization, affected the social behavior of people who originally belonged to tied communities (or rural settings). Consider Tonnies' (1963) concepts of gemeinschaft (community) and gesellschaft (society). Gemeinschaft is defined as "a spontaneously arising organic social relationship characterized by strong reciprocal bonds of sentiments and kinship within a common tradition" ("gemeinschaft," *Merriam-Webster's Collegiate Dictionary*, 11th ed.). Tonnies adopts this view of social relationships in a "community" as organic and suggests that in rural habitats, there is more contact, so one expects their habits to be more exposed. Community, according to Tonnies, is structured by "common understanding, folkways, and beliefs" (224); the threat of shunning is inescapable and undesirable if you depend on the community for your livelihood.

Gesellschaft (society), which refers to a "rationally developed mechanistic type of relationship characterized by impersonally contrasted association between persons," ("gesellschaft," *Merriam-Webster*) explains that industrialization and urbanization created more individualistic and merchant-like personalities. This is compared to those in a community (or rural setting) where the relationships were more personal and dependent on reciprocal relationships. In a community, the issue of honor and respect (Tonnies 1963, 42–43) is constantly being reinforced. In the urban setting, the interaction between people is based on freedom of choice (44, 46); what this freedom does is create a false sense of commonality. The "society" is a civilized state of nature where everyone is trying to secure and maintain a position and commodities at the expense of others. Unlike the organic nature of relationships in communities, those in "societies" are seen as mechanical, according to Tonnies.

Durkheim ([1933] 1997), however, reversed Tonnies' terms and gave them the opposite definitions in order to explain how, indeed, social interaction among those from rural areas (or communities, in Tonnies' terms) could be described as mechanical. According to Durkheim, mechanical solidarity occurs in small and homogenous communities where a series of values are shared, and the members of the community are subject to social expectations. The high level of social homogeneity and the sense of being alike help the community members develop a collective conscience, in which the people do not think of themselves as individuals, but as members of a group. Durkheim ([1933] 1997) also explained how a society (or those who live in urban settings) does not necessarily act as a collection of extremely self-interested individuals, but that they do indeed belong to a more macro interdependent relationship with other members of society due to the dependency in an urban setting on the division of labor. This means that the more people specialize in their own occupations, the more they depend on other members of the same society who develop other specializations. He referred to this relationship as organic. Durkheim's concept of organic solidarity in urban settings becomes important in this book because later I argue that small communities (in Tonnies' term) can also develop in urban places of origin. I call those small communities peer groups.

Luis Wirth's classic work on urbanism also showed that urban communities can be complex and that the high population density and heterogeneity that develop in large urban areas can alter the behavior of their inhabitants by influencing them to be more individualistic than those who live in rural areas, where people tend to be more homogeneous. According to Wirth (1938), the larger the size of a community, the less likely that people can interact with each other on a more personal level, which produces the "segmentalization of human relationships," increases the level of anonymity within relationships, and produces a state of *anomie* (12, emphasis in original). Wirth also states that the higher the population density, the higher the level of friction among individuals due to the "frequent close physical contact, coupled with great social distance," which "accentuates the reserve of unattached individuals towards one another and, unless compensated for by other opportunities for response, gives rise to loneliness" (16). Finally, heterogeneity "tends to break down rigid social structures" and produces "increased mobility, instability, and insecurity, and the affiliation of the individuals with a variety of intersecting and tangential social groups with a high rate of membership turnover" (1).

More recent studies of the behavior of urban dwellers have found that the acquisition of social capital can be selective as people draw their friends and acquaintances from their neighborhood, place of work, church, sports, or social clubs, and the like, rather than from the whole community, as happens in small rural settings (Fischer 1972, 1975, 1982, 1995). Others have argued that family, friends, and neighbors can fulfill different roles as companions or as providers of support depending on how and under what circumstances they interact with each other (Wellman and Wortley 1990). The more complex process in which urban dwellers find social relations may limit the number of lifelong relationships and the number of strong ties available to them. This may mean that urban dwellers have less "community-based" social capital related to international migration available to them (Roberts, Frank, and Lozano-Ascencio 1999; Fussell and Massey 2004). The type of ties available to prospective international migrants from rural and urban areas may differ significantly given the complexity of social relations in both settings.

In this book, I examine social network dynamics that develop from each setting, rural and urban, in order to better understand how social networks operate. Studies in the area of international migration have discovered very important facts about these social networks when looking at migration from Latin America, but more explicitly, Mexico (i.e., Massey et al. 1987; and Massey and Espinosa 1997; Zahniser 1999; Flores 1999, 2000, 2005; García 2005; Smith 2006; Fitzgerald 2008). As scholars began to recognize the power of social networks, their theories of international migration began to reflect the importance of these networks in the reproduction of already established international migratory flows. It also became customary to include social network measures as explanatory variables on regression models predicting international migration outcomes (i.e., Massey and Espinosa 1997; Flores, Hernandez-León, and Massey 2004).

Scholars have analyzed the structure of such social networks of migration (Bashi 2007), and the social dynamics that take place at the micro (Massey et al. 1987) and macro levels (Massey et al. 1993, 1998) in order to understand how social networks function, develop, and keep helping their members. However, studies have simplified the complexity of the social relationships that take place within the social networks and how these relationships develop, function, and foster trust and solidarity between international migrants, especially among those disadvantaged, such as the undocumented. The purpose of this scholarly work is therefore twofold. The first purpose is to address the following questions: What are the specific social dynamics that operate in social networks of international migration from Mexico to the United States at the micro and at the macro levels of analysis? What are the similarities and differences with regard to those social dynamics if one takes into account the context in which the social networks develop, rural or urban? The second purpose is to introduce the concept of Migration-Trust Networks as an extension of existing theories of social networks of international migration. The concept contributes by defining the particularities that characterize the social networks of migration framed by this "new regime," in which a large number of migrants from Mexico to the United States lack legal documentation.

Methodology

In order to address the aforementioned issues, I mainly utilize ethnographic data collected in four communities in Guanajuato, Mexico, and in several receiving communities in the United States over thirteen years (from 1997 to 2010).[1] I conducted this research using a multisite, multimethod, and longitudinal approach in two rural villages, a medium-sized town, and a working-class neighborhood within a city in the state of Guanajuato, Mexico. I build on the research methodology of the MMP, the Mexican Migration Project.[2] The ethnographic data was collected by administering both the MMP and Solidarity questionnaires for a total of 605 households (550 in Mexico and 55 in the United States).[3] I designed the Solidarity questionnaire with the intention of assessing the extent to which migrants helped each other not only at the place of origin, but also at the place of destination and in the transnational context (both at the place of origin and the place of destination). From those 605, we surveyed 85 households in each of two rural villages in the municipality of Abasolo, Guanajuato, which were about two miles apart. Those who lived in the two rural villages mainly depended on agriculture for daily survival. There were also several other villages located nearby and they were all accessible through a paved access road in which public transportation buses often transported people from one community to the next. We used those buses to move from one village to the next, as the two villages were not within walking distance. In addition, 200 heads of households were surveyed in a medium-sized town of about 10,000 inhabitants located near the two rural villages. The medium-sized town offered a broader variety of jobs to local inhabitants besides agriculture, including some local garment factory jobs created as a result of NAFTA. Otherwise, there were not many opportunities for work. Finally, 200 household heads were interviewed in a working-class urban neighborhood in a larger city also in Guanajuato, Mexico, near the municipio of Abasolo. The town and the urban neighborhood were chosen for their proximity to the two rural villages in order to capture the same macroeconomic effects for that specific region in Guanajuato. I drew a simple random sample of each place, following the method of the MMP, and then compiled snowball samples[4] of migrants at the places of destination in the United States. The snowball samples were 10 percent of the ones collected in each Mexican community. In the United States, the team collected extensive ethnographic data and conducted interviews.[5]

I collected the data in the two rural villages during the winter of 1997, in the urban neighborhood during the summer of 2001, and in the small town during the winter break of 2001. I did the fieldwork in the United States during the summers of 1998 and 2002. Extensive ethnographic work was also carried out in all sites, including participant observation of several community activities as well as long unstructured interviews with the migrants themselves, the family members of the migrants, those who had never migrated, government officials, community leaders, and other residents from each community and nearby communities. Questions were asked about the functionality of the local social networks as well as those related to international migration. The questions also covered other issues related to the local economy, strategies for survival, the availability of jobs, local political issues, access to educational and governmental resources, and the difficulty of acquiring legal documentation to migrate to the United States, among other topics.

Apart from the survey data collected using the MMP and the Solidarity questionnaire, the ethnographic work of this study consisted of an additional 235 pages of typed ethnographic notes and 65 open-ended interviews with migrants (30 in Mexico and 35 in the United States). Additionally, there were twenty-five open-ended interviews done with governmental officials and town leaders over time. I was able to follow a total of twenty individuals and/or families over time (five for each of the four communities). From the individuals/families with whom I kept permanent contact, I also learned indirectly about the development of the networks of several other individuals/families from those communities whom I had met during the earlier years of the study.[6] During these years I visited the towns several times to follow the families as they traveled back and forth from Mexico to the United States. Since 2005 I have been able to establish direct contact with these families, governmental officials, and other community leaders via the Internet by using regular e-mail, MSN messenger, Web cameras, chat rooms, and blogs.

The main purpose of the data collection was to identify specific social dynamics by which favors were exchanged, so most of the ethnographic fieldwork focused on tracking how network participants at the places of origin and destination received the social capital necessary to migrate, settle, and find work. Additional information came through interviews with politicians, coyotes, church authorities, educational authorities, and community leaders in both the places of origin and destination. During the fieldwork, I was invited to events in surrounding communities in Mexico, which allowed me to expand the perspective of research beyond those communities of origin in this study. I also engaged in participant observation in each community and studied social interactions among network participants by attending local events, political meetings and gatherings, *fiestas patronales* (religious community celebrations), weddings, quinceañeras, baptisms, first communions, Christmas and New Year's celebrations, school community meetings, and other community events at places of origin and destination. In addition, in order to monitor more accurately any important developments from a distance, in recent years I also participated in Internet discussions through websites and blogs in which the community members participated. My active participation via cyberspace, which included content analysis of the discussion and any videos or pictures posted among the blog participants, allowed me to collect additional data about how the social networks in these communities were developed, maintained, and perpetuated through time.

Given the undocumented status of many of the respondents, the issue of trust became a challenge during the beginning stages of this project. For example, in the first rural village where I began interviewing, no one wanted to speak with me or to any of the other four members of my interview team. On the first day, the interviewers returned that evening and were very worried because no one wanted to speak with them at all. The interviewers stated that people made up all kinds of excuses that made them unavailable for interviews; they refused to provide any answers to our survey. Realizing we needed to gain the trust of the people in the rural village, I decided to speak with the priest of the local church because he would be the most important source of trust. If we could demonstrate that the local priest trusted us, then the villagers would also.

The next day I introduced myself to the priest of the only Catholic church in the village and asked him to introduce me to the community as someone who was not going to do any harm. The priest accepted only after I explained the purpose of the study, presented all my credentials explaining who I was, my forms of identification, letters from the universities I represented in Mexico and in the United States, and answered all other questions he asked. He was very understanding and showed no signs of rejection. The main problem for the people, as the priest explained to us, was that people knew we were from the United States. Therefore, we represented a threat to their loved ones who had no legal status in the United States. I asked the priest to introduce the entire team to the people in the town during mass the next day, which was a Sunday. He did so, and explained that we were not there to harm anyone. The priest pleaded with the community to assist us and welcome us with open arms. We were surprised the next day when we began knocking on doors once again to implement the survey and perform the ethnographic work. Not only did people answer our questions, but they warmly welcomed us into their homes and even invited us to eat with them at their tables. Also, most people tried to give us small presents, such as homemade bread, homemade tamales, fruit, and so forth. We realized that the priest did indeed have a lot of influence over the people; they trusted him, and therefore accepted those he trusted.

During our visit and during the fieldwork afterwards, we often attended mass and were invited to several religious celebrations, including the three-year-old presentation, which is a mass performed in honor of a child who turns three years of age. Given the low survival rate of young children in the past, it became a tradition to celebrate the first three years of life. People believe that after the child passes the first three years, their probability of survival is very high. For that reason, the child is presented to God in the church, followed by a large religious celebration to thank God for the miracle of that child's survival and future. This religious practice is also performed for children residing in the United States.

After completing the first round of fieldwork, we visited the church to give thanks to everyone for their great hospitality. I was shocked by what happened next. As I stood next to the priest, people began to form a line to give us gifts, such as *empanaditas* (homemade bread), homemade candy, crafts for my children, and so forth. We were overwhelmed by the affection and gratitude from the people of the community. It was an unforgettable experience.

After we finished the research in that community, we went to another small rural village nearby (about two miles away from the first one) where we tried to implement the same process of first speaking with the priest and asking him to speak on our behalf to gain people's trust. Surprisingly, this priest refused to introduce us the community. We had no other option but to begin the interviews without his formal introduction. We were astonished to discover that people began to answer our questions just as in the first rural village after the priest introduced us. During our interviews, we asked respondents why they were not hesitant to answer our survey. They shared that family members and friends in the previous village informed them that we meant no harm.

In another effort to gain the trust of respondents, I tried to connect migrants in the United States with family and friends left behind in Mexico by tracking network members via snowball referrals. For example, I took pictures of respondents left behind in Mexico and brought the photos and letters from them to their family members in the United States. I also took pictures of the homes they were building and the new infrastructural improvements in the town that had been financed by collective remittances. Several of the respondents who were contacted in the United States told me that they had called their friends and family members in their hometown in order to verify if I indeed had visited their community, and to ask them if I could be trusted. Once I gained the trust of at least one family who lived in the immigrant enclave in the United States, it then became very easy to gain the trust of the rest of the community members who lived in the enclave communities.

In addition, I also conducted the follow-up interviews in several of the daughter communities around the United States, either by phone or in person. The main purpose of these follow-up sessions was to explore whether the same solidarity relations continued to identify any network fragmentations over the years, and to investigate the ways in which the social networks ruptured or were maintained and perpetuated. I was also able to follow the evolution of the community projects financed by collective remittances throughout the years.

I believe this multisite, multimethod, and longitudinal methodological approach has allowed me to explore in more detail the social, economic, cultural, and structural dynamics that drive social networks of international migration from Mexico to the United States. This approach also enabled me to observe the geographical expansion of both origin and destination places and the maintenance or dissolution of migrant networks. I was, therefore, able to collect data regarding macro level processes of how those social networks grow and expand.

Theoretical Framework at the Micro Level

Scholars of international migration have identified social networks as one of the most powerful processes causing the perpetuation of international migration flows around the world (i.e., Massey et al. 1987; Massey and Espinosa 1997; Massey et al. 1993, 1998; Zahniser 1999; Flores 1999, 2000, 2005). In the past, the term *chain migration* was used to explain how international migrants from communities in Europe were able to help members of their community migrate and settle in the United States, forming immigrant enclaves (mostly composed of settlers who shared the same community of origin) (Hatton and Williamson 1994; Yu 2008). To begin the chain, all that was needed was for one or two people from a single community to migrate internationally. Those pioneer migrants then served as a connection to inform friends and family members back home about the job opportunities, resources, and housing options available at the place of destination. Migrant pioneers also shared important information about how to migrate to the United States. This information facilitated the migration of their family members and friends who eventually settled near them. These new migrants then shared the information with more friends and family back home, continuing the pattern and forming a migration chain.

In the past, other groups of immigrants in the United States have also experienced waves of discrimination, such as the Chinese in the nineteenth century and Europeans (such as Italians and Russian Jews) at the turn of the twentieth century (Foner 2000). Because most of the new arrivals wanted to continue receiving support from their contacts in the host country, they settled in housing near the rest of the pioneer migrants and created immigrant enclaves such as Little Italy, as exemplified by Gans' classic study, *The Urban Villagers* (Gans 1962). Immigrant communities are found all over the United States where European immigrants supported each other in various ways and maintained strong relations with those in home countries (Thomas and Znaniechki 1918).

Sociologists such as Gans (1962) have documented that European migrants had a tendency to segregate in Boston to more easily adapt to the American society. Some arrived to the West End because they could no longer cope with racial discrimination, others because of poverty, or other aspects of social disadvantage. The new arrivals moved within Boston to share cultural practices from back home. Gans describes how immigrant enclaves formed in the West End of Boston and subsequently moved to the suburbs in hopes of integration into American society and upward mobility. While the members of one immigrant group, such as the Irish, were leaving the West End, a different group was arriving; the arrival and nature of new groups depended on the immigration policies implemented at specific times in history. For example, the Immigration Act of 1924 restricted migration from Eastern and Southern Europe and prohibited the migration of Asian Indians and East Asians (Foner 2000). Gans narrates that the "Jews dominated the West End until the 1930s. In the late 20s, Italians and Poles began to arrive" (7). This is important because it shows two things: first, international migrants have relied heavily on social networks in the past, and second, that they ultimately overcame their dependency on those networks.

I argue in this book that there is a fundamental difference between the international migration networks of Europeans and those of Latin Americans. Although during the nineteenth century Europeans also arrived without legal documents and many returned to Europe, the majority were able to become legal residents of the United States once the immigration station at Ellis Island was established in 1892. Therefore, the majority of European immigrants were legal residents of the United States and did not have to enter the country clandestinely. After they arrived they used their social networks for shorter periods of time than more contemporary immigrants in order to adapt in the midst of poverty, exploitation, and discrimination. On the other hand, a majority of today's immigrants from Latin America lack legal status (Massey, Durand, and Malone 2002). Very few Europeans were returned to their countries once they arrived at Ellis Island. Therefore, the majority of Europeans did not have to worry about applying for a legal visa before attempting the journey to the United States; the only requirement was for them to pass the disease and criminal background inspections at Ellis Island. Once clear, they were allowed to stay and work legally in the United States (Foner 2000; Chomsky 2007).

During the second major wave of migration to the United States at the turn of the twenty-first century, which was primarily from Latin America, scholars identified the important role of social networks in reducing the cost and risk of migration for undocumented migrants and facilitating their movement across international borders (Massey et al. 1987; Massey and Espinosa 1997). Given the power of social networks on international migration around the world, scholars have developed theories that incorporate the role of social networks as a possible direct cause of international migration and/ or the strongest possible cause for the perpetuation of international migration flows (Massey et al. 1993, 1998).

Unfortunately, today's US immigration policy discriminates against prospective migrants from most Latin American countries, hindering them from acquiring legal means to migrate to the United States (Massey, Durand, and Malone 2002). Since the Bracero Program, there have been very few opportunities for immigrants from Latin America (and especially from Mexico) to gain legal status to work in the United States, especially if they lack high levels of education. For this reason, the majority of arrivals from Mexico lack legal documentation (Massey, Durand, and Malone 2002). Their unauthorized status creates a new, modern threat for immigrants, and therefore, social networks of migration now depend almost completely on relationships of trust. Without trustworthy sources of information, international migrants risk their lives and risk being caught, jailed, and deported by immigration authorities. Thus, Migration-Trust Networks are specific types of networks in which undocumented migrants participate.

Migration-Trust Networks consist of social relationships based on an exchange of support, trust, and sustenance between residents from the place of origin and those at the place of destination. These ties are based on social homogeneity, similar religious beliefs, and the commonality that migrants share from migratory experiences and/or struggles back home. Network members carry social expectations of each other and encourage certain behaviors and values. Most, if not all, participants in this network depend on a stringent level of trust due to some members' unauthorized status in the United States. Due to the complexity of this concept of Migration-Trust Networks, I first discuss the related theoretical framework in which this concept is based. I provide an elaborated definition of this concept in chapter 6.

The participants in this specific network share resources for securing a successful migration journey, job search, and settlement at the place of destination. The fact that some or most of the participants lack legal documentation places everyone in the network at risk, even those who are legal residents or US citizens. For example, because most of the network participants belong to mixed families (composed of legal and undocumented migrants), the risk of deportation would be present at all times and family separation may be inevitable.

Table 1.1 presents the possible similarities and differences between the social networks of regular international migrants exemplified by the European migrant networks, and those networks in which some of the members lack legal status. Gans' (1962) accounts of the immigrant enclaves of European migrants exemplify normative migration networks and how their social dynamics could differ from those of a MTN. As shown in table 1.1, the main difference between the two types of migrant networks lies in the fact that the Migration-Trust Network has to rely on members for more risky matters, such as providing information on how to get to the border. This may be very challenging for those who have never been out of their hometown, especially those from rural areas. Once in the United States, those from the MTN provide necessary information to prospective migrants to minimize their risk while being transported to their destination. Once at the place of destination, the MTN provides social support to new arrivals. Examples of support involve helping them overcome the barriers of being undocumented, including not having an official ID, being unable to get a driver's license, bank account, or access to credit, and so forth. The MTN helps the new arrivals gain access to information to help them circumvent their lack of legal rights.

Therefore, social networks are important for international migrants' social adaptation and survival at the place of destination. However, MTNs are more important for undocumented migrants, as they serve as a safe haven for both new arrivals and returning migrants who have no legal recourse for assistance or protection. The MTNs may function differently for new and returning undocumented migrants, but they are based on the common ground of trust and loyalty from all its members.

Table 1.1   Similarities and differences between the types of support offered by a
Migration-Trust Network versus a Regular Migration Network

Types of Support Offered	
Migration-Trust Networks	**Regular Migration Network**
Support for traveling to the place of destination:	Support for traveling to the place of destination:
Information about how to get to the border and how to be safe	Information about how to get to the place of destination
Financial assistance to get to the border	Financial assistance to get to the place of destination (US)
Information about how to find a trustful coyote or smuggler	Support once at the place of destination:
Money for the coyote or smuggler	Help with social adaptation
Picking up the immigrant from a safe house and paying the coyote or smuggler	Assistance learning English language
Support once at the place of destination:	Help coping with discrimination
Help with social adaptation	Help finding jobs and resources
Assistance learning English language	Minimizing exploitation
Help coping with discrimination	Sharing cultural practices from back home
Help finding jobs and resources	Providing psychological support
Minimizing exploitation	Provision of lodging to new arrivals
Sharing cultural practices from back home	Provide assistance getting a job
Providing psychological support	
Provision of lodging to new arrivals	
Provide assistance getting a job without legal documents, including having access to counterfeit documents, knowing what to say to employers, etc.	
Helping those who lack legal status function in society despite their lack of rights	
Daily protecting those who lack legal status from deportation	

Note: Text in italics indicates the types of support that differs between the Migration-Trust
Network participants and those who belong to a regular migration network.

Social Capital and Theories of International Migration

Experts in international migration theory and the economic sociology of migration tend to address the social, noneconomic reasons for migration such as social networks and social capital. International migration scholars have borrowed the concept of social capital to refer to the benefits (tangible and intangible) acquired by international migrants as a result of having personal contacts at the place of destination. The contemporary meaning of social capital was first introduced by Loury (1977) and theoretically developed by Bourdieu (1986) and Coleman (1988). Although sociologists disagree about what constitutes social capital, migration researchers generally agree that it refers to the tangible and intangible resources provided by relatives, friends, and *paisanos* to facilitate migration, settlement, and employment in a foreign country (see Massey et al. 1987; Massey and Espinosa 1997). At this point, the field recognizes two international migration theories related to social networks: the *cumulative causation theory* and the *social capital theory*. Actually, the social capital theory is considered part of the cumulative causation theory (see Massey et al. 1993, 1998). The theory of cumulative causation refers to the tendency of migration to self-perpetuate, regardless of what initially caused the migration to begin (Myrdal 1957; Massey 1990). This theory takes into account the changes in context and social culture in the transnational context, at the place of origin, as well as at the place of destination. For example, it claims that a culture of migration develops among the members of the sending community due to the benefits they observe from international migration and remittances. After seeing the benefits others receive as a result of international migration, more people decide to migrate internationally for the same reasons. This process is also called relative deprivation (Stark and Taylor 1989).

The social capital theory, on the other hand, has to do with the concept of the benefits provided to prospective migrants having contacts at the place of destination. According to this network theory, migration becomes easier, less costly, and less risky over time because of a growing network of social contacts in the receiving community. These contacts share information and resources with future migrants, whether family, friends, or people from the same community, aiding in the process of migrating, settling, and searching for employment in the host country. These resources and connections are a form of social capital that dramatically increases the likelihood of additional migration among persons with family or friends living in the United States (Massey et al. 1987; Massey 1990). Sociologists view such social structures and interpersonal networks as potential sources of social capital.

As described earlier, social capital drives social networks and at the same time, the social networks help the process of cumulative causation to take place. Therefore, my contribution through this book is to extend social network theories by expanding our knowledge of how social networks develop and function. I am not focusing on the decision-making process, but instead, on the process that takes place after the decision to migrate internationally has been made.

The Role of Trust in Social Networks of International Migration

Given the vulnerability of the undocumented migrant members of the MTN, the reliance on trusted relationships becomes one of the most important features of the social interactions within the network. In the organizational literature, Schlenker, Helm, and Tedeschi (1973) define trust as the "reliance upon information received from another person about uncertain environmental states and their trust to be accompanying outcomes in a risky situation" (1149). Also, Kramer and Tyler (1996) argue that

> [T]he situation must contain the following components for trust to be demonstrated: (a) a risky situation with regard to whether certain outcomes will be derived in the future; (b) the presence of cues that provide some information as to the probability of various uncertain environmental states occurring, such as the communication of another's intentions; and (c) the resulting behavior of the person demonstrating reliance on this uncertain information. (116)

Game theory has explored ways in which strangers can gain the trust of others. Game theorists Macy and Skvoretz (1998) have found empirical evidence that

> [M]oral sentiments originate in ongoing relationships where they help players resist the temptation to cheat so that they may secure the benefits of more far-sided behavior. Players with such moral sentiments thus outperform those who lack the moral fiber needed to overcome short-sided temptation causing the sentiments to spread across the population. (640–41)

Frank (1988) proposes that "moral sentiment such as sympathy, compassion, or remorse, provide 'telltale signs' that make cooperation between strangers viable in human populations" (640). Frank (1993) "reviews strong evidence indicating the physociological links between emotional states and involuntary nonverbal behavior, especially facial expressions and voice tone" (165). For example, Frank (1993) reveals that certain facial expressions made with the eyebrows cannot be produced on demand by individuals. Instead, they are spontaneously produced when individuals experience sadness, grief, or concern. He also states that other elements such as "the pitch and timbre of the voice, the rate of respiration, and even the cadence of speech are systematically linked to underlying affective states" (165–66).

According to Cook (2005), the observance of the degree of social reciprocity, fairness, trustworthiness, and perceptions of satisfaction are also important when identifying or building trust relations among individuals. Cook (2005) argues that an initial assessment can be based on "status characteristics (visible markers of group membership), on kinship status, or on stereotypical judgments of those who are similar or dissimilar to us" (11). Although she also warns the readers that such initial assessment may be wrong from the very beginning, they are still important, especially among those who have weak ties. If one demonstrates from the beginning that he or she can be trusted and develops a good reputation, other MTN members will begin to trust him or her. Trust is enforced through social expectations and punishment, so members, especially new ones, do not want to ruin their reputations with other members. Therefore, when new members join the network, the relationship between them and existing members is tenuous until they are assured the new members can be trusted.

Tilly (2005) introduced the concept of Trust Networks in his writings on state formation where he declares:

> Trust networks, then, consist of ramified interpersonal connections, consisting mainly of strong ties, within which people set valued, consequential, long-term resources and enterprises at risk to the malfeasance, mistakes, or failures of others. (chapter 1, Kindle loc 336)

Tilly (2007) applied the concept of trust networks[7] to the case of economic exchanges and the exchanges of favors in the transnational context among international migrants. Despite his connection between trust networks and international migration, Tilly did not identify the trust networks as a concept that could be applied to the vulnerability that undocumented migrants face. This particular trust network is about creating a form of social organization for social adaptation and economic survival at the place of destination. More importantly, the trust network is used to create a safe haven for migrants who lack legal status. For the migrant trust network to work effectively, network participants should be in a relationship with one another to some extent prior to migrating. This is typically the case as people migrate from small, rural communities where people know one another or from established peer groups in urban areas. In this way, people learn to exchange trust under uncertain conditions. These preexisting relations are then converted into more intense and intimate social relationships of trust, allowing for a greater level of reliability within the context of international migration.

Existing Studies of Social Networks of Migration

Detailed data on the characteristics of social networks within existing data sets (e.g., demographic characteristics of those who provided the help to survey respondents, depth of the relationship, or frequency of contact) is scarce, perhaps because of the extremely laborious job of collecting such data. As a result, most studies have neglected to identify the social dynamics that occur at the micro level within social networks that drive international migration flows. Most scholarly work makes only abstract references to social networks and social capital (Burt 2001). This scholarly work emphasizes the importance of these networks but fails to explain exactly how they operate and how social support is exchanged, not only at the micro level of analysis, but also at the macro level.

In the field of international migration and social networks experts have claimed that networks are not necessarily static entities, but that they change and transform over time (Boyd 1989; Granovetter 1985; Hagan 1998; Mahler 1995; Menjívar 2000). For example, Boyd (1989) found that those who participate in social networks meet specific roles and functions (such as those networks used simply to get to the United States as a first-time migrant), while others participate in networks that are used later, once the migrant is more established. In addition, studies of social networks among migrants have found that competition among immigrants or exploitation of fellow countrymen may disintegrate ethnic solidarity and cohesiveness among network participants (i.e., Mahler 1995; Menjívar 2000).

Other scholars have looked more closely at the social dynamics that take place among network participants. For example, Bashi (2007) explored the social structure of the networks of migration of West Indians. She collected data on the contacts of migrants and has helped expand our knowledge of social network structure by defining and describing the role of the *hubs*, or those who become the gatekeepers of the social network as they select and facilitate the future migration of others. She goes on to describe the role of the *spokes*, those who migrate and settle, but do not perform any of the roles of the hubs in migrant networks. Bashi contributes to the transnational migration literature by showing that pioneer migrants—who she suggests could also become the hubs—are the ones who actively recruit migrants from the place of destination, and therefore, help activate the migration network from the very beginning. Furthermore, she argues that altruistic behavior and the willingness to help others exists only among the hubs, but she fails to identify any altruistic behavior among the spokes in her study. There is too much emphasis on the hub's role and the hub's benefits from showing altruistic behavior toward the spokes. Any help or support provided by the spokes toward others, Bashi attributes to the attachment or loyalty they have to the hub who helped them migrate. Bashi's work is important for our understanding of social networks of migration, but her hubs and spokes dichotomy does not allow for the possibility that spokes could also directly or indirectly provide migration social capital to others in the social network. She fails to explain why altruistic behavior could only be attributed to the hubs and not to the spokes.

The Sources of Social Capital and International Migration

Using examples related to international migration, Portes and Sensenbrenner (1993) defined social capital as "collective expectations affecting individual economic behavior" (1326). They used classic sociological concepts and introduced four sources of social capital based on the collective behavior of people:

1. Value introjections: "socialization into consensually established beliefs" that prompt behavior that is not simply out of naked greed
2. Reciprocity exchanges: this is when the favor is returned to the same person who provided the help.
3. Bounded solidarity: "situational reactive sentiments," which result in collective conscience
4. Enforceable trust: "pluralistic rewards and sanctions linked to group membership" (1326)

Immigration scholars have used such sources of social capital primarily to examine economic enterprises formed by immigrant entrepreneurs. In fact, Portes and Sensenbrenner (1993) expounded the above concepts of social capital using examples chiefly related to immigrant ethnic entrepreneurship enterprises. Not included are examples of social support in order to migrate and settle in the United States. Unfortunately, studies of social networks among unskilled and undocumented immigrants have neglected to examine closely the sources of social capital formulated by Portes and Sensenbrenner, due to the generalization that undocumented immigrants do not tend to form economic enterprises (see Valdez 2011). The concept of MTN provides an avenue for further developing the sources of social capital proposed by Portes and Sensenbrenner (1993), especially reciprocity, bounded solidarity, and enforceable trust. Throughout the book, I adapt and apply these concepts to the case of Mexican immigrants to the United States, focusing especially on those who lack legal documentation in the United States.

Portes and Sensenbrenner (1993) proposed the concept of *bounded solidarity* as a source of social capital that "focuses on those situational circumstances that can lead to the emergence of principled group-oriented behavior quite apart from any early value introjections" (1324). In other words, the members of the group develop certain expectations of collective behavior in which any actions or decisions made should benefit not just the individual but all the members of the group. Portes and Sensenbrenner argue that one example of the situational circumstances immigrants face that leads to such bounded solidarity behavior is the extent to which they are subjected to racial or ethnic discrimination once they arrive to the United States.

Similar to the mechanical solidarity concept, the idea of *enforceable trust*, also proposed by Portes and Sensenbrenner (1993), refers to a set of social expectations to follow that will be enforced through social monitoring, which can result in the rejection or punishment of those who do not conform to those agreed-upon values and behaviors. The similarity of experiences, such as crossing the border clandestinely, feeling discriminated against, sharing the fear of being caught by the border patrol, being exploited in the United States, and so forth, gives rise to the enforceable trust social mechanism among migrants once they identify each other in the United States. Tilly (2007) has argued that international migrants help each other through bounded solidarity due to a series of expectations from the members of the rest of their group, and that the social networks of migration from transnational communities are based on trust networks. I also argue that the social expectations of behavior at the community of origin are transferred to the place of destination, and that the transnational relations of trust among migrants and nonmigrants create the fundamental conditions for the MTN to effectively provide social capital to its members.

Portes and Sensenbrenner (1993) also took into account that reciprocity was an important source of social capital and assumed it was directly associated with the exchange of favors among immigrants; that is, those who received favors later returned them to the same givers. The findings in this book challenge this assumption. I find instead that those who receive the favors, later return those favors by helping others. I refer to this type of social exchange as "risk-pooling." The findings in this book challenge Portes and Sensenbrenner's (1993) assumption of direct reciprocity as scholars, for example, have argued that social capital exchange is not necessarily the same as economic exchange (Cook 2005). This has not been previously explored in the international migration literature due to a lack of detailed data about how favors are exchanged.

The Paisano Sentiment

The concept of paisano also plays a very important role in the creation of social networks from smaller communities. According to Massey et al. (1987), the term "paisano" has no meaning at the place of origin of the migrants, but it becomes very important when two migrants find each other in the United States. In many instances, not only have they known each other all their lives, but they know the reality and struggles of the people back in the community and share the same migratory experience.[8] Therefore, paisanos tend to develop a sense of commonality and social cohesiveness as well as enforceable trust once they find each other in the United States. Also, paisanos are subject to the expectations of the rest of the members of the community. According to Tilly (2007),

> For the purpose of studying migration . . . labels such as kinsman, *compadre*, *paisano*, fellow believer, and co-member of a craft provide a first indication of a trust relationship . . . trust networks, then consist of ramified interpersonal connections, consisting mainly of strong ties, within which people set valued, consequential, long-term resources and enterprises at risk to the malfeasance, mistakes, or failures of others. (6–7, emphasis in original)

Paisano ties are formed from trust relationships and can become essential in the absence of any other ties, like kin ties or friendship ties. Therefore, any type of tie can become a strong tie if international migrants develop a sense of commonality with each other, even between those who have just met in the United States, such as José and Pancho from the foreword of this book. Once they identify with each other and become part of the MTN, they are transformed into strong ties and begin exchanging trust and social capital.

The Paisanaje Sentiment

Rural or urban MTNs can also be a form of social support based on ties of *paisanaje*. Paisanos or countrymen who are from the same rural community of origin have usually lived there for the majority of their lives. They probably attended the same school, the same church, played sports together, or at a minimum heard each other's name at least once. As pointed out by Levitt (2001), members of rural villages throughout their lifetime have the opportunity to meet everyone in their communities of origin; therefore, this increases their chances to acquire social capital from anyone in the community, including friends and paisanos from the place of origin at the time of migration, even if those ties are not relatives.

When paisanos consider helping each other migrate, they do so out of a sense of solidarity—a paisanaje sentiment. According to Massey et al. (1987), *paisanaje* is the "feeling of belonging to a common community of origin . . . it is a latent dimension of association in the home community" (142 – 43). Massey and colleagues state that the concept of paisanaje

> [I]s not a meaningful concept until two paisanos encounter each other outside their home community. Then the strength of the paisanaje tie depends on the strangeness of the environment and the nature of their prior relationships in the community. (143)

In general, the term paisano is used to describe those who migrate from small communities of origin; but for other migrants, like those who migrate from urban communities of origin, paisano can mean being from the same metropolis, state, or country. For some, the commonality of a geographical area of origin is enough to activate the bonds and the paisanaje sentiment at the place of destination. The common immigration experience and the alienation that the immigrants experience during migration also influence the paisanaje sentiment. Massey et al. (1987) also suggest that the term paisano could encompass those outside the community of origin who marry migrants in the United States.

Paisanos understand the harsh reality of life back home, and that makes them more understanding and loyal to others in the MTN. For example, Oscar, a respondent who migrated from one of the rural villages, was interviewed in the United States and stated:

We really like our hometown. Maybe you didn't think much of it but we like it a lot. The problem is that we just don't want life to be so difficult. Do you know how much money people make there? About 30 pesos a day, while 1 kg of meat costs 50 pesos. People have to work two days in order to buy just one kg of meat. The situation is too difficult to even survive. Like if I go visit, I bring my money with me and I'm pretty comfortable with that, but for the people who live there and haven't been back to the US in a while it's really tough. For them it's a struggle because they have to survive and it's really hard there. That's why a lot of people are coming now.

Oscar understands the struggles that people face back home and demonstrates empathy for his fellow migrants who leave for the North. In addition, Oscar's statement explains why more migrants are leaving for the North or are forced to perform circulatory patterns of international migration. Those with prior migration experience must eventually leave again for the North after spending time with their families because of the lack of economic opportunities in their hometown. Urban-origin migrants also understand the struggles that others are suffering at home and throughout the country.

Therefore, paisano ties are very important for the functionality of the MTNs. Paisano ties can serve as substitutes for other ties when prospective migrants do not have close contacts in the United States, such as close friends or family members. Paisanos do not need to have close ties to prospective migrants in the past. Instead, the sole fact that they were born in the same town or region makes them loyal and supportive to prospective migrants. The paisano sentiment is strengthened even more in an MTN. During my interviews, I noticed that the *paisano sentiment* was very strong, as migrants called themselves paisanos in a certain tone of voice that implied respect, loyalty, and partnership. Because it is difficult to portray this tone, I provide examples of how paisanos cared for one other.

Paisanaje ties are activated most deeply when members of the MTN, either abroad or at home, are in trouble. This was the case when migrants were from rural or urban areas. I observed that every time someone was very sick, whether at the origin or destination, the paisanos demonstrated solidarity by providing social and financial support to the family of the person who was sick, regardless of their relationship to the person needing help. One of the major challenges for the members of the MTN was that they were not able to easily return to Mexico given their lack of legal status. This was especially problematic if an immediate family member passed away; they were not able to attend their funeral. Therefore, having a paisano in the US provided some level of comfort for the family member who could not participate in the grieving ritual directly.

Members of the MTN, especially the paisanos, also united for other causes. On one occasion, I attended a soccer game where one of the players got hurt and went to the hospital. Given that he was not able to work for a few days, the members from the MTN made a *coperacha* or *colecta* (a cooperation) in order to give financial support to the wife and children of the player until he could work again. The members of the MTN raised $500 to give to his wife. The soccer player recovered from his injuries after a month or so and returned to work. He and his wife were very thankful to everyone who helped during that difficult time.

On another occasion, someone died, and the body needed to be returned to the family in Mexico. Again, the members of the MTN demonstrated solidarity by raising the money to send the body back to the hometown. As I followed this situation, they needed about $4,000 to send his body to the state of Guanajuato from Chicago. Because of the high cost, the paisanos made an announcement on the Spanish-speaking radio station in Chicago. I listened to the announcement during my visit and was told about the sudden death of a forty-year-old husband and father of three children, all of whom lived back in the medium-sized town that I studied. I entered Mi Ranchito, a Mexican produce store, and was amazed to see all the people who came to donate a dollar or two. People would say, "Here goes for my paisano." This is how they referred to him if they did not know him personally. Again, I noticed the sweet emotion in the tone of their voice when they said the word "paisano."

Paisanos share common experiences of joblessness, poverty, a lack of resources and government benefits, and a lack of credit and credit markets in their hometowns. They understand the desperate needs of one another's families. This shared understanding, made up of shared migratory experience, expectations of the community, and religious beliefs, makes the formation of an MTN automatic. It is driven by the paisanaje sentiment.

Collective Efficacy

In order to address how social networks of international migration function at the place of origin, as well as at the place of destination, and how the MTNs become effective social entities in which undocumented international migrants find safety and continuous social support, I rely on the theory of *collective efficacy*. Robert Sampson (2006), in his studies in the area of criminology, has been working on the development of the *collective efficacy* theory in order to explain "how tight-knit urban neighborhoods produce safety because of the rich supply of social networks" (150). Collective efficacy is an unobserved social mechanism driven by the cohesion of social ties, which helps to explain how collective action can function as a problem-solving mechanism "under specific kind of social contextual conditions" (164). One of the most important components of collective efficacy is mutual trust. Sampson argues that collective efficacy is created by "a particular kind of social structure (cohesion, with an emphasis on working trust and mutual support) with the culturally tinged dimension of *shared expectations* for social control" (152). In fact, Sampson (2008) was able to make the connection between his theory of collective efficacy and neighborhoods in Chicago in which a large proportion of its residents were recent immigrants. The larger the percentage of foreign-born in those areas, the lower the crime rate. In this book, I make the proposition that collective efficacy takes place within the social structure of MTNs.

Therefore, a Migration-Trust Network can consist of various types of social ties, such as kinship, friendship, paisanaje, *compadrazgo, cuatismo*, coworkers, neighbors, and others.[9] For the MTN to begin to feed itself and function effectively, the majority of its members should have preexisting relations of trust in which they help one another. Outsiders can become members of the MTN as long as they follow the social and behavioral expectations of the network and remain trustworthy. These outsiders may be residents from other areas, employers, coyotes, labor recruiters, city officials, or others. New members, if they are legal residents (e.g., employers or city officials), may also be vulnerable and jeopardize their reputations because they are associated with undocumented migrants.

On one hand, the Migration-Trust Networks can develop more readily among rural-origin migrants because of social homogeneity, cohesiveness, and relationships of trust. In addition, they share a set of social expectations to maintain certain values and behaviors. Rural-origin prospective migrants have also developed a collective conscience, and those who do not behave according to a community's expectations are subject to rejection or punishment. On the other hand, urban-origin migrants may or may not already belong to a peer group (i.e., close friends, neighbors, or family) before migration who have specific values and expectations of one another. This is why migrants from urban communities of origin may not be able to join an MTN as easily as those who migrate from rural areas. The social structure of an MTN, the dependency on relationships of trust among its members, and the specific circumstances of the members allow for collective efficacy to form. The structure addresses the specific needs of the undocumented migrants throughout the entire migratory process, but especially once the migrants settle at the place of destination.

I also argue that MTNs function at the macro level via a series of additional social mechanisms that connect the places of origin with the places of destination (also referred as the transnational context). In the following section, I introduce the macro level social forces that can affect MTNs at the macro level.

Theoretical Framework at the Macro Level

Social networks and relationships of trust can also influence or be influenced by macro-level factors, such as the social, cultural, and economic conditions at context of reception or at the place of origin. Collective behavior, such as the sending of collective remittances to the place of origin, is another form of solidarity at the macro level that helps fuel social networks of migration. For this reason, it is important to delineate how macro-level factors affect and influence social networks of migration.

Tilly (2007) summarizes the connection between trust networks and macro-level forces that perpetuate international migration, though he was not necessarily thinking of undocumented migrants. Tilly provides six main points:

1. Within the wide range of interpersonal networks that play some part in long-distance migration, trust networks figure importantly in solidarity between people at the origin and destination.
2. Members of such networks typically acquire long-term rights and obligations, binding themselves to each other, which means networks operate simultaneously as sites of social insurance and social control.
3. For that very reason, migration streams attached to trust networks tend to concentrate in relatively specialized economic, geographic, and social niches as compared with all streams of migration.
4. The operation of migrants' trust networks creates and depends on boundaries that separate members from outsiders; as a result, membership in-

hibits assimilation of migrants at the destination and poses sharp choices for the second and later generations.

5. In the long run, the survival of transnational trust networks through the second generation and beyond depends heavily on the social segregation or integration of the immigrant stream at the destination. Whether segregated through self-selection or exclusion, segregated immigrant communities more frequently maintain transnational trust networks.

6. That segregation, however, generally confines members of trust networks to a relatively narrow range of opportunities for work, housing, sociability, and welfare. If those opportunities connect members with rich rewards, the network prospers. If not, it often suffers. (5–6)

Tilly's six points justify the connection between relations of trust at the micro level and other contextual and transnational factors at the macro level. He explains the functionality of social networks of migration and their successful expansion and longevity through time and even through generations. Most importantly, he takes the transnational context into account by observing the social, cultural, economic, political, and geographic transformations at both the place of origin and the place of destination. As a result, I cannot limit the concept of MTNs to micro-level factors that affect social networks of migration. In the following sections, I introduce the theoretical framework at the macro level and examine factors that contribute to the functionality and expansion of social networks of international migration, such as transnationalism, the context of reception, collective remittances, and cumulative causation.

Transnationalism

Transnational theory looks closely at the social, economic, political, and cultural transformations that take place at both the sending community and the receiving community (Smith 2006). When newcomers arrive at the place of destination, they have to adapt their customs, cultural practices, and social interactions to the new social arrangements, conditions, and characteristics of the context of reception. Conversely, those who return to the place of origin tend to bring new customs, cultural practices, and forms of social interactions, consequently transforming the culture and practices in the sending community. Any form of communication, whether by visiting, telephone or text messaging, sending pictures, letters, or Internet, can have an impact in both places. Communication can affect a large number of factors, such as cultural beliefs and practices, religion, social values, social behavior, language, political practices, and social roles, to name a few (see Smith 2006). To pay attention to such behavioral transformations is important, given that these changes can alter the behavior of social network participants at the origin and destination and can even affect migration decisions. Furthermore, I argue that collective efficacy also happens at the transnational level. That is, the social structure that creates the collective efficacy among the MTN members is driven by social forces in both contexts, in the origin and in the destination.

Context of Reception

Most international migration theories take into account not only the characteristics, social composition, and transformations of the sending community, but also the context at the receiving community, which is what Massey and Durand refer to generally as "a daughter community" (i.e., Massey et al. 1987). This community is composed of migrants from the same place of origin who settle next door to each other to both give and receive support or exchange social capital. In most cases, international migrants tend to segregate themselves in immigrant enclaves in the place of destination. The tendency to arrive and form immigrant enclaves happens for several reasons. Immigrants share information about lodging, finding schools for their children, going to the doctor, where to buy groceries or do the laundry, and so forth. The migrants' lack of English language skills also calls for them to settle near each other and minimize communication problems that would arise were they to settle outside the immigrant enclave.

According to international migration theories, one of the most important determinants for the continuation of the migration flow is the existence of pull factors, such as the availability of jobs and affordable housing as well as transportation to job locations (Korinek, Entwisle, and Jampaklay 2005). As mentioned previously, Menjívar's work made the connection between the cohesion of a social network and the conditions found at the context of reception. Menjívar suggested that one of the reasons, among other structural factors, for why Salvadorans' ties ruptured once they arrived at the place of destination in her study was the unavailability of jobs for future migrants. Therefore, without the necessary conditions at the place of destination to attract migrants, even with social contacts being available to help, the international migration network would not be able to keep fueling itself and continue its growth.

Krissman (2002, 2005) argues that the social network of migration needs to be conceptualized as having participants who play different roles within the network, not just the international migrant members themselves. He argues that nonmigrants who are located in the United States, such as employers, should also be considered part of the social networks of international migration. Therefore, the context of reception also has the potential to add other network participants into the MTN who may play a crucial role for the MTN to continue its function. Without the direct or indirect participation of these members, the MTN would not function correctly. While Krissman, for example, has demonstrated how employers participate in the social network as outsiders, he does not focus on the specific aspect of undocumented migration. That is, he has not considered the extent to which trust relations operate among network members in order to accept outsiders as part of their social network, and how or why such a social dynamic occurs.

Relative Deprivation and Remittances

Remittances transform the economic behavior of people at the place of origin and can generate what Massey et al. (1993, 1998) call *relative deprivation* among some members of the community (also see Stark and Taylor 1989). Feelings of inequality and deprivation are exacerbated when households receiving remittances conspicuously build mansion-like homes and purchase expensive possessions such as name-brand clothes and imported vehicles. As a result, those who live in the community of origin feel deprived and decide to migrate as well, ultimately creating a new "culture of migration" that is transmitted throughout generations and social networks (Kandel and Massey 2002). Such social dynamics help transform the community, the cultural practices, and the values, and most importantly, they allow for the creation of greater social and economic stratification. Migration becomes the vehicle through which some people improve their social status in reference to themselves and to other members of the community. Through the act of migration, and the flow of remittances that ensues, they may even consider themselves superior to everyone else, or may be seen as superior by others in both the community of origin and at the places of destination. Therefore, once international migration begins, social and economic stratification also begins to change, especially among those left at the community of origin (Flores-Yeffal and Martinez 2010).

The Role of Collective Remittances

In addition to family remittances, collective remittances are an important way social network participants offer support to those at the place of origin (i.e., Smith 2006; Fitzgerald 2008). Collective remittances result from solidarity and cooperation between those at the destination who choose to send money back to their hometown to improve its infrastructure. In most cases, the migrants themselves decide how the funds will be used rather than local and municipal leaders, and they assign priorities to specific projects, such as paving streets, building a church or a plaza for social gatherings, installing sewage systems and electricity, and/or planning the fiestas patronales every year. Similar to how family remittances can cause feelings of deprivation for nonmigrant families who do not receive them, I argue that such infrastructural improvements funded by collective remittances can cause a similar effect among surrounding communities lacking similar support. Such a scenario changes the social and economic stratification of the communities, improving the status of those who receive collective remittances while lowering the status of those who do not. Therefore, I argue that members of the communities who do not receive collective remittances feel deprived, and they too, begin to migrate and organize in the same way, or sometimes even more effectively than the first community. This creates a sort of competition between surrounding communities, which further exacerbates and perpetuates the cycle of migration and expands the social networks to a larger geographical area.

Cumulative Causation

Cumulative causation refers to the tendency of migration to self-perpetuate, regardless of what causes the migration to begin in the first place (Myrdal 1957; Massey 1990). According to the social network theory of international migration, migration becomes easier and less risky over time because of a growing network of social contacts in the receiving community (Massey et al. 1993, 1998). Social capital (tangible and intangible benefits) is shared in the form of information and resources with future migrants—whether family, friends, or people from the same community—who aid in the process of migration and search for employment in the host country. These resources and connections are forms of social capital that dramatically increase the likelihood of additional migration of persons who have family, friends, or community members already living in the United States (Massey et al. 1987). Therefore, the social networks theory and the social capital concept are both part of the theory of cumulative causation. In order to understand how social capital is exchanged through social networks of international migration, one has to consider numerous factors that can influence how these social networks are created, maintained, and reproduced, and in turn, how they sustain and perpetuate the international migration streams. One of the most important factors is the cohesiveness and relationships of trust among network participants — especially if one considers the high prevalence of Mexican immigrants in the United States who lack legal authorization to live and work there. An analysis of the Mexican Migration Project data reveals that as many as 90 percent of the international migrants in the sample (MMP 128) were undocumented (Flores-Yeffal and Aysa-Lastra 2011). This fact differentiates contemporary Mexican and most Latin American immigrants from European immigrants who migrated at the turn of the twentieth century.

Other important factors should be taken into consideration, such as the context of the sending community (whether rural or urban), the context of the receiving community, and the transnational dynamics occurring in both, as migrants and nonmigrants exchange old and new cultural and behavioral practices. The effects of cumulative causation and relative deprivation at the individual, family, and community levels are also important for understanding how social networks grow and develop. Therefore, when looking at social networks in the context of international migration, scholars should consider both micro and macro levels of analysis in the transnational context to understand how social networks are created, perpetuated, or extinguished over time.

Using primarily ethnographic data collected in four communities of different sizes in the state of Guanajuato, Mexico, and in their daughter communities in the Unites States, this book unveils the impact that the rural or urban context of the sending community has on the formation, composition, and development of social networks of migration in the transnational context. The main purpose of this book, which consolidates the findings of thirteen years of continuous research work, is to unveil how social networks of migration function while taking into account the social cohesiveness and trust relationships that take place within these networks. To do this, I argue that one has to understand the micro level of analysis in combination with the macro level. This means linking the context of origin with the context of reception and observing how these transnational dynamics can either intensify or slow down the cumulative causation effects of those international migration flows.

Furthermore, I introduce the concept of Migration-Trust Networks in which I present, from a transnational perspective, a series of factors that drive social networks of migration. I take into account the particularities of this new migratory flow of Mexican migrants, such as the lack of legal documentation and other contemporary issues that place them in a position of greater disadvantage. In addition to describing the solidarity relations among migrants at the micro level, I argue from a macro perspective that the social and physical transformations caused by a mass migration from one community can have a domino effect in surrounding communities. This activates the social networks in those communities, thus expanding the source of the international migration flow to a broader geographical area in Mexico.

In chapter 2, I provide empirical evidence in support of the concepts that I claim provide the theoretical basis for why the Migration Trust-Networks function appropriately for undocumented migrants. I describe the membership requirements to participate in a MTN in rural and urban settings. I discuss how religion can influence the behavior of network participants so that they act collectively, trust others, and offer mutual support to others in need; in particular, paisano sentiment is important and becomes a crucial behavioral component of the MTNs. Other components of MTNs are bounded solidarity and enforceable trust forms that are manifested among MTN participants. Assisting others is expected of MTN members but reciprocal exchange is not; instead, a form of "risk-pooling" occurs in which migrants "return" favors by helping others in the future. I go on to provide examples of social control and social punishment in rural and urban settings. Finally, I elaborate on the role of different types of ties, including fictitious ties such as compadres and cuates, in becoming providers of social capital. I argue that a form of collective efficacy is created through a series of social dynamics and norms.

In chapter 3, I provide examples of the help provided to the Migration-Trust Network participants. I divide the types of help into the following: help to arrive in the United States and then help to settle and become established at the destination, such as providing lodging, transportation, child care, and job hunting. One of the rewards for providing social capital to others is acquisition of a higher social status and respect. I differentiate how social status manifests at the place of origin, as well as at the place of destination, which may lead to a new form of noneconomic social stratification among the MTN participants in the transnational context.

In chapter 4 I provide a theoretical and empirical proposition of how and why the Migration-Trust Networks are able to expand by absorbing new members through a process I call "the MTN effect." I also elaborate on this process and provide a set of different examples of how urban migrants or orphan migrants are absorbed by Migration-Trust Networks in the United States. Finally, I present the argument of how and why other nonmigrant strangers may become part of the MTN.

I provide empirical evidence in chapter 5 of how macro-level processes are driven by trust relations among the MTN participants. I provide examples of relative deprivation at the micro (among community residents) and at the macro levels (among entire communities). I also provide examples of how the culture of migration influences most to leave, but also some to stay in the community; usually the youngest sibling is left behind. The context of reception is also important for the MTN to work properly. Factors such as affordable housing, available means of transportation, the availability of housing amenities, schools for children, medical services, and means for entertainment and culture can be important for the MTN, but not totally essential depending on the type of social environment. The most important requirement for the MTN to function properly and expand is the demand for labor. I discuss the role of collective remittances on the preservation and expansion of MTNs. Exogenous ties connect people from other nearby communities to the MTN, creating a domino effect of expansion of the MTN or the creation of new MTNs. Finally, I conclude chapter 5 by providing examples of how technological advances, such as cell phones and the use of computers (through cybercafés, community websites, and networking sites) provide the right conditions for Migration-Trust Networks to function and continue expanding via the transnational context.

In chapter 6, I provide a summary of the findings from chapters 2, 3, 4, and 5 and explain in detail how the concept of MTNs operates and functions in the transnational context. I show that MTNs can develop in both rural and urban places of origin given the right conditions. Micro and macro social forces presented in this book function simultaneously in the transnational context in order to develop, expand, and/or transplant MTNs.

I present examples of the advantages and disadvantages of MTNs in chapter 7. I argue that assessments of advantages and disadvantages differ depending on who is analyzing the issue: the migrant or someone outside the MTN. In most cases, I argue that the migrants themselves would assess their membership in the MTN as positive and advantageous, while outsiders would generally see membership as a great disadvantage. Migration-Trust Network participants who are undocumented (together with their family members who have legal documents) depend permanently on MTNs even if they are able to assimilate, adopt the culture, learn English, and get a college education. Existing without legal documents does not allow them to become part of the broader US society, as European migrants did at the turn of the twentieth century.

Finally, I present concluding remarks and policy recommendations in chapter 8. This book provides a framework for thinking about the nuances of cumulative causation when participants of the migratory flow lack legal documentation at the place of destination. I recommend that policymakers take advantage of the cohesive bonds and collective efficacy manifested among participants of MTNs to distribute important information related to health, educational prospects, new laws, and so forth. In addition, policymakers working on immigration laws should consider the long-term effects of a population living in the shadows of the United States and permanently dependent on MTNs, as they cannot become fully integrated into American society. Instead, policymakers should find ways to regularize the status of the millions of undocumented immigrants now permanently living in the United States.

Notes

1. I may occasionally borrow some examples from my ethnographic work in the country of El Salvador to help make further generalizations; but for the most part, this book focuses on the social networks among Mexican migrants.

2. Survey data was also collected but not extensively used in this book. The primary research instrument used was the ethnosurvey (Massey 1987). This semistructured questionnaire gathers social, economic, demographic, and migratory information on household members in Mexico and in the United States. In order to study such networks of migration more deeply, I appended to the standard MMP instrument a separate module I designed to reconstruct migratory networks, which I call the Solidarity questionnaire. This part of the survey employed the egocentric network methodology developed by Burt (1984) and applied by the General Social Survey (GSS). In addition to asking migrants about their social network connections, the module included a set of questions about social contacts in the sending community in order to assess daily living strategies at the place of origin. Although these samples are only representative of the four communities from which they were drawn, the state of Guanajuato has historically been a large source of migrants to the United States. It thus offers an attractive setting to study migratory behavior (see Massey and Zenteno 2000).

3. The version of the solidarity questionnaire used for the two rural villages differs from the one used for the town and the urban neighborhood. The version applied to the two rural villages does not include a name generator. See Flores (1999) for the first version of the solidarity questionnaire. The most recent version of the Solidarity questionaire is available upon request by contacting the author directly.

4. A snowball sample is collected by a chain of references instead of simple random methodology.

5. For details on sampling procedures, see Massey et al. (1987), and Massey and Durand (2004).

6. In this book, I use fictitious names for when I cite the views or answers to my questions from the respondents interviewed in order to protect their identities. In addition, I cannot reveal the localities where I did my research in Mexico and the United States given the vulnerability of the respondents who participated in this study.

7. Karen Cook (2005) observed the concept of "trust networks" around the same time as Charles Tilly. It appears that Cook's vision of trust networks was also very similar to that of Tilly (2005). I am mainly using Tilly's work here because he utilized the concept and applied it to transnational migrant networks.

8. Paisanos are defined not only as the countrymen from the same rural village or small community, but also as those who migrate from the same city or country. Therefore, paisanos can also be two complete strangers who only have in common the fact that they were born in the same region. They only become paisanos once they meet each other in the United States.

9. Compadrazgo refers to "the reciprocal relationship or the social institution of such relationship existing between a godparent or godparents and the godchild and its parents in the Spanish-speaking world (as in So. America)" (*Merriam-Webster*). Personal relations among cuates is called cuatismo. "Cuate (from the Náhuatl word meaning twin brother) is used throughout Mexico to describe a special male friend or group of friends with whom one spends considerable leisure time and who can be trusted with intimate information. Cuate groups can include up to ten members who share common interests, who are bound by intense friendship and personal relations, and who commit themselves to assisting each other in case of need" (http://countrystudies.us/mexico/59.htm).

CHAPTER TWO

The Social and Contextual Components of Migration-Trust Networks

This book extends the concept of Tilly (2005) in his work, *Trust and Rule*, where he states, "Trust Networks consist of ramified interpersonal connections within which people set valued, consequential, long term resources and enterprises at risk to the malfeasance of others" (5). As mentioned in chapter 1, it is unclear whether or not Tilly was able to make the connection between his concept of Trust Networks and undocumented migration. His applications of the concept of Trust Networks to international migration looked at international migration as a more general social process in which migrants needed to rely on trust relationships, but not necessarily because they were undocumented. An extension of Tilly's concept of Trust Networks are MTNs, which consist of members who lack legal status at the place of destination, which in this case includes the majority of Mexican migrants in the United States. I argue that the risk associated with international migration is different for legal and undocumented migration. Undocumented migrants have to depend on higher levels of trust than regular (or legal) migrants do. Even after arriving successfully, settling, and gaining employment, undocumented migrants still face high levels of risk, such as deportation.

Therefore, the Trust Networks of Tilly and the MTNs described in this book are different in that those who participate in MTNs are forced to use the MTN as a safe haven, while those who participate in a regular Trust Network require only support. They may leave or be ejected from the Trust Network, but those who belong to the MTNs do not have such options. Also, the requirements for belonging to a regular Trust Network for legal migrants may be more relaxed compared to the requirements for belonging to an MTN. The level of trust required among members of an MTN is higher, and the risk of malfeasance is greater. Therefore, the membership within an MTN would be more exclusive, but at the same time more inclusive to those who are vulnerable, that is, the undocumented migrants.

Migration-Trust Networks are based on behavior in which migrants help each other without necessarily expecting material return. Social homogeneity and the commonality from their international migration experience and social struggle helps them identify with each other (i.e., enabling their bonded solidarity and enforceable trust). Similar experiences help them develop a collective conscience in which all the members of the network see themselves as a group and not as individuals. A set of social expectations develops among network participants in which social support, social cohesion, and trust is expected. Any betrayal could place everyone in the social network at risk because many lack legal documentation. For this reason, protecting the legal status of the community members becomes one of their social obligations. Given the high levels of social cohesion, cooperation, and trust needed to sustain the MTN, a form of collective efficacy develops within the structure of the network. This means that the MTN's main function is to help its members circumvent their undocumented status. Mutual trust plays a very important role in this relationship. Offering social capital to others may also be driven by religious beliefs that encourage fellowship among both migrants and nonmigrants.

Paisanos understand fellowship. Once migrants reach the United States, they become paisanos, creating a sentimental bond with other paisanos and prospective migrants. The paisano sentiment is driven by likeness of the migratory experience represented in bonded solidarity and maintained by enforceable trust via social surveillance, as explained through Durkheim's mechanical solidarity. The migrants' experience, along with religious faith, encourages them to assist one another.

There is no direct reciprocal response when receiving assistance because the person receiving the help does not return the favor directly to the person giving it. Instead, those who receive help are expected to help other new arrivals in the future. The reason for this is that those who first provide help are generally already established migrants who have been successful getting a job and settling in the United States; they do not need the favor to be returned to them. Instead, the favor is bestowed on new migrants. I refer to this process as "risk-pooling."

One of the most powerful properties of MTNs is that they can provide social capital without regards to the type of social tie (strong or weak) between the prospective migrant and the person providing help. This is important for migrants who lack assistance from family or close friends. Membership to the MTN is not limited to those from the same hometown. Anyone can be absorbed by the MTN if at least one member of the MTN gains that person's trust and the new member adopts the social obligations and relationships of trust within the network. As elaborated later in this book, the new member can be another international migrant or a nonmigrant (but one who actively participates in the functionality of the social network, such as an American employer, coyote, labor recruiter, neighbor, worker, friend, government official, etc.). For example, during fieldwork in the United States, I met a Guatemalan migrant who was living in the same home and working in the same restaurant as some of the migrants from the medium-sized town in Mexico that I studied. I interviewed the Guatemalan migrant, and he stated that the "Mexicans" (what he called them) wanted to help him. They found him a job and let him live with them.

Finally, the members of an MTN are subject to social rejection or punishment if the social expectations of behavior are not followed and/or the relationships of trust are not kept. Such behavior could jeopardize the rest of the members of the MTN. In the following section, I present the membership requirements for someone to belong to an MTN, taking into account the context of the place of origin of the prospective migrant, whether rural or urban.

Rural Community's Migration-Trust Network Membership

The migrants who are helped and those who provide the help do not necessarily have to know each other before meeting at the destination. For someone to qualify to receive help to migrate and settle in the United States, a number of conditions apply. Such conditions have nothing to do with whether the migrant is a close or weak tie to the person who is providing the help. Instead, the conditions depend on whether or not the migrant is from the same community of origin as the person providing help, or from a smaller community nearby. This is especially true for those who migrate from rural villages. These conditions can be met if the prospective migrant meets certain requirements, which may include (but are not limited to) one or more of the following:

1. The community of origin is small enough for everyone to know each other in order to allow social monitoring between community members to take place effectively.
2. The prospective migrant was born in the community of origin of the person providing help.

3. The prospective migrant was born in a small village or town that is located near the rural village or hometown of the person providing the help.

4. The prospective migrant married a person who was born in the rural village or hometown of the person providing the help.

5. The prospective migrant previously traveled with the person providing the help, or with a friend or family member of this person, while crossing to the United States.

6. The prospective migrant has no ties whatsoever to the person providing the help, but they met each other in the United States by working in the same place or living in the same apartment complex and have developed some sort of trust relationship, for example.

7. Both migrants share similar migratory experiences, and/or struggles back home, which cause them to identify with each other.

For all the above conditions, the reputation of those who need help becomes very important. Those who have violated the social expectations and values of the community members or peer group in the past, would be rejected from their membership in the MTN.

Urban Community's Migration-Trust Network Membership

To belong to an MTN, urban-origin migrants usually need to have been members of some kind of clique-like network, peer group, or intimate group before their international migration trip. These groups will already have at least one member who is a migrant in the United States. Some of the circumstances in which urban-origin migrants can access MTNs are:

1. The prospective migrant originally migrated from a rural area to an urban area (within Mexico), allowing him or her access to the MTN from his or her original rural community of origin (Massey et al. 1987).

2. The prospective migrant has a family member in the United States who is willing to help him or her migrate and who is already a member of an MTN in the United States.

3. The prospective migrant has a coworker, friend, paisano, compadre, or cuate who is a member of an MTN in the United States and with whom he or she had an intimate relationship of trust in the urban place of origin.

4. The prospective migrant meets someone (not necessarily someone who he or she has met before) upon arrival in the United States who has member-

ship in an MTN in the United States and is able to gain the trust of that person.

Only those urban-dwellers who are able to access a well-established MTN will receive support to migrate and settle in the United States. On the other hand, those who are helped either by family members or through other ties who do not belong to MTNs may suffer the fragmentation of those ties (Menjívar 2000). In other words, the relationships migrants have with those who originally helped them tend to rupture after some time if these people are family members or other nonnetwork ties. This rupture of ties can be due to the nature of social relationships in urban areas, where more individualistic behavior is practiced and there is a lack of social monitoring among the members of an MTN. When the rupture of ties occurs, the urban-dwellers, in most cases, are able to gain access to another MTN via a process I call "the MTN Effect," which is explained in detail in chapter 4. This is when the urban-dweller is absorbed by another, already established MTN to which he or she has access via his or her job, or any other social stage such as the church.

The Social Forces Driving the Migration-Trust Networks

The Role of Religion in Migration-Trust Networks

Hagan (2008) provides a new perspective of international migration, arguing that religion plays an important role both in the decision to migrate and during the international migration experience. She emphasizes the dangerous journey that immigrants from Latin America and Mexico face and argues that religion often helps them gather the strength to get through the difficult journey. Levitt (2007), in her recent book, *God Needs No Passport*, presents evidence of the extent to which immigrants transcend national borders through the practice of religion. Other scholars prior to Hagan and Levitt introduced the importance of religion in the international migration experience, such as Durand and Massey (1995) in their study on *retablo* art.

Important to migrants and nonmigrants in the transnational context are faith, fellowship, and trust in others. These practices are very much interrelated. During my ethnographic work, I found no rural or urban difference in how people discussed or approached their religious faith. God was appealed to for physical and emotional sustenance in both contexts in similar ways, although religious celebrations were practiced more often in the rural areas of origin. During my interviews, most people described a fellowship in which they would help others in need. Respondents in Mexico as well as in the United States commonly stated, "We have to help others, so God will help us," or, "it's better to give than to receive [*es mejor dar que recibir*]."

Migrants and nonmigrants really believe that if they do good things for other people, then good things are going to happen for them as well. Even if people have very little, they still offer to share what they have with others. One lady said, "If I have a piece of bread, I will keep half and give the other half to others." Not only do migrants regularly hear this in Mexico and in the United States, but they also see it lived out. During all the years I observed the practices of the migrants and nonmigrants from the four communities, I witnessed several instances when people did not have very much and shared what little they had with others. Once I arrived to a home for an interview, and the family was just about to eat a late dinner. In order to accommodate me, I noticed that they had very little food on their plates. I was very embarrassed and did not know how to respond. I refused their invitation for dinner multiple times, but they kept saying, "Where two people eat, three can eat as well." This is also a very common saying in Mexico and in other Latin American countries, as I had the exact same experience in El Salvador. It was often difficult to interpret such practices as religious or just a part of the culture. I identified it as religious because people would often mention God during our conversations.

When I asked about their decision to migrate under extremely dangerous conditions, most migrants answered, "[B]ecause I knew God would protect me that is why I decided to take such a dangerous journey. . . .We are all in the hands of God, so I placed myself on God's hands." Several migrants shared the same sentiments in Mexico and in El Salvador, which indicated that they were driven by their faith in God. They trusted that God was going to protect them from any harm throughout their dangerous journey and beyond, as they also trusted that they were going to do well in the United States. Doing well largely meant they would be safe and able to eventually send money back home to their loved ones.

Religious beliefs and the values associated with migrant and nonmigrant culture leads to mutual cooperation in the transnational context. A large part of the individual and/or collective remittances are designated for the church and for religious practices back home. In most rural villages and towns, the first money sent by migrants in the form of collective remittances usually goes to the local community's church. Migrants want to build a church, make improvements to an existing one, or build a plaza in front of a church in order to celebrate the annual fiestas patronales back in their community of origin. Even in the United States, migrants celebrate their fiestas patronales—for example, in "Casa Guanajuato" in Dallas, Texas—but on a smaller scale than is done at the place of origin. I experienced the celebrations in both places, at the origin and at the destination, and in both places, religious faith (including prayer) was one of the most important components.

Fiestas patronales is a religious event in which those living in eight surrounding communities are chosen to embark on a novenary, or a nine-day pilgrimage to honor the saint of a main community. On different days, members from different villages carry an effigy of the patron saint to the main community and leave. Honoring the saint involves praying directly to the saint, reciting the prayers of the rosary, and prayer for everything else that affects the people's lives, including international migration. Women pray that they will have something to eat at the table that day; men pray to have a job. Prayers are offered for those who left for the United States so they may have a good life and be able to find work in order to send remittances.

On the ninth day, peripheral communities travel once again to the main community for a mass, followed by a grand festival. The fiestas patronales then becomes the epitome of how religious faith is expressed by international migrants in the transnational context. Through the fiestas patronales, migrants also demonstrate their comparative success to those at the place of origin and to members of other communities at the periphery as they endeavor to host a nice event for those visiting from surrounding communities.

Other activities also take place during the fiestas patronales. International migrants generally return home for the celebrations, so a number of first communions and baptisms are also observed. With many family members present, everyone assists in these very important religious celebrations. Fiestas patronales also provides an opportunity for some community members to benefit by selling cultural crafts or food to the visitors. Everyone in the community takes an active role. Religion is practiced in different ways through cultural events and/or religious manifestations, which take place in the transnational context through social transformations of social behavior. Religious practices occur at the places of origin as well as at the places of destination regardless of where the migrants are or the obstacles they may confront through migration.

Religion and Its Relationship with Trust

Unquestioningly, religion is influential in social networks for the procuring of trust. For example, in the methodology in chapter 1 I explained how in order to implement the survey in the first rural village, we needed to ask the priest for help. It was not until the priest of the church introduced the research team to those who attended Sunday mass that people then began to answer our survey questions. Later, it was very easy to gain access to the second village nearby as the word had already spread from one village to the next that we represented no threat to the people in those communities. From that experience it was clear that the people in those communities trusted the priest and anyone else the priest trusted as well.

Also during the visits to the area in the following years, I witnessed the community connection, not only in those two villages, but also in villages within the surrounding fifteen miles or so. I was regularly invited to celebrations that took place in nearby villages, which revealed how connected people were from one rural village to the next in terms of distributing information via friends and family ties, and the extent to which they all shared the same religious faith, fellowship, spirit, and trust in others through their faith in God.

Another cultural practice in which I was able to observe the deep social connection between the villages and religion was through the practice of soccer. Migrants in the United States not only sent money to fix the churches and to support the priests, but they also sent the trophies they won playing soccer to the local church in their community. Altars in churches at the place of origin were decorated with soccer trophies as offerings. Near the trophies were pictures of the teams where one could see that migrants from different villages in Guanajuato were members of soccer teams in the United States, providing evidence that the people from different villages were migrating to the same places of destination. Thus, this phenomenon demonstrates how important religion and the church are for those who left, and for those who stayed behind.

It was more difficult to connect the issues of trust to religion in a medium-sized town or in the city. However, during the church services we attended, I observed the same devotion to God and to the Virgin of Guadalupe as I saw in the rural villages. The priests in urban areas offered the same sermon messages, which very often centered on caring for and helping others.

In the United States, the people attended church with the same devotion as they did back home; it did not matter if their place of origin was rural or urban. I also attended church in the barrios where I did my fieldwork, and I observed the same atmosphere of devotion as I observed in Mexico. Most of the rituals and administrative formalities at the church in the United States that serve immigrant communities are conducted the same way as in Mexico. The services in these churches are different from those that serve the English-speaking population in the United States. For example, in Mexico, people attend church and no one is aware of how much money people donate to the church during the mass, as envelopes are not distributed with names on them. In contrast, when I attended English-speaking masses, attendees returned their envelopes with their family names printed on them (and even account numbers on them).

In addition, the Spanish-speaking masses allowed for more informality than the English-speaking masses. For example, people do not have to be members of the Spanish churches to receive services such as catechism classes for the children, baptisms, first communion, or wedding celebrations. In the English-speaking churches, people had to be members to receive such services. However, English-speaking churches would often relax these requirements for Spanish-speaking immigrants according to their needs. When I visited English-speaking churches and took part in mass, I was often asked to exhibit more formality. This was not the case when I visited Spanish-speaking churches. I interpret such informality from the churches that serve the Hispanic community as a way to help people feel more comfortable joining and practicing their religion in the United States.

In some cases, people changed their religious affiliation after coming to the United States, but they maintained a strong faith in either case. This is exemplified in the case of Guadalupe. In the summer of 2002, I interviewed Guadalupe, a middle-aged woman from a large city in Guanajuato. She lived with her family in Dallas, specifically in the Oak Lift neighborhood, a segregated immigrant Latino community. A couple and their baby, who had just arrived from Mexico, were living with her at the time of the interview. Guadalupe, her husband, and her seven children had been living in the United States for ten years. Several other relatives, all of whom I visited, also lived in the same neighborhood, about four to five blocks away. Their distance from Guadalupe's home was unlike the people from smaller places of origin who lived in the same apartment complexes or next door to each other in clusters. Most of Guadalupe's relatives had emigrated and lived

first at Guadalupe's home and then began living on their own, so I identified Guadalupe and her husband as the pioneers of that particular MTN
to Dallas from the city. Setting an interview with Guadalupe was difficult
because she said she had to go to church. When I asked for any free time
for the interview, she said she had to be at church every single evening on
weekdays and all day Saturdays and Sundays. I had never met anyone who
spent so much time at a church, so I decided to ask her why she was going
to church that much. Guadalupe responded,

> When we lived in Mexico and when we [her family] arrived to the US we
> all used to be Catholic, and so we had faith in Jesus Christ, and we went to
> church every Sunday. Then suddenly right after we arrived to the US, my son
> was very, very sick, and so we were introduced to the Christian [Protestant]
> church by a friend who worked in the same factory with me. We began at-
> tending that church and we all became Christian when my son got well. No
> doctor could do anything for him, but at the Christian church, we all prayed
> for him to get well, and he did. Now my whole family and I are dedicated
> to that church. We never imagined that we would ever leave the Catholic
> church, but after this miracle happened, we all agreed to do so. We go there
> to attend mass and to volunteer every day. There we all help each other as
> brothers and sisters. We now dedicate our lives to the church.

Most migrants from Mexico and Latin America are Catholic (Saenz 2005).
For Guadalupe and her family, the event they considered to be a miracle
became the catalyst that caused them to decide to join a Protestant church.
As a result, they changed the way they practiced religion.

Religion plays an extremely important role throughout the international
migratory experience of the migrants. Their faith is what helps them believe
they will survive at the end of their dangerous journey and that they will
be successful at the destination. One important way in which international
migrants portray their faith regarding international migration is through
the retablo art culture and folklore, as seen in Jorge Durand and Douglas Massey's book, *Miracles at the Border* (1995). Retablos are very small
paintings on laminate sheets, no larger than four by six inches, that portray
the occurrence of miracles. People place them at the church as an offering
to the saint they believe is responsible for the miracle. Most international
migrants attribute the miracles to either La Virgin de Guadalupe or to La
Virgin de San Juan de los Lagos. They ask an artist to paint an illustration

of the miracle and to write the text describing the story of how it happened. The migrants' religious faith becomes extremely important, enabling them with the courage to begin their journey (Hagan 2008).

Participation in an MTN is also born from religious faith. It is often believed that by helping others, God will be with them and will multiply and return what they give to others. A typical phrase heard not only in Mexico, but also in El Salvador, describes this: *"Hoy por ti, Mañana por mí,"* which translates to "Today for you, and tomorrow for me." For example, a woman from the medium-sized town who I interviewed in Chicago added to one of her responses:

"Es que cuando uno le ayuda a sus padres o a otra gente, el dinero se le multiplica a uno."

("The thing is, that when you help your parents or others, the money will multiply for you.")

"Lo que yo tenga, yo lo comparto con los demás, que al cabo que Dios provee más adelante."

("Whatever I have, I share it with others, because in the end, God will keep providing for us.")

For this reason, migrants also attend church once they arrive in the United States. They carry with them religious images, make altars in their homes, or even make elaborate altars outside their homes in order to express their religious faith and feel more protected. Ricardo Arjona and the Intocables also reflect such faith in popular songs such as "El Mojado," where they sing:

Dijo adiós con una mueca disfrazada de sonrisa,
(Said goodbye with an expression faked as a smile,)
Y le suplico a su Dios crucificado en la repisa, el resguardo de los suyos.
(and asked his God crucified on the wall to look after his family.)

The lyrics of this popular song, which has been broadcast on radio stations and TV programs throughout Latin America and the United States, reflect the way in which undocumented migrants leave their homelands and how they leave and arrive with their faith. The lyrics are a great example of how religious beliefs play a very important role in the international migration process.[1] They reflect migrants' trust in God to take care of their family members left behind. Not only will the family be safe, but the person leaving for the North will also be able to cross the border successfully, quickly find a job in the United States, and begin providing for the family back home.

The following passages from the Bible were regularly mentioned at church by priests during my fieldwork and discussed among the people during everyday conversations. These passages reflect how migrants and nonmigrants are encouraged to increase their faith through Bible teachings:

Do not be afraid any longer, only believe. (Mark 5:36, NIV)

In God, whose word I praise, in God I trust; I will not be afraid. What can mortal man do to me? (Psalm 56:4, NIV)

Jesus said, "What do you want Me to do for you?" And the blind man said to Him, "Teacher, I want to regain my sight!" And Jesus said to him, "Go your way; your faith has made you well." And immediately he received his sight and began following Him on the road. (Mark 10:51–52, NIV)

The LORD your God, who is going before you, will fight for you, as he did for you in Egypt, before your very eyes, and in the desert. There you saw how the LORD your God carried you, as a father carries his son, all the way you went until you reached this place. In spite of this, you did not trust in the LORD your God, who went ahead of you on your journey, in fire by night and in a cloud by day, to search out places for you to camp and to show you the way you should go. (Deuteronomy 1:30–33, NIV)

They also pray for their family members to be protected while they are away.

In addition, trust can be driven by religious faith. One of the most important principles of any religion is the emphasis on brotherhood and trusting in others. God trusts us, and we trust God; therefore, we should trust others. Bible teachings, especially in Catholicism, emphasize trust and loyalty to others even when they are considered enemies. For example, the following Bible passage encourages helping others in need:

Do not take advantage of a hired man who is poor and needy, whether he is a brother Israelite or an alien living in one of your towns. (Deuteronomy 24:14, NIV)

The Bible also teaches that if you are slapped on one cheek, you should turn to be slapped on the other cheek. As I attended church regularly in both places, in Mexico and in the United States, members were often reminded of these passages. For example, the passage in Mathew states:

You have heard that it was said, "Eye for eye, and tooth for tooth." But I tell you, do not resist an evil person. If anyone slaps you on the right cheek, turn to them the other cheek also. And if anyone wants to sue you and take your shirt, hand over your coat as well. If anyone forces you to go one mile, go with them two miles. Give to the one who asks you, and do not turn away from the one who wants to borrow from you. (Mathew 5:38 – 42, NIV)

Jesus answered, "If you want to be perfect, go, sell your possessions and give to the poor, and you will have treasure in heaven. Then come, follow me." (Matthew 19:21, NIV)

The Bible emphasizes that we need to love and trust others because we are all sons and daughters of God. It also teaches to forgive others of their mistakes in the same way that God forgives us from our own sins. For example:

On the contrary: If your enemy is hungry, feed him; if he is thirsty, give him something to drink. (Romans 12:20, NIV)

Therefore, thinking badly of others or not trusting others can also be against religious teachings.

Religious faith expresses several things, such as the belief that the migrant will arrive safely to the United States, find a job, settle, and send money back to his or her family members. They have faith that the migrant's family will be safe back home and that they will receive everything they need for their daily subsistence. In addition, whatever help or resources they provide to others, God will multiply those resources back to them. Most importantly, religious faith can encourage people to trust others and to think of them as brothers and sisters in Christ. Therefore, groups of people (or even entire communities) who follow such religious beliefs and Bible teachings create a set of norms, social values, and social expectations for others based on those beliefs, emphasizing faith, fellowship, and trust in others.

The act of international migration for most people is such a difficult and dangerous journey that it requires the magic of religious faith and the strong belief in God and in other religious images, such as the faith in La Virgen de Guadalupe, or La Virgen de San Juan de Los Lagos. It is through the same faith and religious practices international migrants are able to make the decision and cope with the struggles and dangers associated with the international migration journey (Hagan 2008; Levitt 2007). Given such strong religious faith, when things go well those events are considered miracles, as is manifested through the retablo painting practices studied by Durand and Massey (1995). In addition, it is also through religious faith that international migrants are able to learn to trust others and engage in altruistic behavior and are able to offer their support to others and become good citizens of a Migration-Trust Network.

Bounded Solidarity

According to Portes and Sensenbrenner, *bounded solidarity* "focuses on those situational circumstances that can lead to the emergence of principled group-oriented behavior quite apart from any early value introjections" (1324). In other words, the members of the group develop certain expectations of collective behavior in which any actions or decisions made should benefit not just the individual, but all the members of the group. Therefore, they no longer think of themselves only as individuals, but as members of a group. The members of the MTN do not mind slowing their upward mobility to help others migrate internationally. Sending individual remittances and collective remittances back home is another example of their collective sentiment. Bounded solidarity also develops from the experience of being vulnerable to exploitation and intimidation because of their undocumented migratory status. Rural migrants have greater chances of becoming victims of exploitation once in the United States given their lower levels of education and possible lack of skills to perform urban-type jobs. As a result, bounded solidarity is especially important for rural-origin migrants. It is also important for urban dwellers, who may have higher levels of human capital, but are vulnerable because they lack legal documents.

Enforceable Trust

Most international migrants feel empathy toward each other because they understand the situation back home and the reasons they had to make the difficult decision to migrate (see quote by Oscar in chapter 1). For most international migrants, the experience of leaving everything behind—friends, family, loved ones, and their own lives—and potentially never seeing them again can be very traumatic. The journey to the United States (or any other country) can be extremely dangerous and result in life-threatening situations, leaving an indelible mark in the minds of migrants. Being ignorant of the customs and language of the destination only adds to their anxiety. Therefore, international migrants empathize with one another and also prospective migrants. According to Portes and Sensenbrenner (1993), such empathy toward other international migrants who have had similar experiences can be the catalyst of a sentiment of solidarity that results in what they call *enforceable trust*. The concept of enforceable trust is related to migration because it provides an explanation for social cohesion among migrants (Weber [1922] 1963). According to Portes and Sensenbrenner, social cohesion emanating from common origins in a small community is reinforced by the enforceable trust that arises from the commonality of the migration experience itself. This creates bonds among immigrants and

> [G]ives rise to a multiplicity of social networks that frequently coalesce into tightly knit ethnic communities. The social capital emerging from the monitoring capacity of these communities is best referred to as enforceable trust. . . . Individuals behave according to expectations not only because they must, but out of fear of punishment or in anticipation of rewards. The predictability in the behavior of members of a group is in direct proportion to its sanctioning capacity. (Portes and Sensenbrenner 1993, 1332)

In other words, when individuals belong to an intimate social group, which is the case for migrants from small rural villages or small communities, they are more likely to experience enforceable trust. On the other hand, those who migrate from urban or larger communities may or may not belong to an intimate group; it depends on the types of relationships they have with other migrants. If a number of individuals belonged to an intimate group at work or on their soccer teams, for example, then it is very likely that if those individuals were to migrate, they would also experience enforceable trust. Given that enforceable trust is also caused by the commonality of the international migration experience, the shared experience may suffice for urban dwellers who meet in the United States to form an intimate group.

It is through bonded solidarity and the enforceable trust mechanisms that the paisanaje sentiment develops and allows the MTN to expand because it fosters cohesive behavior, even among those who have never met before, such as Pancho and Jose at the beginning of this book. Pancho decided to support and help Jose get settled. Jose, without the help of Pancho, would have struggled even more. Their shared migratory experiences and their struggles joined them to the same MTN once they met each other in the United States. The reciprocal relations that result from the cohesion created by the enforceable trust and bonded solidarity mechanisms results in a form of risk-pooling behavior in which favors are not returned, but passed on to future prospective migrants. I elaborate on this form of behavior in the forthcoming chapters.

Social Consequences for Breaking the Trust and Social Values

Social Punishment in Rural Areas of Origin and for Rural-Origin Migrants

What were the social consequences for those who did not agree to meet the expectations of other community members and help others migrate? Three interviewees from the rural areas of origin told me that they did not ask anyone for help to migrate. They recalled how difficult it was for them to get to the United States by themselves, sleeping in an abandoned car for several days in the middle of an abandoned field, not eating for several days, and wearing the same clothes until finding a job. I did not initially understand why they were so disconnected from the rest of the social network of paisanos and family members from their origin community. In fact, these respondents mentioned having migrated to an area where no one else from their community of origin had ever migrated before.

I discovered that these few individuals had difficulty finding social capital to migrate internationally because they had been rejected by the community members prior to their first migratory trip. In some way, they violated or did not meet the expectations of the rest of the community before migrating. They may have done something immoral like assaulting someone or robbing a local home or store. I found out what happened in those isolated cases through casual conversations with other community members. Clearly, those who had violated the social expectations were also victims of social gossip. When people referred to the violators, they did not hesitate to tell me all the details of what they had done wrong. For example, a lady told me that one of them traveled by himself to Fresno, California, where nobody else from their community had migrated; I call him Sergio. As part of an unrelated conversation, she said,

> One day a ten-year-old child was playing near Sergio's backyard, and he saw that Sergio had in his trash some of the empty boxes of some of the electronics which were missing at the local store. The boy told his parents, and then the

boy's parents told the store owner. The store owner then reported the case to the authorities of the local municipality who came to town and did a crime investigation within the next few days of the report. The authorities found that Sergio still had some of the missing electronics at his home. Sergio was sent to jail for a couple of years, and when he got out, he left to the US. Now he is back, but people don't talk to him, only his very close family, like his parents and his wife and children. His far family members like his cousins and uncles don't talk to him after he did that.

After this conversation, I heard the same story about Sergio from his distant relatives, so I realized that the gossip was true. It was very interesting for me to learn that even the family members stopped talking to Sergio after he committed the crime. Later, I learned the history of the robbery and realized it coincided with the date Sergio said he left for the United States. Sergio only spent four months in the United States because his situation there was very precarious. He was not able to find a way to save money to send back to his family because he had to pay a lot of money for rent after finding a job, and this caused him to return to Mexico. In Sergio's case, it was very difficult to settle in the United States, at least temporarily, because he lacked social capital from others.

Since there is no formal policing in these rural villages, people enforce values and norms by social punishment. Individuals who want to migrate know they would be denied help because of prior immoral behavior; so those like Sergio, who have become stigmatized, decide not to ask for help in the first place and attempt to migrate on their own. This example is important because it shows the impact of social punishment in the transnational context. Those in the community of origin, as well as those living in the United States, generally learn about the social violation, so in both places the punishment is effective. For this reason, Sergio was not able to contact anyone in the United States for help to migrate. He was afraid that he was going to be denied the help due to his criminal act from the past. Even after he returned, the punishment was still in effect. However, those very close to him decided to support him. The other two individuals who were punished also had experienced rejection from people in the community for different reasons that had to do with violations to the moral values and expectations from the village residents. One of the respondents had cheated on his wife with her sister, which was considered a huge violation of the moral values of the community. The other individual was considered very irresponsible because he had become a drunk and used drugs, so nobody trusted that he would be able to maintain his job in the United States if someone recommended him. For the same reason, he was denied support from others in regards to a place to stay, food, clothing, and so forth.

Another instance of social punishment surfaced when international migrants did not send remittances to their family members at the place of origin who were in need. The following quote from my field notes reflects such a scenario:

> In some cases, I found people who had nothing to eat and whose family members abroad had stopped sending remittances. A few young men had left the pueblo [town] and forgotten about their family members, or their mother after a few years or sometimes after getting married. Some people mentioned that they never heard from their family members again. Those who failed to send remittances to their family members were seen very negatively by the rest of the people in the rancho and were stigmatized.

I learned over the years that only those young migrants who got married once in the United States were excused for not sending remittances to their other family members, especially to their parents. Remittances are expected more so from male or female migrants who are not yet married. Once they marry, people understand they have other expenses, such as trying to support their own family, especially if they have children. I also learned that the punishment for those who never sent remittances back to their families was greater than for those who started but then stopped sending money completely. The single migrants who never sent money but had jobs in the United States, and were known to spend the money on themselves, buying beer or engaging in other types of selfish spending, were stigmatized if their family members back home were in need. Sending money back home in the form of remittances is an informal commitment, so if one does not try to do so and their family is in need, the situation is judged as a violation of the social expectations of those left behind in the community.

Those who stopped sending money because they no longer had a job were excused, but those who had the means to do so faced stigmatization and gossip, particularly at the place of origin. The violators were humiliated repeatedly by being told directly they were irresponsible where their parents were concerned. The punishment was harsher at the place of origin because those who stayed behind had to cope with the suffering and impoverishment of the parents because they did not receive remittances, and many community members themselves had to provide help to the migrant's parents. These members witnessed firsthand the consequences of the young migrants' irresponsibility. International migrants are subject to punishment in the transnational context, but the level of punishment in each place, the origin or destination, may vary depending on the type of violation and how those who stay behind and those who are in the United States understand the consequences of any particular type of violation.

A respondent shared how much she had to comply with the social expectations of the community members at the place of origin: "Here, people are scared of one another." This lady spoke about being stigmatized because her daughter had gotten pregnant in the United States. Again, social monitoring is not restricted to the place of origin alone; it also occurs at the place of destination. Social monitoring has a transnational nature in which those at the place of origin judge those abroad, and those abroad also judge those at the place of origin.

Social punishment not only crossed international boundaries, but extended to the nearby communities as well. I learned of instances in which people from nearby villages were ostracized, but in general, social control was exercised in the community where migrants were from. The place of origin set the moral course for others from a different location to follow if they used that network in the transnational context.

Punishment for Those from Urban Origins

It was more difficult in urban origins to detect social punishment from others given the lack of social monitoring in such areas. The punishment, if any, was ejection from the group and only occurred among those who belonged to peer groups or clique-like groups, such as coworkers at the urban place of origin, the members of a sports team, and so forth. During the time I monitored the peer groups in Mexico, as well as in the United States, there were no rejections.

Although I never witnessed anyone rejected from a peer group over the years, I did witness instances where urban dwellers experienced shameful rejection from others. For example, Sofia, from the Chicago area, was difficult to interview. After several requests, she told me over the phone,

The truth is that I don't want to meet with you because I am scared that others from my family and my (city neighborhood) will find out that my husband is in jail. Also, I am afraid because I am undocumented and I am scared for me and my children. We don't want to get deported, so I feel very scared to meet with you because I cannot trust you.

I had received her contact information through a family member when I visited her neighborhood in the city. Sofia went on to explain that she lived isolated from her other family members and friends because she was trying to hide the unfortunate situation of her husband. When I asked if she could give me information about another family I could interview in the area, she answered,

No, we don't know anyone here. We used to live in San Francisco where some of our neighborhood friends lived, but we left because my husband had problems at his job. One of his friends from the neighborhood had recommended him for the job and my husband got to work late all the time, so he got fired. Then his friends from our neighborhood back in Mexico whom had recommended him for the job stop talking to him for that reason. We then moved here to Chicago because my husband found a job on his own as he had heard of another company who needed workers over here, and so he got the phone number and contacted them directly. Then my husband got in trouble at his job selling drugs, and so now he is in jail. I don't want nobody to find out from back home because I am very ashamed.

Sofia's husband was ejected from his MTN in San Francisco due to his work ethic violations on the job where he had received a recommendation. This is a very good example of social expectations of behavior also including work ethics, especially if another MTN member recommended him for the job. Her husband being in jail was even worse than the loss of his job, and for that reason she was very afraid if others back home found out about their situation.

Among urban-origin migrants, I learned of people being very supportive at the beginning of the migratory career of the prospective migrant. They assisted migrants on their journey to the United States by providing housing, transportation, food, and help finding employment. However, as described in chapter 4 as part of "the MTN effect," in some cases, the migrant and the person who first offered the help (usually a family member) in many instances experienced conflict among themselves. This resulted from fragile social bonds at the outset. Conflicts, brought on by individualist mind-sets, were so extreme that migrants and their helpers stopped talking to each other. This usually happened to those who migrated from urban origin areas and who were helped strictly by family members, rather than the clique-like networks of peer groups I described earlier. The lack of social monitoring among the urban dwellers who were not members of preexisting relationships of trust did not allow for the social networks to be maintained and perpetuated in the same way as the rural-based networks or the urban-based peer groups did. More details of such conflicts are presented in chapter 4.

To summarize, social punishment due to social monitoring was usually effective among those from rural areas of origin or among those urban origin dwellers where preexisting social relations of cohesiveness and trust were central. The enforcement of social norms usually took place in the transnational context, although the degree of enforcement varied depending on the nature of the violation and how the social violation was received in the area of origin and at the place of destination. Social monitoring and punishment appears to exist in both settings, rural and urban, but only among those who belong to peer groups at the place of origin, or to MTNs at the place of destination. Those with more individualist mind-sets were not able to acquire the same quality social capital and support as those who were part of Migration-Trust Networks.

Types of Ties

In an MTN, most of the ties function similarly as a result of the social mechanisms that reinforce the social support and behavior of the members of the network. For this reason, kin ties, friends, paisanos, compadres, *cuates*, and even strangers join the MTN and become strong ties. As mentioned at the beginning of chapter 2, paisanos play a crucial role in MTNs given their important role as pioneers and also because their ties strengthen as members of the MTN arrive to the United States and begin to support others. In this section, I elaborate on the other possible type of ties among MTN members besides the paisano, which are *compadrazgo*, cuates, friends, and kin ties.

One very important way in which both rural- or urban-origin international migrants increase their chances of receiving social support at the time of migration is through the use of fictitious ties. *Cuatismo* is a type of fictitious tie practiced with the purpose of strengthening social relation-ships, especially among males. Cuatismo is a form of friendship, but stron-ger. Cuates usually get together more often than normal friends, share in-timate information, and support each other more strongly. Migrants who are cuates get together on Sundays, for example, to watch soccer games and drink beer, plan vacation trips together, spend holiday celebrations together, and also become compadres in order to further strengthen their relationship. I found most of these types of relationships among migrants and their coworkers. Migrants often said to me, *"el es mi cuate del trabajo"* ("he is my buddy from work"). Such ties may be even stronger than those among best friends or family members. When two migrants became cuates, I understood that they were potential members of the same MTN.

In Mexico and other parts of Latin America, compadrazgo is a way to build stronger relationships of trust, or to convert a weak relationship into a strong relationship in which participants grow closer (see Lomnitz 1977). Becoming a compadre can mean even more than being a cuate; it is a stronger relationship and more focused on family. One way to become a person's compadre or comadre is to baptize his or her child, thereby assum-ing responsibility for the child if something were to happen to the parents. This demonstrates trust and care, which in turn strengthens their existing relationship and upgrades it to something similar to a kinship tie, or even stronger in certain cases.

Compadres and comadres tend to interact with each other with more fre-quency and spend more time together than with their own family members. Through compadrasgo, even those who have never met before can trans-form their social relationship into a strong relationship of trust and loyalty in the future. Migrants benefit from those types of fictitious ties because more social support and social capital becomes available to them.

For example, during visits to a family in San Francisco who were origi-nally from the city in this study, I noticed that two of the brothers who I had met in Mexico later on became compadres because one baptized the son of the other. It was interesting that the brothers called each other "compa-dres" instead of calling themselves brothers, or simply using their names. It seemed that for them, it was more important to be compadres than broth-ers, thereby strengthening their relationship. The same happened among friends who became compadres. The new relationship meant more to them even if they had been best friends in the past.

I noticed, for example, that once two friends who claimed to have been cuates for a long time became compadres, they began to visit each other more often to spend time with each other's families. I also noticed an increase in the level of commitment and social support they provided each other. For example, Juan, who was single and from a medium-sized town, became a compadre of Miguel who was originally from Mexico City. After having met each other in the United States at their jobs, they became compadres after three years. Juan told me about his relationship with Miguel after they became compadres:

> We were cuates for a long time and spent a lot of time together playing soccer and getting together to have a beer after work all the time. Our relationship grew stronger when we became compadres. I got married and Miguel became my compadre as he baptized my son, Carlos. At that point we began to see each other more often, go to church together on Sundays, go on vacations together, spend the holidays together. Now our relationship is stronger than if he was part of my family. I see him more often than I see my own brothers.

This example of Juan and Miguel exemplifies the extent to which fictitious ties can be strong ties—sometimes stronger than family ties.

Friendships are very important for the members of an MTN, as they are sources of social capital. Flores-Yeffal and Aysa-Lastra (2011) found that about 30 to 40 percent of migrants' friends in rural and urban areas helped by providing them with accommodation. According to the solidarity survey (conducted in both a town and city), 20 to 30 percent of friends assisted migrants.

After family members, friends provide most of the help migrants need. This is the case especially in urban settings where migrants have to diversify their ties more than in rural settings in order to gain access to social capital. Table 2.1 shows the mean statistics of the four communities surveyed for this study. One can see that the type of context dictates the number of friends one may have available in the United States at the time of migration. Rural residents report having about ten friends ever in the United States for each head of household, while migrants from the city report approximately two friends, and migrants from the medium-sized town report about seven friends. However, in preliminary statistical analysis using the Mexican Migration Project data (MMP 128), Flores-Yeffal and Aysa-Lastra found that in the medium-sized towns the number of friends who provided help was a lot greater than in any other setting (small rural areas and larger cities). More

Table 2.1   Mean Statistics for Heads of Household with Migration Experience

Variables	City	Town	Rural 1	Rural 2
Sex	89	95	100	94
Years of education	5.47	5.38	3.17	2.31
Number of friends in the US	1.76	5.42	4.43	4.65
Number of friends ever in US	2.40	7.29	9.22	10.94
Contacted relatives	51.11	50.63	50.77	60.78
Number of US trips	1.49	1.78	4.88	4.75
Months of US experience	57.51	59.00	80.77	114.80
N	45	79	65	51

research is needed to investigate the role of friends in medium-sized towns versus other types of localities.

Family members are usually considered strong ties and are very close to the migrants. Family members feel more obligated to help other family members. In addition, the tie is considered a relationship for life. Wierzbicki (2004) explains the differences between friendship and family ties. She states:

> We can pick our neighbors, to the extent that income and other social constraints allow us mobility. We can pick our co-workers, to some degree, in that we have some choice of occupation and job and thus the type of people with whom we work. We can pick our friends, subject to constraints of time and the availability of persons with sufficiently common interests. But we cannot pick our kin. The only choice regarding kin is how (and how often) we interact with them . . . kinship ties are permanent, whereas other types of ties can be dropped. (67–68)

Therefore, kin ties play the most important role in providing social capital to prospective migrants in the MTN. As shown in table 4.1 (chapter 4, this volume) and as found by Flores-Yeffal and Aysa-Lastra (2011), family members provide about 50 to 60 percent of the help migrants need. Family members, however, are not always able to help prospective migrants, especially at the beginning of the migratory career of the community and in urban areas of origin. Other ties then have to serve as substitutes, especially paisanos (see Flores-Yeffal and Aysa-Lastra 2011). Paisanos, compadres, and cuates may substitute and reach a similar level of strength as that of kinship ties.

Following are my field notes from the United States about Manuel, a thirty-year-old married man from one of the rural villages:

> He didn't put in any of his own money, nor did he sell any of his belongings in order to go to the US. His brothers paid all the expenses. There is a tradition in which money borrowed from brothers is not paid back. If a paisano lends money, he does require the money paid back but only the expense of the coyote fee. This is not the case for brothers. A migrant does not have to pay back his brother for all the expenses incurred in his first migratory trip, but for all subsequent trips, he needs to find his own financial arrangements.

From this example, one can appreciate how the social commitment may be stronger for kin ties since Manuel's brothers do not require him to pay the money back, but paisanos do. Manuel goes on to explain that paisanos only expect migrants to pay back the money for the coyote, but they do not ask for all the other expenses they have while providing lodging and other help to the new arrivals. When asked if those who had helped expected favors to be returned when they provided help to migrants and nonmigrants without regard to how they were related, 54 percent of migrants said they did not expect favors returned. Of those who had never migrated, 47 percent would not expect the favor to be returned. Notice that the percentage was higher for those with migratory experience. This may mean that those who have not yet migrated are not fully aware of the challenges international migrants face. More research must be done to explore these issues.

I followed several families over the years and observed how they provided help to their kin. The MTN members did not seem to discriminate by the type of tie in the level of assistance they provided each other. I observed that friends and paisanos or compadres and cuates provided the same level of affection and care to the new arrivals as family members did. They all seemed to consider one another family members.

In some cases, family members were more insensitive to prospective migrants than nonblood relatives. Although family members provide social capital, our ethnographic work revealed that a greater degree of conflict may also exist among family members when those who provide the help are isolated migrants who have not joined an MTN.

I discuss this issue in detail in chapter 4, in a section entitled "The MTN effect": I present the scenarios of how family ties for urban-origin migrants were found to be more fragile than their ties with friends or paisanos, which was not the case for migrants from smaller places of origin. Family members did help urban-origin migrants at the beginning of their journey, but once they arrived in the United States, the increased needs of the new arrivals and lack of social monitoring from other community members caused the kin relationship to weaken. In contrast, family ties for migrants from smaller communities and for those belonging to peer groups in urban settings before migrating seem to be subject to the same social monitoring as their paisano and friend ties. This means that all the members of the community, including family members, are being judged and are subject to the same kind of expectations. If rural-origin migrants were to detach themselves from the MTN and isolate themselves, their social ties might also become fragmented due to the lack of social monitoring by other members of the network.

Notes

1. The rest of the lyrics of the song can be found online in Spanish at http://www.lyrics box.com/ricardo-arjona-lyrics-mojado-1gsd7zs.html

CHAPTER THREE

"Hoy por mí, Mañana por ti": Social Capital Shared via Migration-Trust Networks

Martin, who migrated from a medium-sized town and was interviewed in a small town in Indiana, was sharing a house with six other migrants who were neither related to him by kin nor by friendship; he met them shortly after arriving to the United States. He said:

When I got here I was surprised because a guy (*un vato*) who lived in this house and who I'd never met before told me, "Let's go to Wal-Mart." When we got there he told me to get a cart, and when we got to the pants section he said, "What is your size?" I said, "I don't know, 32 in Mexico, here I don't know." He looked at me closely and grabbed a pair of pants. Then he asked me, "What size underwear do you wear?" Then he asked me about socks and he also asked me if I needed a jacket; and he even got me a jacket (*Y hasta una chamarrita me compró*). That impressed me a lot and I felt very good about it. I did the same thing for others who arrived later on. I took them to Wal-Mart like they did for me when I arrived. I did not return the favor directly, but I returned it by helping others like I was once helped.

This quote exemplifies how social ties get transformed from weak ties into strong ties through *migrant solidarity* shared among those who participate in a Migration-Trust Network and how the MTN operates: first, the commonalities with the international migration experience are shared and the bounded solidarity and paisanaje sentiment are created. One person helps the next person and so on without regard to their relationship with the person in the past. In most cases, no direct reciprocity is expected; instead, a form of risk-pooling takes place where the person who received the help is expected to help others in the future. Even if the new migrant wanted to return the favor directly to the person who helped him or her, the need for help would be greater for the new arrivals than for the person who provided the help because he or she was more likely to already be settled.

As exemplified in the previous quote, most international migrants who come to the United States, especially the undocumented, arrive with no possessions and little or no money. Given the difficulty of crossing the border, they come with only the clothes on their backs; they arrive *"con una mano atrás y otra adelante"* ("with one hand in the back and the other one at front"), as it is commonly said in Spanish. The metaphor describes how they arrive without possessions or even clothes, so they have to cover their private parts with one hand in the front and the other one behind. They refer to their situation with humor, joking and making fun of the sad reality of arriving with nothing.

Undocumented international migrants need all types of information, economic assistance, and social support, even if the trip is not their first. They need help to get to the border between Mexico and the United States, then they need to find a trustful smuggler or coyote. Once they arrive in the United States, not only do new arrivals need a place to stay, food to eat, clothes to wear (since they could not carry much with them when they crossed the border), and information such as where to buy groceries, they have a greater need to know how to protect themselves from being caught by the immigration authorities. At the time of arrival at the place of destination, undocumented immigrants also need trustworthy information about the place they are going to reside because of their vulnerability to be deported by immigration authorities. For this reason, in most cases they end up staying with someone they trust in an immigrant enclave where there are many people from the same place of origin (whether urban or rural) who live next door to each other in order to offer support to get going in the new country. In the following sections, I explain the types of help that undocumented international migrants need to both enter and settle in the United States.

The Trip to the United States

The sacrifices made in order to migrate internationally are often underestimated. Testimonies from ethnographic interviews in Mexico and in El Salvador alike describe how some people sold most of their possessions in order to get enough money to begin their migration journey, especially when they left for the first time to the United States. One often heard story is "I sold everything I had, all my furniture, my jewelry, my piece of land with my adobe house, my chickens, my cows . . . so I could get enough money to leave to the north."

The first step is to get to the border between Mexico and the United States, and then find the coyote. In many instances, coyotes will travel with the migrants the entire way from their home community to the United States. For those who do not have such a coyote, the first step is always to find the right information to get to the US-Mexico border. That becomes a real challenge, especially for those who have never traveled to the border. Border towns can be very dangerous since predators know that migrants carry money and that in most instances they are naive and inexperienced about the dangers they may confront in a border city: possible assault, extortion, kidnapping, and rape, among several other types of dangers. For example, one of the respondents told me:

> If you look lost when you arrive, you can become a target, especially if you are in a Mexican bus terminal of a border town, for example. There can be many predators there looking for victims as many of those who arrive to the bus terminals have plans on crossing to the US, and those who are looking to physically assault or take advantage of someone knows that.

Therefore, prospective migrants not only need money to get to the border, but also correct information in terms of where to go, what to say, who to talk to, and how to act along the journey so they can avoid any type of danger.

Crossing the Border

The next step is to cross the border into the United States successfully. If repeatedly unsuccessful, then the prospective migrant usually returns to the home community with thoughts of trying again at a later point, depending on the difficulty of their past experiences. Migrants have reported that if they had a very difficult and/or traumatizing experience, they would not try crossing the border again for a few months. For others, especially women, the psychological trauma was too great, so they never tried to cross again.

Respondents went on to describe how they had been caught by the *migra* several times and had to return home with nothing to come back to. Those who had difficulty soon realized that they had to begin making use of their social networks in order to migrate. Most, however, used their MTNs from the start so that they would not have to sell all their possessions in the first place. Mexican migrants seldomly had to sell all their possessions in order to pay for their trip to the border, but in El Salvador about half of those who

I interviewed stated that they had sold everything they had to leave for the United States. In general, however, especially in the case of Mexican migrants, the members of the MTN would provide all the necessary help for them to make their international journey.

Not only do migrants need to make it to the border or cross several borders, as in the case of Salvadorans, but they also need a good *coyote*, a trustworthy smuggler to help them cross the border(s) successfully and finally arrive to the place of destination (Spener 2009). More importantly, they need to *survive* this journey. For this reason, international migrants, especially if they are undocumented, need trustworthy information and network connections. The information they acquire about a smuggler can mean the difference between living and dying on the way to the United States. Smugglers are well-known for robbing people, raping women, and kidnapping children, but most importantly, they are known for not caring about the lives of their *pollos*, or migrants. It is widely known that coyotes will leave the migrants behind in the desert if they (the migrants) cannot continue with the journey or keep up the pace with the rest of the group. They also place the lives of the migrants at risk by transporting them inside cargo trains, trucks without ventilation, and using them as mules to pass drugs. For that reason, immigrants cannot use just any coyote to cross the border without documents; they need to find a trustworthy smuggler. A greater level of trust is necessary when women and children need to be taken across the border. Women are at risk of being sexually assaulted and children risk getting lost or becoming too weak for the undocumented journey. Thus the question is, how do they find a coyote who can be trusted?

The answer is through social capital. According to David Spener (2009), international migrants learn to trust coyotes or the *coyotaje* practice through social capital, bounded solidarity, and enforceable trust social mechanisms. He describes how, if a coyote does not do a good job, then his reputation is ruined and he may not get anymore business from that specific community. The coyote may also be denounced to the police or to the immigration authorities. As mentioned in chapter 1, social capital refers to the benefits that international migrants acquire from having contacts. In this case, the benefits are acquired from contacts with prior international migration experience to the United States. The best thing prospective migrants can do for themselves is to ask someone with firsthand experience to help them find a trustworthy coyote. Members of MTNs will provide reliable information to others and also will believe and trust the information given by

MTN members. There are different types of coyotes. Some are people from the same town or small rural village who gain knowledge on how to cross from crossing themselves several times. They learn the routes and how and when to cross. During the interviews, I learned that women and children generally crossed the border with this type of coyote, though it was still very difficult for many of them. These types of coyotes were not as useful after the border patrol increased its resources and changed its tactics (Massey and Pren 2012). Migrants needed smugglers that were more professional. This is when social capital became more essential; the coyote had to come from an even more reliable source because the coyote was more likely to be a stranger and the migrants faced even greater danger.

Only someone who has relied on a specific smuggler in a previous migration experience in which the crossing was successful would be able to make such a referral. For many, this is the difference between life and death, so prospective migrants should trust the source of the information. Many prospective migrants contact those in the United States who have crossed successfully to request information about trustworthy smugglers. In general, the people providing the information will not share any of the specifics about the struggles they faced, such as walking long distances or getting bitten by a snake, and so forth. They will simply say, "Well, the coyote was trustworthy and he was able to get me here safe." For the most part, no other details will be shared since those providing the information want to also sound trustworthy. If they are recommending the smuggler then that means that they believe the prospective migrant will be safe in the hands of the smuggler they are recommending (also see Spener 2009). As a member of an MTN, it would be very risky to recommend a dangerous or an irresponsible coyote since the reputation of the person giving the information is also at stake.

Paying the Coyote Fees

The next issue to face is how the new migrant will pay the coyote fees. According to the ethnographic interviews in Mexico and the Mexican Migration Project's data, coyote fees varied depending on the time period in which migrants crossed the border. During the early 1980s fees ranged from $250 to $350, and during the early 1990s the fees went up to $500 to $700. After the increase of border enforcement such as the border blockades during the late 1990s and early 2000s, the coyote fees escalated to between

$1,200 and $2,500. Finally, during the late 2000s, the coyote fees increased to a $2,500 to $3,500 range. Therefore, it has become more difficult for the newcomers' contacts to help them out by paying their coyote or smuggler fees. Smuggler fees for those who migrated from El Salvador ranged from $5,000 to $8,000 and some people even paid up to $10,000, depending on the way they were smuggled: the less life-threatening the crossing (by the inspection point, for example, instead of crossing the desert by foot or in the back of a truck), the more expensive the coyote fee. This was also true for those from Mexico. Many of the respondents from Mexico reported to having paid more than $5,000 to be crossed through the inspection points without any life-threatening risks. Most respondents preferred to pay a higher smuggling price to minimize the risks for their loved ones, particularly for their children and wives. According to Spener (2009) coyote fees did not necessarily go up because of the increased border enforcement, but also because of the changes in the law that punished the coyotes by increasing the probability for them to get caught and the amount of time spent in prison if they do.

Who pays the coyote or smuggler fees? It can vary, as the help can come from either one person, a couple of people, or from several individuals. An international migrant can have different kinds of needs, such as money to get to the US-Mexico border, money to pay for the smuggler, a place to stay upon arrival, and so forth. The helper (or helpers) provides substantial financial support and time, making this a significant commitment, especially if the migrant is from Central or South America. A mere acquaintance would not provide so much; therefore, the type of tie (or ties) providing the help is usually strong, such as a family member, a very good friend, or someone who feels obligated to provide the help (e.g., a paisano, coworker, cuate or compadre). The burden would be enormous if only one person provided all the help needed by the newcomer, so in many instances several people from the MTN organize themselves and/or cooperate in order to cover all the financial, lodging, and any other needs of the newcomer or newcomers since sometimes they also arrive in groups or as entire families.

In most instances, the person migrating already has a contact or a set of contacts that will help him or her migrate. Only in the absence of such contacts at the place of destination would that person have to rely on strangers, like in the example of Pancho and José mentioned at the beginning of the book. They became acquaintances when José arrived in the United States, but their relationship probably evolved and became stronger with time. Ethnographic data shows that such a relationship—in which bonds of affection come about automatically—is possible under certain circumstances. For example, this might occur when the individuals involved are both migrants and have had similar experiences risking their lives crossing the border or similar backgrounds of struggle in their home countries, and therefore identify with each other.

The person who told the migrant how to find a coyote or smuggler commonly provided the money to pay for the smuggler and for the migrant's trip to the US-Mexico border. Then, the same person (or maybe someone else) would provide lodging and other amenities once the person arrived to the place of destination. Of those interviewed who migrated from Mexico, only a few said they sold most of their belongings. In the case of Salvadorans, the majority reported selling most of their personal belongings since their trip was so expensive. Those who provided help to Salvadorans could not afford the whole cost of the trip plus the smuggling costs.

But how and why would a paisano or a countryman provide financial help and lodging for a newcomer? This is where the size of the place of origin becomes important: the smaller the community of origin, the more probable that the members of the community share bonded solidarity and enforceable trust, as well as a number of social values and social expectations from fellow migrants and the remaining members of the community. Most importantly, rural-origin migrants are more likely to belong to an MTN, which allows them to feel safe once they arrive to the United States. Those who do not behave according to expectations and social monitoring may be rejected or punished by others. Therefore, as we saw in the beginning of this chapter, those who are helped are expected to help others, and these expectations are passed along to newcomers. The MTN grows as the international migration chain continues to grow as well. Those migrants from urban places of origin are more likely to support others if they had participated in a peer group or in a clique-like network back home. While those who come from urban areas may have social expectations of one another, the paisanaje and enforceable trust mechanisms may also build solidarity. That is, the migrants believe they are in the same boat, and the similarity of their experiences makes them want to support each other and develop a form of solidarity with the same kind of social expectations as those from smaller places of origin. Therefore, paisanos and friends are transformed into strong ties and are all part of clique-like networks in which trust relations make everyone in the MTN feel safe, especially given the risky circumstances they confront during the international migration and settlement processes.

Types of Help Given to Settle in the United States

There are many challenges upon arrival to a new country for any international migrant, especially during their first trip, but undocumented immigrants in particular face some extremely difficult challenges due to their lack of legal status.

Once in the United States, another issue is that of survival. Arriving without possessions means newcomers have to get by with nothing but the clothes on their back, which are in poor condition given that they were the only clothes they wore during the long trip to the United States. For that reason, migrants need new clothes, even if secondhand, or at least money to buy used clothes at the local thrift store. Martin's anecdote at the beginning of the chapter recalled someone taking him to Wal-Mart upon arrival, but in most cases, newcomers reported they were taken to the thrift shop. They will need at least one or two more changes of clothes, especially to find a job. In responding to how they helped migrants, several of the respondents told me, "The first thing you do is to take them to buy some clothes at the thrift store." They all seemed to know where to shop for the best deals to help new arrivals until they could purchase their own clothes.

Once clothes are bought, the next issue the migrant faces is where to stay. If the new arrival has family members at the place of destination, it is more likely that the family member will aid the new arrival with a place to stay, but if not, then another person from his or her community, or a paisano or friend, will provide the aid. This occurs especially when the migration flow is new. Not everyone has family members at the place of destination, so others provide a place to stay—in most cases, paisanos (Massey 1986; Massey et al. 1987; Flores-Yeffal and Aysa-Lastra 2011). According to Massey et al., paisanos are the pioneers. They are the first to arrive at the place of destination and initiate the social networks that help launch the flow of migration. After the flow begins to mature, prospective migrants begin to have family members and friends available in the United States to provide them a place to stay. Ethnographic work showed that even when migrants were struggling to make a living at the destination, most still found ways to help others. They were willing to help others even if their salaries were very low and they were working only part time. However, in order for a household in the United States to welcome a newcomer, at least one person living in that household must be employed.

Living arrangements depend on the characteristics of the migrants. Wives and children who joined family members in the United States (and also joined the MTN) often lived in their own homes. If the new arrivals were single women or men who left their families behind, they usually found accommodation in the living rooms of a network member's home and slept on the sofa. I did not meet any new arrivals who had their own room with their own bed. As a result, the rest of the family or those living in the same apartment adjust to less privacy, especially in the evenings since they can no longer, for example, stay up late and watch TV, have friends over, or simply get up in the middle of the night to make a snack in the kitchen. It is also typical, when visiting some immigrant homes, to see beds in the middle of the living room or in a corner. Some of them are daybeds and are reconfigured as sofas during the day and as beds at night. Some other living arrangements, especially when hosting entire families or couples, even set up curtains to divide the living room for privacy. Single women posed a greater challenge since it was less appropriate to place them in the living room, especially if other men were living in the house. Under such circumstances, the women shared rooms with the hosts' children.

Most respondents acknowledged that they received a place to stay for periods ranging from three months to a year before they could get out on their own. Those who moved out settled in nearby apartments no farther than one or two blocks away in order to maintain contact with the rest of the people from the community of origin and to keep supporting each other.

One commonly mentioned challenge regarding living arrangements was if the host or newcomer worked the night shift while others did not. Under such circumstances, everyone was stressed as it suddenly became more difficult for all to continue their normal routines, such as watching TV during the day. Other living arrangements, such as sharing the bathroom, also caused stress. The following quote from Maria exemplifies this. She was interviewed in California and was from a medium-sized town. Maria's brother-in-law and two of his close friends from the same town were staying with her. She said:

> It is very stressful to get ready in the morning to go to work because the boys, "los muchachos," also have to leave at the same time and we only have one

bathroom to take a shower. So, I have to either take the shower the night before, or wake up and get ready very early in the morning so I don't have to rush to use the bathroom to get ready.

Other than simply timing the use of the bathroom, women who had male residents had to take extra precautions. Maria explained,

> It is also difficult because I need to be careful with what I am wearing all the time, as I have to cover myself and worry about it. I cannot necessarily be comfortable in my own house and wear anything I want, such as a pair of shorts for example. Also, I need to be very careful with my personal hygiene products, not to leave them in the bathroom, so I experience a lot of lack of privacy.

The people I visited in their homes did not necessarily demonstrate in front of others being uncomfortable as a result of their living arrangements. Not only did they offer the help, but they also had to keep to themselves any inconveniences and avoid complaining, instead showing to others that they enjoyed helping the newcomers. As a member of an MTN it seemed to me that it was also important to show the willingness to help by portraying a good attitude about it. Making the newcomers feel as comfortable as possible in every single way was important to demonstrate their solidarity to the rest of the members of the MTN.

In most cases, those who offered the new arrivals a place to stay also provided food for them until they were able to find a job and then help contribute to the grocery money. It seemed very rude to ask the newcomers for any money, especially for food, when they had just started working. For this reason, those helping the new arrivals had to make big sacrifices and share their food with the newcomers without asking for any compensation, at least until the newcomers could afford to contribute. More people in the house also meant the need to buy more food, which led to a more difficult trip to the store every week, and a more careful planning of what to buy, what to cook, and how to stretch the money to feed everyone. Usually if a woman lived in the household, she went shopping for everyone. If no woman lived there, then the men would take turns going to the grocery store.

Cooking also became a challenge since not everyone had the same eating habits, and cooking responsibilities were not fairly distributed. In most cases, however, interviewees had no problems with the cooking arrangements. Wives who did not work outside the home would cook for everyone. Where there were only men living in the household, they shared the responsibility evenly. For example, one group of respondents discussed living arrangements in response to the following question: "When migrant men live together in one apartment, who does the cooking?"

> Whoever gets there first and is hungry cooks for everyone and himself. He brings the food and cooks for everybody. Friends bring the food; whoever's hungry has to help with the kitchen. They're neutral. There are NO rules for who does what. They don't order each other to do anything.

Most men I interviewed knew how to cook, or at least the basics. I was invited to eat often during the interviews in the United States. I have to say that no matter who cooked, males or females, the food was very good! I noticed that when males cooked, they usually made just one thing, often only meat, and then ate it with tortillas. When a female cooked, the meal was more complete; for example, it included beans and rice or a salad. It seemed that those households in which women cooked had more balanced meals and healthier eating habits.

In most cases, new arrivals did not have to help with rent, mortgage, or utility bills for the household. This represented a burden for the hosts, as an extra person meant more water, more gas, and more electricity and therefore higher utility bills. Again, complaining about it was not accepted behavior, so those who provided any amenities had a good attitude about it in order to demonstrate their solidarity since when they were helped in the past, those who helped also did so with a good attitude.

Most US states do not allow undocumented immigrants to have a driver's license without a Social Security card and proof of legal residency in the United States. For this reason, most undocumented immigrants in the United States do not have a license to drive to work. In most cases, the person or family providing the lodging to others also provided transportation to the new arrivals. These hosts had to spend time taking the new arrivals to work, the store, the doctor's office, and so forth, which translated into higher gasoline costs. One way many new arrivals have dealt with this situation is by riding a bike to work. Still, just the simple task of riding a bike can become quite a challenge for a new arrival since they can be detained by the police if they do not follow the city regulations for riding a bicycle, such as having a headlight at night. If the immigrant is detained by driving without a driver's license, for example, he or she would be at risk of deportation if the police officer reports him or her to the immigration authorities after an arrest.

Bringing children provided a greater strain on the household since babies cry and children make noise and break things around the house. Mothers who work or need to be outside of the home for any reason (doctor's appointments, etc.) also require babysitting for their children, which in most cases is provided by the members of the household. Therefore, the transition for new female arrivals was much more difficult with children given their unique needs and circumstances. However, I found that many single men who were staying in the households were willing to babysit in order to help the new female arrival get going.

Providing temporary living arrangements for someone can become very complicated for everyone in the household, even for the new arrivals. Patience was required of everyone. Most of the difficulties and complexities mentioned earlier faded after the new arrivals found a job and were able to contribute financially to the household. This did not happen right away, however, due to their small salaries (especially if they lacked legal documents). With their newly earned money, they had to immediately begin paying back those they borrowed from to travel, the smuggler's fees, and/ or send money back home. Therefore, new arrivals usually made very, very small contributions to their hosts' households. It was, in most cases, not enough to pay even a third of the extra expenses associated with having an additional person living in the household.

The data suggests that men and women have different needs and exchange and receive social capital in different ways. I concluded from my own observations that a different set of arrangements needs to be made to help women migrate regardless of their age and marital status due to their vulnerability of being raped or their greater risk of dying while trying to cross the border clandestinely. Therefore, the level of risk is greater for women and children than for men who are trying to get to the United States without legal documents. Living arrangements are also different since women have different needs. They often require more privacy, childcare arrangements, and additional information most men do not need to settle in the new society.

Unfortunately, I did not find many single women in my study, as most of the women I observed and interviewed were married. Throughout the years, however, I did observe that daughters of the first-generation immigrants who arrived as children to the United States were absorbed into Migration-Trust Networks. They learned the norms and social expectations from their parents and seemed to comply with the nuances of the living arrangements when their parents offered help to other newcomers. The girls cooked for the newcomers without any complaints, cleaned the house after school, and seemed to understand how and why their privacy had to suffer. Households with young girls received, in most cases, couples or entire families as new arrivals rather than single men. Gender is a complex issue that deserves individualized attention. More qualitative research is needed regarding gender social capital exchange in order to better understand the social dynamics of gendered social networks.

For all the reasons previously mentioned, one may assume only specific types of ties will provide lodging arrangements to prospective migrants. The person providing the help would have to be someone the migrant is close to, someone the migrant trusts, and someone willing to handle the lack of privacy and additional economic strain in the household that comes with helping the newcomer. I found that place of origin, whether rural or urban, made a difference in the way such living arrangements were handled and tolerated. In general, those who migrated from smaller places of origin did not complain and tolerated most of the inconveniences. I discuss in chapter 4 (see concept of "the MTN effect") that when hosts are urban-origin migrants, their level of tolerance may be low, potentially leading to conflict and fragmented ties. Such fragmentation occurs since the person providing help lacks the social monitoring of other migrants from the home community.

Newly arrived and undocumented immigrants need reliable information to find work. Most of these jobs require them to show some kind of documentation to prospective employers. They must learn where to obtain fake documents from a trustworthy source, where and how to find employment in which their legal status will not be questioned, and what to say and what not to say to prospective employers in order to hide their status. Most newcomers who lack legal documents find themselves in trouble when they try to cash their checks from work. They cannot get a driver's license or a state ID. The MTN members then become crucial for teaching the newcomers what to do. For example, they can either go to the corner store or pay high interests for cashing their check, or they can go to the Mexican Consulate and get a *mica consular*, which is now accepted as identification by several financial institutions across the United States. Not having an ID also leads to the limitation of opening bank accounts, the ability to access any form of credit, renting an apartment in their name, buying a cell phone, and so forth. For this reason, newcomers have to learn what to do in these situations so they can at least cash their check and send money to their loved ones back home. The MTN members often teach the newcomers all the strategies to circumvent their lack of legality in the United States.

Finally, given that undocumented migrants are subject to exploitation and abuse from their employers, it is important that they find a job that pays reasonable wages and has working conditions that will not be too harsh or too dangerous.

In most cases, undocumented immigrants already have a job waiting for them upon arrival. This happens when employers notice the good work ethic of the community of migrants and ask them to recommend friends when there are openings. Because of their recruiting role, scholars have argued that employers should also be considered part of the social networks of migration (Krissman 2002, 2005). Employers expect new arrivals to possess the same work ethic as their family, friends, or paisanos. In most cases, this is true. Employers know about MTNs and how to access them. In fact, many of the "new destinations" in the United States have been generated through the recruitment of pioneer migrants who belong to MTNs (see Zúñiga and Hernandez-León 2006; Singer, Hardwick, and Brettell 2008).

Undocumented immigrants must learn how to get around from place to place without getting caught by immigration authorities. Respondents stated that most of them ride with family, friends, paisanos, or coworkers, given that many of them work at the same place and live in the same quarters, so they all share the gasoline costs. In most cases, they make arrangements with their employers to work the same hours as the people who give them rides to work.

Another important location they must learn is where to go for medical care. In most cases, they find out about a local clinic where Spanish is spoken so that they can describe their symptoms to the doctor and communicate effectively. Other community members who have navigated the system and know what to do usually escort them. Given the lack of medical insurance opportunities for undocumented immigrants from their employment, access to low-cost medical clinics is critical for their family's survival. At the time of this writing, prenatal care is offered at no cost to undocumented women in the United States because their children will become US citizens if born in the United States; however, many are unaware of such an option and do not take advantage of it.

Female immigrants need to know how to enroll the children in school and what to say to school authorities. In most cases, they are personally taken to the schools by other women and are helped through the whole process of enrolling the children. Since the majority of new arrivals do not have a receipt or any proof of residence, the neighbors provide either testimony or a letter saying they share the same quarters, making it possible for the children to be enrolled in a nearby school.

Other basic situations new arrivals often must learn to navigate include: how to cross a street light, how to catch a bus, how to shop at the supermarket, how to do laundry at the laundromat, and many other basic things for everyday survival. More importantly, new arrivals have to know what to do in case of emergencies, and whether or not to call the police. Any mistake could uncover their undocumented status and subject them to deportation. The following excerpt from my field notes portrays the extent to which migrants need help from each other at the place of destination:

"When I got to Modesto, I didn't like it and didn't feel comfortable being there because I didn't know anyone. There were only two families there and I had never met either of them before. I'm from Rancho 1 and they were from Rancho 2. I felt really lonely there. I didn't know anyone there and at home I did. But then I became very comfortable. Some of the ladies helped me and took me to the doctor when I got pregnant. They helped me get Medical and told me what I had to know. When I got here we came with Maria and she personally took me everywhere I needed to go. My husband never took long to find a job, somewhere around three weeks. Here we've hosted a lot of people who arrive. We've let them stay with us and they never take long to find work, never more than around three weeks."

The husband was cooking while I interviewed the wife. He said Manuel helped him find work. Manuel's wife also worked, taking care of a girl for forty dollars a week from six in the morning to eight at night. She said she feels sorry for the girl's mother because she had an operation. She also said that she lived one week with Laura until her husband got the key to live in the one bedroom apartment next door to Maria. Maria helped her go to the doctor and get medical and everything. She said that she was also helped to put the children in school too.

To this family, not only was it important to have received support upon arrival, but when their turn came to help others, they felt obligated to do so, even if it was a sacrifice. Sometimes when a whole family arrives, it is more difficult to navigate the network because of the special needs of a family. They generally settle near the ones who helped them, as in the case with Maria. Such a living arrangement allowed this new family to continue participating actively in the MTN.

Migrant Social Status Resulting from Participation in the Migration-Trust Networks

Migrant Status at the Place of Origin

International migrants can increase their social status at the place of origin in many ways. At the beginning of the migratory career of a community, most people in smaller communities and rural villages are culturally and economically homogeneous, given that the majority of them work in agriculture. The more urban the place of origin, the more social and economic stratification exists among community members. Nevertheless, it is very likely that the social sphere of even urban individuals is homogeneous; for example, his or her social contacts and family members back home would probably be from the same socioeconomic status. Therefore, most international migrants from both rural and urban places of origin tend to belong to very homogeneous social groups before their international migratory career.

Once international migration begins, the individuals who left begin to send remittances back home to their families, and the signs of international migration begin to manifest in forms of social and economic discrepancies between the households that receive remittances and those that do not. For example, those who receive remittances from the United States begin to wear better clothes, buy more or better food, buy new furniture, build a new home or improve their existing one, begin a local business, and so forth. By contrast, the households that do not receive remittances continue to live as they always have, while watching others improve their living standards. Nonmigrant residents usually tend to give households receiving remittances greater respect in the community as a result of the consequences of international migration.

Many migrants return from the United States with expensive cars or trucks, nice clothes, nice television sets, stereos, DVD players, and other electronics that are uncommon possessions among those who live in the sending community. As a result, the community grants such migrants a high social status, even higher than their family members who receive the remittances. The higher status of returning migrants is also influenced by the increased human capital they have gained from the international migratory experience. They are more likely to become international migrants again and to experience success whether they choose to migrate again or stay home. Returning migrants who have acquired legal status in the United States and who are able to travel internationally more often acquire an even higher status than migrants who have not.

International migration creates a social and economic hierarchy in the sending community, creating gaps between members of the community depending on their status: migrant households that receive remittances and those that do not, returning migrants, legal migrants, and US citizens. In most cases, migrant status is often reflected in the economic assets of the migrant household. There tends to be a strong, direct correlation between human capital acquired through the international migration experience (including legal status in the United States) and the economic assets of households—more years of migration translate into more household assets. Legal or US citizenship status tends to result in more household assets and a higher socioeconomic status compared to others in the community.

Migration-Trust Networks are also affected by the hierarchical socioeconomic structure that results from migration. Those at the higher end of the spectrum provide help to the new international migrants. Some become hubs (in Bashi's terms, refering to those who help many prospective migrants), which gives them an even higher social status in both the community of origin and destination. Many hubs or higher-status members of the community who help other migrants are not necessarily residing in the United States when helping other migrants, though most are.

Migrant Status at the Place of Destination

International migrants also acquire status at the place of destination, but it manifests itself in different ways compared to the community of origin. Social status at the community of origin is largely measured by physical and economic assets, but at the place of destination, social factors determine status, such as the type of job, knowledge of the English language, and legal status. Most importantly, social status is manifested in the amount of social capital provided. That is, the more migrants this person assists to come to the United States, the higher the social status he or she gains among the rest of the people in the community, regardless of job, legal status, salary, or assets in the United States and/or in Mexico. Such migrants are the *hubs* in the research of Bashi (2007).

Ethnographic evidence from interviews conducted in immigrant enclaves in the United States confirms this. One example is the testimony of El Tío (the uncle). He helped more than thirty people migrate; when asked, he did not even know the number. He was a modest man and most people in his US community greatly respected him. When I asked him the number of people he helped to migrate, not only by providing them money for the smuggler, but also by providing a place to stay, food, transportation, and employment, I sensed that he had not kept track. More importantly, he did not want to say the number of people he helped. His demeanor suggested that by admitting it, he would be guilty of being proud or boastful. In other words, if he said it aloud, it would be the same as asking to be admired. My research notes while interviewing him state:

> He answered, "Lots of people. I've lost count. I've helped them by lending money, paying the coyote fees, sometimes even the coyotes wait for me to pay them the coyote fees until I get my check."
>
> As long as he could help, he would. They don't have to be relatives, nor do they have to be from the same hometown. They just have to know each other. He doesn't expect anything in return and he keeps having a very good relationship with the people who owe him. The most he's ever lent was a thousand dollars and the least was one dollar.

When I asked him why he helped so many, he replied, "I just like to help others in the same way I was helped when I first arrived." He seemed to feel obligated to help those in need out of religious conviction and also because he had the means. The testimony of Armando, interviewed in the United States, reflects the same behavior in helping many new arrivals:

> Yes, I've helped about six in total. I've lent them money and have paid their coyote fees. They're still paying me back for the coyote in installments. I've also helped four people find work, including Alex. When they stay with me, I pay everything for them: clothes, food, transportation and everything they need when they arrive. The only thing they've paid me back for is the coyote fee, in installments.

It is important to mention that those who Tío and Armando helped were not their family members, but paisanos through the risk-pooling mechanism, since later on those new arrivals helped other newcomers and so on and so forth. Most of those I interviewed helped others to migrate, but there were some who helped several migrate. Those who provided help to many were more highly respected by the rest of the people of the community and especially by those who had received help from them. Again, becoming arrogant as a result of helping many newcomers is against the social values and behavioral expectations of the MTN. Therefore, the higher social status is usually not recognized by those providing the help, but by those who receive it and by the rest of the members of the community.

In general, favors were not returned directly to those who provided the help, but there was always an expectation that the newcomer would engage in risk pooling and help other newcomers in the future. In most cases, only the coyote fees were paid back, though not necessarily to family members. All other help, such as food, lodging, and transportation, is generally provided without the expectation of monetary repayment. Therefore, reciprocity is rarely expected and rarely occurs. Instead, favors are expected to be paid forward to others. The functionality of the MTN depends on such arrangements in which the new arrivals and even the returning migrants are always guaranteed social capital support to get to the United States, to get a job, and to settle. Once they settle, they are also expected to participate as active members of the MTN in helping other newcomers.

I found in my research that awarding higher social status to those who provided the most assistance occurred among those who migrated from smaller communities, especially from rural villages, but not with those from urban areas. For those who migrated from urban areas, higher social and economic status was awarded for more traditional reasons—to those who had better jobs, were legal, spoke more English, and had more migratory experience. Helping others did not necessarily improve their social standing. Urban dwellers with higher socioeconomic status usually were able to navigate the difficulties of being undocumented and find better job opportunities than those who arrived with lower levels of education from rural or urban areas. They still needed the support of the MTN, but they (for example) knew English already upon arrival and so the opportunities for upward mobility were more available to them due to the greater amount of human capital they brought with them.

In this chapter, I have presented how MTNs function at the micro level and listed the ways in which social network participants exchange social capital to migrate successfully and settle in the United States. In the next chapter, I explain how MTNs expand and absorb new migrants, taking into account the context of the place of origin, whether rural or urban.

CHAPTER FOUR

Expanding Networks

After arriving with a tourist visa in San Francisco, Carlos, who was from a city in Guanajuato, was able to find a job in a Mexican restaurant washing dishes. Upon arrival he stayed with his brother, who was married and had two kids. After a month of staying at his brother's place Carlos began to have problems because his sister-in-law complained of the lack of privacy she experienced with Carlos' presence at their house. She also complained about the extra burden of having to cook for Carlos, make him lunch early in the mornings, spend more money on food, and so forth. Carlos was then told by his brother that he had to find another place to stay because he no longer could stay at their house. Carlos' friends at work said, "Don't worry, come over to our house and we will get you all taken care of." Carlos moved to a house that was shared by three paisanos from the same village near Acapulco, Guerrero, Mexico. At the time of the interview with him, we got together at the house of these paisanos from Guerrero. He had already been living with them for three years and I was able to meet them. They all acted as if they were all family and demonstrated a huge affection for Carlos. Carlos told me during the interview that the best thing that had happened to him was to find these three paisanos who offered him their home and support as a new arrival. He stated, "I felt so fortunate of being able to get to meet them and learn from them how to help others without expecting anything in return. We became best friends with time, and since I am living with them I have felt like living at home, not like I felt while living with my brother and his wife, like an *arrimado* [a stranger]. I also got to know all the other people who live here in San Francisco and who are from their same rural village. They are always very good to me and have supported me as if I was also part of their family. I feel very blessed to have gotten to know them."

The story of Carlos exemplifies orphan urban migrants who have experienced tie fragmentation from family ties once in the United States as a result of their family members not belonging to an MTN. I will describe in this chapter how MTNs can expand and absorbe orphan migrants through the process I call "the MTN effect," as well as how other outsiders may also be absorbed into MTNs, which are characterized by a clique-like network structure.

The network structure of the Migration-Trust Network can be compared to that of a clique-like network, or a peer group. The clique-like networks are composed of three or more individuals who maintain strong ties with each other, interact often, and most importantly, support each other collectively. In the *transnational* context, individuals who belong to MTNs do not necessarily have to live or be in the same geographical area. For example, participants of this network can include: (1) migrants at the place of destination; (2) nonmigrants at the place of origin; and (3) returning migrants at the place of origin. The MTN may also extend to more than one place of destination or more than one place of origin. The MTN participants maintain their relationships at the transnational level via telephone calls, text messages, letters, and more recently, the Internet. Blogs, community websites, and online networking tools such as Skype, MSN messenger, and Facebook are very accommodating. Those who have legal documents visit family and friends whenever possible, while others mail packages or send gifts back home with other travelers. Among nonmigrants, those who already belong to peer groups at the place of origin are more likely to engage in MTNs, given the social cohesion within the peer groups.

Most of the members of an MTN respect a series of norms and expectations imposed by the other members. Therefore, social surveillance takes place at both the place of origin and destination. The MTN is structured to benefit everyone, and they judge selfishness through social rejection. The sending of individual remittances and/or collective remittances exemplifies a relationship of trust and fellowship at the transnational level.

Outside the sphere of international migration, it is usually very difficult for a clique-like network to expand. Membership is considered exclusive and newcomers are less likely to be able to fulfill all the necessary expectations and functions that already exist among the members of the circle. One of the biggest obstacles for the expansion of such clique-like networks is the lack of trust in newcomers. Although newcomers may gain the trust of some of the members, they are less likely to gain the trust of all the members. For this reason, the expansion of a clique-like network is not a common social event in any regular circumstances in life. Consider a peer group of coworkers in a job place. The participants of such peer groups may have exclusive access to their clique-like network, maintain strong ties with each other, and have frequency of contact, and so forth. Under these circumstances, the risk associated with allowing a newcomer to enter the clique-like network can be higher because the new participant may behave as a member of the peer group and cause dissension within the group or bring a social stigma. A newcomer could potentially leak information shared within the clique-like network or peer group — including inappropriate comments or actions in the workplace — and possibly even cause one or more members in the group to lose their jobs. In other words, the chances that a newcomer would penetrate such a job-related peer group are often very slim since the relationship between the members of the group may be too established. This is not necessarily the case for MTNs.

In fact, the chances of being accepted as a new member of an MTN are greater than that of a normal clique-like network, while the risk also associated with participation in an MTN is much higher than that of a regular clique-like network, due to the lack of legal status of many of the MTN participants. The MTNs initiate an exclusive, yet inclusive, domain in international migration. Its participants meet the characteristics and the behavior of a regular clique-like network in terms of being an exclusive circle, difficult to access, having exclusive benefits, cohesiveness, strong relationships, and so on and so forth. However, the membership requirements for an MTN may differ enormously from that of a regular clique-like network in the sense that membership requirements can be more welcoming to new members of an MTN due to the particular nature of undocumented migration.

As discussed in chapter 1, the context of origin — in this case, either rural or urban — can be important in order to understand how MTNs are formed, and can determine the kind of social behavior that people adopt in each setting. From the ethnographic work in this study, it seemed that the type of place of origin of the migrant was more influential than the type of place of destination. Therefore, when I refer to urban or rural in this chapter, I am referring to the type of community of origin of the migrants, and not to their place of destination. Whether the place of destination is rural or urban becomes irrelevant given that in most of the research, it was found that migrants still created social clusters at the place of destination (also referred to as immigrant enclaves) during the formation of the MTN, regardless of whether the setting was rural or urban. Through empirical evidence, Sampson (2008) implies that collective efficacy develops in urban destinations in the United States, confirming the assumption that the context of the place of origin is more important when the MTNs are formed, but as the migrants settle in the United States, the type of context (rural or urban) of the place of destination becomes less relevant.

Flores-Yeffal and Aysa-Lastra (2011) found that social capital is more likely to be provided to prospective migrants if those providing the help have migrated from rural communities in Mexico of less than 3,000 inhabitants. The small size of the community makes it easier to monitor the social behavior and, therefore, enforce the social values and expectations of the members of the community. Given that the members of an MTN tend to think of themselves as a group and not as individuals, they are also able to create new social bonds with those who they identify as fellow migrants— those going through similar experiences both in the host country and back home. By acting in accordance with religious sentiments to welcome and help others who are struggling, members also create the right conditions for an MTN to form, expand, and absorb other members who were once considered strangers, especially those lacking legal documentation.

An MTN based in a larger town or urban location would probably be sourced by a group of individuals who were previously members of a non-migration-related peer group at a smaller scale. Clique-like networks or peer groups develop among those who have had very long relationships in the past and have shared large amounts of trust with each other. Ruben Hernandez-León gives examples of this, such as the gang members in Monterrey, or those subjects who lived in the same neighborhood and worked in the same factory or job for many, many years. In urban places of origin, once a few members of the peer-group begin to migrate, the original peer group subsequently transitions into an MTN after the individuals arrive at a specific geographic area or immigrant enclave.

There are several factors that allow for newcomers to be absorbed into the MTN even though these newcomers are knowingly taking great risks (i.e., possible death when crossing the border by trusting given information on which coyote to hire, losing a job if employers find out about undocumented status, possible deportation, etc.). The factors that allow new members to be absorbed by an MTN include (but are not limited to) the following:

1. The new members may also be undocumented and, therefore, need the social capital exchanged between the members of the MTN. Given this situation, the existing members of the MTN may feel sympathy for the

stranger (perhaps partly rooted in religious faith and beliefs) and allow him or her to become part of the MTN.

2. The existing members of the MTN may identify with the struggles and migratory experience of the newcomer and therefore, develop a solidarity sentiment and welcome him or her into the MTN.

3. For the existing members of the MTN—given that they have prior experience with peer group relationships of trust before migration and after migration—it may be easier to cognitively identify the facial and behavioral signs of someone they can trust to join the MTN.

In both rural-based and urban-based scenarios, preexisting relationships of trust and social monitoring establish the right conditions for peer groups to continually employ these values at the destination. In the absence of relatives or friends with migratory experience, some migrants of urban origin would likely begin settling next to each other, exchanging resources and favors at the place of destination. The MTNs at the place of destination consist of: (1) residents of the enclave; (2) those from the community of origin who interact in the transnational context; and (3) the new members who join the network at the place of destination, such as new husbands or wives of existing members who are not necessarily from the same place of origin. In this way, the MTN of either rural or urban origin begins to gain foothold and grow at the place of destination.

The urban settings fieldwork for the present study revealed that peer groups developed among those who worked in the same taxi or cab agency (*sitio de taxis*) for many years or in other jobs, such as factory work, restaurant service occupations, and hotel janitorial services, among others. When respondents described their prior relationships of trust during the interview process, they always mentioned how the people in their peer group had developed a close relationship with each other and had developed at least a good degree of trust in each other. Therefore, relationships of trust do form in urban settings under certain conditions. The commonalities of the international migration experience are transmitted to those with no prior migration experience at the origin.

Another important factor for mutual cooperation is social homogeneity in the rural and urban areas of origin. However, people who live in a rural area of origin are more homogeneous because they are more likely to perform the same occupations, have the same standard of living, the same levels of education, and so forth (see Flores-Yeffal and Aysa-Lastra 2011). Their cultural and religious practices also remain homogeneous. Therefore, those who migrate from rural areas, due to their high level of homogeneity, are more likely to develop a sense of collective sentiment and empathy. Social homogeneity among rural-origin migrants is an added bonus in terms of quick absorption into an MTN.

It is considered that urban settings develop higher levels of heterogeneity; still, the division of labor in society and labor specialization can also provide an opportunity for people in urban settings to cluster in more homogenous groups, as suggested by Durkheim ([1933] 1997). For example, those in urban settings who work in the same occupation are more likely to have the same income, live near the same neighborhoods, be around the same age, and so forth. (see Hernandez-León 1999, 2008). The amount of time the relationships have been established is also a factor that determines the strength of trust between individuals. Working for many years in the same job and sharing the same experiences during that time allows for sentiments of social bonding and relationships of social trust to develop even in urban settings. Thus, even when lacking social network contacts to migrate internationally from an urban setting, the urban-origin migrant resorts to contacts that are likely to be part of an urban-origin clique-like network or peer group whose members have access to an MTN. In most cases, however, family members help international migrants from urban areas. Only in the absence of family members at the place of destination do urban dwellers look to non-kin for social support to migrate, such as someone who belongs to some sort of clique-like or a peer group network in the urban setting. Those who live in urban areas before international migration but are originally from rural areas are more likely to use rural-based MTNs (Massey et al. 1987; Flores-Yeffal and Aysa-Lastra 2011). Flores-Yeffal and Aysa-Lastra found that approximately 60 percent of those who migrate from rural and urban areas for the first time are helped by family members. Table 4.1, which analyzes data collected from a medium-sized town and a city, shows a similar percentage. The ethnographic work in the places of origin as well as the places of destination showed that family members from urban origins tend to have very fragile ties with each other if they do not belong to an MTN. That is, if those urban dwellers did not belong to a peer group or clique-like network at the place of origin, they were more likely to be on their own when they chose to migrate.

These migrants are more likely to be helped by family members. The problem is that when the family members (most likely extended family

Table 4.1   Percentages of Times Relationship Was Named First and Second in Name Generator by Type of Place (First Relationship Mentioned)

	First named		Second named		All contacts	
	Town	City	Town	City	Town	City
Husband or wife	5.50	3.08	0.00	0.00	3.75	1.71
Mother or father	5.50	1.54	12.12	0.00	6.88	1.71
Brother or sister	21.10	13.85	9.09	15.38	18.75	13.68
Son or daughter	1.83	0.00	3.03	3.85	2.50	0.85
Uncle or aunt/nephew	18.35	20.00	12.12	23.08	17.50	18.80
Other family member	3.67	3.08	3.03	11.54	3.13	5.13
Other family/political	11.01	9.23	6.06	0.00	8.75	8.55
Percent of family helping	66.97	50.77	45.45	53.85	61.25	50.43
Paisano	3.67	1.54	9.09	7.69	5.00	4.27
from work	3.67	6.15	0.00	0.00	2.50	3.42
Same organization	0.00	0.00	0.00	0.00	0.00	0.00
Neighbor	1.83	0.00	9.09	0.00	3.13	0.00
Friend	21.10	33.85	18.18	26.92	21.25	32.48
Godfather or godmother	0.00	0.00	3.03	0.00	1.25	0.00
Acquaintance	0.00	4.62	6.06	3.85	1.25	4.27
Other	2.75	3.08	9.09	7.69	4.38	5.13
N	109	65	33	26	160	117

members such as uncles and cousins, or sometimes even brothers and sisters; see table 4.1) are asked for help to migrate, they feel obligated to help the prospective migrant if they have the resources to do so. Thus, they are not helping their family member under the same social pressures as the members of the MTNs are. The family members are not always subject to the same social values and social expectations of specific behavior as are those who belong to the MTNs. Therefore, given the lack of social monitoring by other clique-like or peer group network members, the family members do not feel obligated to continue providing help after a while and their social ties begin to deteriorate with time. Also, as shown in chapter 2, after a while of taking care of family members and providing them with shelter, food, transportation, and so forth, this dependence becomes way too much of a burden, not only socially, but also economically. The family members begin to feel tired of having to provide so much. While those who belong to an MTN might have adopted as a part of their culture the willingness to help others without much in return, the urban dwellers (especially those family members who are not subject to such expectations) might not be used to having to provide so much and they get tired more easily of doing so. As a result, social conflict begins to develop between the family member providing the help and the person receiving it. The relationship begins to deteriorate and disintegrate, leaving the new arrival without any social support or social capital to continue surviving at the place of destination.

This chapter explains and provides empirical evidence for a social process in which those international migrants who migrate without being part of an MTN become victims of fragile urban family networks. Urban migrants who are in the United States and left with no social capital seek to diversify their networks by connecting to rural-based or other urban-based MTNs. In most cases, these orphaned urban-based migrants end up absorbed by rural-based MTNs given that rural-origin networks are more likely to be composed of interpersonal connections that perpetuate themselves through relations of solidarity and the enforcement of norms. Once orphan urban migrants identify these MTNs, they can be incorporated into them through a process I call "the MTN effect."

As in the story of Martin in chapter 3, where he was taken to Wal-Mart by a stranger who bought him new clothes upon arrival, I found evidence of the following forms of help provided to migrants, which are described in more detail in chapter 3: money for traveling to the Mexican border and surviving until a successful crossing, information about finding a coyote (from a trustworthy source), money to pay the coyote (anywhere from $300 to $2,000 in US dollars), lodging (food and a place to stay), money to buy clothes, transportation, help finding a job, information about buying false documents, enrolling the kids in schools, and where to go to the doctor. As expected, I generally found that rural migrants have less knowledge about urban places of destinations. Therefore, membership to MTNs becomes essential to prospective migrants in order to be able to safely and successfully migrate and settle in the United States. It is very important to state here that urban-origin migrants who were able to obtain tourist visas because of their high levels of human capital—such as higher levels of education, better professional occupations, more economic resources to migrate, and greater access to tourist visas—are still very vulnerable after overstaying their visas. Because these urban-origin migrants have no access to any of the advantages or rights of a legal citizen, they become as vulnerable as any other member of the MTN and are likewise subject to possible exploitation, discrimination, and more importantly, possible deportation. In fact, from the urban-origin interviews, I learned that most of the undocumented urban-origin migrants with higher levels of human capital were not able to transfer their human capital once they arrived to the United States. They were more likely to experience downward mobility rather than obtaining a job that matched their human capital skills (see Flores 2010). Therefore, this particular group could also greatly depend on the support of an MTN for their daily survival at the place of destination. Still, compared to the migrants who arrived from rural areas of origin, who traveled with no legal documents, and who had very low levels of education, those urban dwellers who arrived with a tourist visa and who had higher levels of education were able to learn English more easily, get better jobs, and get ahead.

The MTN Effect

Migration-Trust Networks are mostly composed of close ties and relationships of trust. The smaller a migrant's place of origin is, the more likely that a prospective migrant from the same area will have social capital available to migrate internationally (Flores-Yeffal and Aysa-Lastra 2011). Therefore, urban-origin international migrants are less likely to belong to an MTN.

The main argument of the MTN effect is that its clique-like network structure and the social capital provided within the MTN serves as a powerful magnet at the place of destination that attracts urban-origin migrants. The MTN is attractive to orphaned urban-origin migrants (who lack social contacts) and to those whose social networks are very fragile and disintegrate once in the United States. The migrants then gravitate toward and are accepted into the rural-based or urban-based MTN.

As stated earlier, without social contacts and relationships of social support, it is almost impossible for such migrants to be able to complete their migratory process successfully—especially if they are undocumented, regardless of the level of human capital with which they arrived in the United States.

In the next few paragraphs, I document the MTN effect using ethnographic and quantitative data from four communities that I surveyed in the state of Guanajuato, Mexico—two small villages, a town, and a working-class neighborhood in a city. I interviewed 560 households in Mexico. I also did a snowball sample in the states of Illinois, Indiana, Texas, and California, yielding fifty-six households in the United States (10 percent of the Mexican sample). The ethnographic fieldwork consisted of several open-ended interviews, fieldwork notes, and participant observation in several different settings.

In my analysis, I assume that having been raised in a rural village, a prospective migrant automatically belongs to an MTN (see Flores 2000; Flores-Yeffal and Aysa-Lastra 2011). This is the case when the rural village's population is less than 3,000 inhabitants. However, this is true only if at least 10 percent of the members of the community have already engaged in international migration measured by the migration prevalence ratio of the community due to the effects of the process of cumulative causation. Lindstrom and Lopez-Ramirez (2010) empirically tested these assumptions and found evidence that once migration had reached more than 10 percent, international migration continued and increased considerably with time. Migrations from rural areas in Mexico are more prominent due to the fact that there is a longer history of rural-origin migration to the United States. In addition, a culture of international migration has already been developed, including the experiencing of relative deprivation among a certain number of inhabitants at the place of origin. (Relative deprivation is felt when some people begin to have more than others because of the flow of individual-level remittances into the community of origin.) Under such conditions, this means that the cumulative causation process has begun and that an MTN has already developed. Therefore, a rural-based social network of international migration is automatically considered an MTN. The MTNs are the most reliable type of networks for undocumented migration and settlement in the United States, not only because of their specific network structure (clique-like), but also because of the social conditions that develop within such a structure, which allow for the relationships of trust to be developed, strengthened, and enforced in such a way that greatly reduces the extreme risk associated with undocumented immigration. As mentioned before, MTNs also develop in urban areas under specific circumstances, such as when people at the urban places of origin already belong to peer groups developed at work, in a sports team, urban neighborhood, gang, and so forth. Urban dwellers are attracted to MTNs because they see them as increasing their odds of successful migration and settlement in the United States. When orphan urban-origin migrants are attracted to rural- or urban-based MTNs and are adopted by one, this social dynamic is called the MTN effect.

Empirical Evidence of the MTN Effect

Massey et al. (1987) found that when urban migrants from a large city in Jalisco, Mexico, wanted to migrate to the United States, they went back to their rural hometowns to acquire the social capital necessary for migration. Through my ethnographic research, I found evidence that even if a person was born in an urban city in Mexico, at some point in his or her life he or she is likely to meet someone in the city from a rural town and use that person's contacts to migrate to the United States. The following quote from Luis, who migrated from a medium-sized town in Mexico to Indiana, instantiates this concept:

> I was able to get the help to migrate from the family of a friend who used to work with me in Mexico. His family is from a *rancho* in Jalisco. He told me all about who to contact at the border so I could get a coyote. Also when I arrived, I stayed with his cousin who lives in this house. The next day after I arrived I was already working.

Luis was able to gain access to a rural-based MTN and therefore have a successful migratory experience because he acquired the necessary social capital to get to the United States and settle. Luis also described how he was later able to access all kinds of information to enjoy a successful settling. He stated:

> Later on I was able to rent my own apartment and bring my wife and children to the US, thanks to the support of the people from the rural village. They also helped me later on to get my family to the US by recommending me a trustable coyote. Also, I received help with paying the coyote. Not only that, but later on the women from the network helped my wife to place the children in school and also helped to babysit the kids so she could also go to work.

Not only was Luis able to bring his wife and children safely to the United States, but his access to the MTN also helped him obtain a job for his wife, a family to stay with at the place of destination, social support, babysitting, and so forth, which all allowed him to successfully settle in the United States. I followed Luis and his family throughout my thirteen years of fieldwork and he not only continued participating in the MTN, but he also adopted the same behavior shown by the other members of the rural-based MTN, even though he had migrated from an urban place of origin. He also helped several other newcomers and their family members in the same way he and his family were helped. This example is illustrated in figure 4.1, scenario 1.

The next scenario that I found shows the MTN effect operating for someone who migrated directly from an urban community to the United States and arrived with a social contact who did not belong to an MTN (either a friend or family member). This is illustrated in Figure 4.1, scenario 3. The first example of this is that of Pablo, who arrived to the United States from a city in Mexico and was interviewed in San Francisco, California. The second example is that of Leonor, from a city in Guanajuato, who was interviewed in Dallas, Texas:

Pablo: "When I arrived in the US, I stayed first with a friend from León. After one week, his wife got tired of me being there, sleeping on the sofa in their living room. She told me that I had to leave. I didn't know what to do. At work, I told my friend Alfredo and he invited me to come and live at his house. He said, 'come to my house and we will accommodate ourselves' (*vente a la casa y ahí nos acomodamos*). He is from a rural village in Guanajuato, Mexico, and he lives with other *paisanos* from the same village. I have been living with them for the last five years. I am very glad I met them."

Leonor: "When my husband and I arrived, we stayed with my brother-in-law. His wife was very mean though. She only wanted to have me as a maid (*sirvienta*). When I cooked, my sister-in-law used to tell me, 'Don't tell my husband that you were the one who cooked.' My husband did not notice because he came too late from work. She pretended that she needed to use the room where we were staying for something else and we had to sleep in the living room. My son is the one who suffered the most. One time they had these men, who came to play pool and I had to be there sitting down, with my son in my arms, till three or four in the morning without being able to lay down on the floor. The worst part was when I wanted to look for a job; she [my sister-in-law] told me that I was not going to find anything because I did not know any English. It was not until my husband met a friend from his job and we moved in with him [that I found a job]. He is from a *rancho* in Guanajuato and his wife helped me find a job. She also took care of my son for me while I worked. After a while, we were able to rent our own place, but we stayed here, in this neighborhood where all the people from that *rancho* live."

1

Luis is an **urban dweller** who is originally from a **rural town**.

He had migrated from his rural hometown to the city…
(internal migration)

When Luis decides to migrate internationally, he goes back to his hometown and utilizes the existing (rural-based) Migration-Trust Network (MTN) in his hometown in order to successfully migrate to the place of destination.

Luis is now part of an urban-based MTN; therefore he is able to migrate. This is called *the MTN effect.*

2

Luis is an **urban dweller.**

He is a member of a peer group in his job, church, sports team, etc. in his city.

One person within that peer group decides to migrate internationally. This first migrant later provides help for other members to migrate too.

Little by little, this peer group evolves into a Migration-Trust Network (MTN).

3

Luis is an **urban dweller** who is **NOT** a member of any peer group or MTN.

Luis can either…

Enter the host country with help from family ties at the place of destination.
i.e. brother in-law

However, *urban* family ties are often fragile and tend to disintegrate over time because of the lack of social surveillance imposed by a larger trust network. His ties then disintegrate.

Enter on a tourist visa or by some other means. He may be travelling alone.
Later the visa expires. He arrived with no social capital, and therefore struggles to settle and survive at the place of destination.

Luis meets someone at his job, church, sports team, or other peer group. This new friend belongs to a Migration-Trust Network (MTN).

Luis gains this friend's trust, and he is eventually absorbed into his friend's MTN. This is called *the MTN effect.*

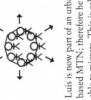

Figure 4.1   "The MTN Effect:" How urban dwellers gain access to Migration-Trust Networks (MTNs).

In both of these scenarios, we see how urban ties, even if they are originally strong (from family members, for example), tend to become very fragile once the immigrants are interacting and living with each other in the United States. Therefore, for urban-origin migrants that do not belong to an MTN, their social ties can break at any stage of the migration process. Urban-origin migrants then find themselves forced to find social support from other sources. In both of these cases, rural-based MTNs absorbed urban migrants as members of their network. According to the testimonies of Pablo and Leonor, I later learned that they, too, adopted the same supportive behavior and social expectations of the members of the MTN they became part of—just like the case of Luis. Both of them later described how they also helped other migrants who came from the same rural village in Mexico that sourced the MTN. In addition, Leonor also brought more people from her own neighborhood in the city of Guanajuato. She brought a friend, who later brought her brother, and then her brother brought another friend from the city. In the end, the MTN effect not only allowed for the adoption of the first migrant, who in this case was Leonor, but also for the absorption of Leonor's new MTN, which was begun by Leonor. In this case, the rural-based MTN merged with an urban-based MTN.

I also came across migrants who were from urban areas of origin, possessed higher levels of human capital, had migrated with a tourist visa, but given their lack of social contacts in the United States for social support, were ultimately absorbed by an MTN after struggling to settle in the United States (see figure 4.1, scenario 3). For example, Rodrigo, interviewed in Houston, Texas, described his frustration as an educated immigrant who experienced downward mobility and whose eventual success in the United States ultimately depended on his participation in an MTN, which he joined soon after his arrival to the United States. He described his struggle in the following quote:

> Upon my arrival to the US, I became very frustrated as I was not able to find a job on my own. I originally traveled with a tourist visa so I didn't need help crossing the border with a coyote and all that. I then arrived to Houston and rented a hotel room during the first few days. I had some money saved. I knew there was a company hiring in Houston which a friend in Mexico had told me about. I went to apply to that company, but they ended up finding out that I had no legal permit to work in the US, since I was a tourist. Nobody had told me what to say or how to handle the situation. I then told my

situation to a cleaning lady in the hotel I was staying at. We used to say hi to each other all the time, and one day we had a long conversation in which we got to know each other better. I then felt confident to tell her my situation. I explained to her that I was a civil engineer in Mexico but that my English was not very good. I also told her that I was running out of cash and that I didn't know what to do. She was married and she told me that she was going to talk to her husband about it. The next day she told me that if I wanted I could stay in a house where her brother was staying until I got on my feet. She also told me that her husband could possibly help me find a job. I then moved in with her brother, Carlos. He was living with three other friends; they were all from a small town in Jalisco. They were sharing a two bedroom apartment. They allowed me to sleep on the sofa. Then Maria's husband helped me find a job in a factory making plastic bags of all kinds. Several people from the same town in Jalisco also worked in that same factory. I became very good friends with all the people from that town and I am very thankful I got to know them during those difficult times. Later on I was able to get on my feet and I also brought my wife and my son to the US. We are now both working in the same factory and we now have a place of our own in this same neighborhood with the people from Jalisco. We like living here because we always have support from our neighbors. The lady next door babysits my son so my wife can also work. I am very thankful for meeting Maria at the hotel when I arrived. We are still very good friends.

Rodrigo's testimony describes how Maria's MTN was able to absorb Rodrigo—practically a stranger—into her MTN based from a small town in Jalisco. Three years after the first interview, I contacted Rodrigo again by phone (in June 2004) and he told me that after we spoke, he had helped a couple of his friends from his urban neighborhood in Guanajuato also migrate to Houston. He said that they came during different times and he helped them get on their feet in the same way he was helped. Both of his friends now worked at the same factory he used to work at when he arrived, and also rented apartments around the corner from where he lived. It was clear to me that Rodrigo had been adopted by Maria's MTN, and it even looked like Rodrigo began an MTN of his own, which also became embedded within Maria's MTN. Even though Rodrigo was originally a stranger, the fact that he began a social tie and a relationship of trust with Maria provided the right conditions for Rodrigo to be absorbed into Maria's MTN. After Rodrigo learned about the benefits of the MTN, he then decided to stay near them and after learning how the MTN operated (regarding behavioral norms and expectations), he then began an MTN of his own.

The next scenario of the MTN effect pertains to Javier, who was born in an urban community in Mexico. He joined a clique-like network or peer group at his workplace in Mexico and obtained access to the social capital necessary to migrate. He ended up moving to a daughter community composed of members of that MTN in the United States. He was interviewed in California (see figure 4.1, scenario 2, for an illustration of this concept).

> We worked driving a taxi together for the same taxi company (*sitio*). We all used to hang around together. One of my taxi driver friends helped me migrate. He let me borrow the money for the coyote and when I arrived I stayed at his house. After one week, he also found me a job. After that, I helped another taxi driver come in the same way my friend helped me.

This scenario offers an example of an MTN formed within an urban community of origin. In most instances, because of their social structure, these urban-based MTNs can offer the same characteristics of rural-based MTNs and tend to perpetuate themselves through relations of social cohesiveness and social trust.

Another example of the peer group, or clique-like network developed in the urban area, is that of Carlos. Carlos received help to migrate from a neighbor, Miguel, from his neighborhood in Mexico. He said that they had attended middle school together when they were younger and they had been very good friends during that time. Later on when he needed to migrate, Carlos heard from another neighbor that Miguel had left for the United States, and even though they had not talked to each other in many years, he decided to approach him for help. Carlos visited Miguel's mother's house across street and asked her for his contact information. He then contacted him and Miguel accepted to provide him with lodging upon arrival, since Carlos already had a tourist visa to enter. Carlos described his arrival experience in the following way:

> It was a little awkward at the beginning when I arrived because I had not spoken to my friend Miguel in many years; I think ten years had passed. He was very welcoming and he even went to pick me up at the airport upon my arrival to Chicago. Since I came on a plane I had all my belongings with me, but Miguel helped me get a job in the same factory where he had been

working the past four years. Then he also took me to work and fed me for a while until I began to get paid. It was not until I arrived there that I realized that other people in the neighborhood were also from the same place I was. In fact, my friend Miguel had himself been helped to migrate by another neighbor, and I didn't even know that until I arrived to the US. Then, once I learned how everything worked, I also began to help other people from the same neighborhood who were also my friends. One knows that people are struggling over there in Mexico, so if it's possible to help others come, why not do it? Now we are also neighbors over here in the US. We all live near each other.

Carlos' testimony provides a perspective of how the preexisting relationships based on trust can be activated for prospective migrants in the urban areas of origin, even after many years have passed. In addition, this testimony also reflects the way in which urban-based clusters of people (such as old neighborhood or school friends) can re-create another cluster in the United States by helping each other to migrate and by also living near each other in the host community. In some instances, urban-origin migrants were able to settle near each other, yet in other instances, I observed that those who could not find nearby housing arrangements at least tried to live as close as possible to each other, even if that meant living a couple of blocks away.

Throughout my ethnographic work, I also observed that once the orphaned urban-origin migrants are attracted and absorbed into rural- or urban-based MTNs, they are able to participate as new MTN members and learn how the MTN functions — including its values, social expectations, and the ways in which social capital is exchanged. Moreover, the new MTN member may also begin to help other newcomers, either from the same MTN (new members of the original MTN), or by forming a new MTN of their own by inviting contacts from their urban hometown (or any other orphaned migrants they may meet in the United States). Then those new members of the MTN who were brought by the pioneer member would continue the cycle by adopting the norms, social expectations, and supportive behavior of the MTN, and subsequently bringing more contacts.

I also noticed that when outsiders are accepted into the MTN, they can be different types of outsiders.

Orphan migrant: An orphan migrant, as described in most of the previous examples, is someone who has never had prior trust-based cohesive relationships with any of the members of the MTN until the person is in the United States and encounters an MTN member in circumstances that allow him or her to engage in some sort of new trust relationship. This happens when the orphan migrant begins to join a peer group in the United States where the MTN member participates as well. The peer group is formed or joined as a result of a specific set of circumstances, for example, that they begin a friendship, become work buddies, or play a sport together. Then the MTN participant would be able to recognize that the orphan migrant is not a threat for the MTN. The MTN member will more readily empathize if the orphan is also undocumented. Enforceable trust, solidarity mechanisms, and religion also factor into the member's decision to accept the orphan migrant. Once the orphan migrant has proven to be trustworthy, he or she is adopted and absorbed into the MTN.

Not only does this new migrant become part of the MTN, but his or her contacts also have the potential to be adopted and absorbed into and assisted by the same MTN. This means that an MTN can be diverse since people from different places of origin, different backgrounds, and even countries can participate together as long as all newcomers learn and respect the social expectations of behavior of the MTN.

Active nonmigrant stranger MTN participants: A nonmigrant stranger—such as an employer, a coyote, a businessperson who serves the members of the MTN, an educator, a local authority, among others—may be welcomed as a participant of the MTN as it depends on their participation to function. For example, it needs employers who will hire undocumented immigrants. In fact, many of these employers are active recruiters themselves. As (Krissman 2002; Garcia 2005) describe in their studies, the employers in many cases identify the effective functionality of the MTNs and the good work ethic of its participants and decide to utilize the MTN to recruit more workers. While the employers need the cheap labor, the members of the MTN also need jobs for prospective and/or returning migrants. Once members of the MTN trust an employer, then the employer becomes a member of the MTN.

After a presentation of some of these findings in a symposium just before submitting this book for publication I was approached by one person in the audience who told me, "I am also part of an MTN." He said he was a salesman from Sprint and he did not understand why he had a long line of people waiting to talk to him all the time, while the other employees in the store had no customers. He learned that he is getting referrals via what he thinks is a Migration-Trust Network. He described how, even though he is not the only salesman who speaks Spanish in the store, he always tries to be loyal to his customers and he believes they trust him more than anyone else in the store. For this reason, he receives many referrals to other immigrants who only speak Spanish. Although he did not say whether they were undocumented immigrants from the clues he gave me during our conversation, I think he knew they were undocumented. He seemed very excited after listening to my talk since he had finally realized what was happening and that he had become part of a Migration-Trust Network.

Other entrepreneurs are also important. The MTNs need coyotes to bring people across the international border without documents. Therefore, once they trust a coyote, that coyote or smuggler becomes an active member of that specific MTN. The owner of the corner store also becomes an active participant. During my fieldwork, I observed that a store owner would find ways to accommodate the MTN members' needs and simultaneously make money. For example, they cashed checks without formal ID and sold beer and cigarettes to immigrants without proper ID. An international form of ID was sufficient, such as a voting registration card or a mica consular (a Mexican form of ID given by Mexican authorities in the United States).

Apartment managers and landlords become active member participants. They are significant in that they do not ask for a Social Security number or run credit checks (as most do not have a SSN or a credit record). Instead of running credit checks, apartment managers require proof of job stability and/or references from other neighbors who already live in the appartment complex. Furthermore, these apartment managers allow immigrants to have extra people living in their homes temporarily, as they begin to understand how the MTN operates. Once the migrant staying in the living room is able, he or she will then rent another apartment unit from that same landlord. The landlords and apartment managers observe the good behavior and ethics of MTN members and come to trust that they will pay their rent on time and take care of the apartment units even if they live under more crowded conditions.

Those just described—the employer, the coyote, the store owner, the apartment manager, and landlord—must somehow demonstrate from the beginning of their interactions with the migrants that they can be trusted and that they do not represent a threat to the undocumented migrants who participate in the MTN. Some argue that they may take advantage of MTN members, but the fact is that they are also cooperating with the network for the effectiveness of its functionality. Without their support and participation, the MTN would not be able to function.

Indirect MTN network participant strangers: Others, such as consumers of goods and services, also participate as indirect members of the MTN. The reason I also consider them as part of the MTN is because they are providers of trust and solidarity to the rest of the members of the MTN even though they are not doing it in a direct way when using the services in which undocumented migrants participate.

If the member who has the relationship of trust with the outsider signals to the rest of the members of the MTN that they can also trust that outsider, then the outsider is absorbed by the MTN. The outsider is obligated to respect the behavioral norms and expectations of the members and, most importantly, to be trustworthy and loyal to all the members.

One of the best examples of this is the fact that members of all the MTNs in which I participated granted me their trust. Initially, it was difficult to gain the trust of some MTNs, but once I gained the trust of at least one of the members, I was then welcomed by everyone else to conduct my interviews. While waiting to interview a migrant in a restaurant, I met a Guatemalan immigrant who also worked in that restaurant. He stated:

> I am here by myself. I came one day looking for a job to this restaurant and once I began to work here, I was then invited by one of the Mexicans to live with them in this house. There are only Mexicans here, and I am the only one from Guatemala. They are good to me and they have helped me with everything since I got here. They allowed me to live with them and they fed me and bought me clothes when I arrived. They are nice to me and they are now like my only family here in the US.

He was obviously very comfortable as a member of that network.

The MTNs, if they are functioning well—that is, the members of the network can find jobs and all the resources necessary for settlement in an immigrant enclave—have the capacity to absorb members from other MTNs under the following circumstances:

Transplanted migrant networks: If members of an MTN are not able to find jobs, then their network is collapsing. Therefore, an MTN in a different geographical location may begin to absorb the members of the collapsing MTN. For this to happen, a member from the collapsing MTN has to know someone from the absorbing MTN. If only one contact or member is able to make the connection between both MTNs, then that will be a sufficient requirement for the well-functioning MTN to be able to absorb all the members from the collapsing MTN. The place of origin of the migrants from any of the MTNs would be irrelevant, given that what is important is that one member is trusted, and that same member shares trust among the members of both MTNs. If even one person is trusted by both, then both MTNs are able to share the trust relations and expand them throughout both MTNs (see figure 6.3 in chapter 6).

Urban migrants possess social capital mostly drawn from family members and friends from their place of origin. These networks, even though they contain some strong and weak ties, tend to be fragile because they are not driven by the enforcement of norms and strong relations of support and bonded relationships of trust. For this reason, urban networks cannot easily perpetuate themselves unless they are formed as clique-like networks or peer groups from the start. Then once their members begin to migrate, they become part of an MTN.

Cumulative causation can take place in urban places of origin (see Fussell and Massey 2004) because the diversification of networks can occur either before migration when the urban origin migrants reach back to their rural community to access the MTN from his or her rural roots. Those ties can be diversified once migrants enter the United States. Urban migrants first draw the social capital necessary to get to the United States using local networks of social support, in most cases composed of family members or members of other preexisting clique-like networks or peer groups that were transformed into urban MTNs after members began to migrate. Once in the United States, however, those who lack preexisting clique network relationships have fragile ties. Their networks do not function very effectively as a result of the lack of social surveillance, which would otherwise enforce those ties to provide the necessary social capital for migrants to properly settle and become employed in the United States. Therefore, urban migrants tend to be attracted to other migrants who already belong to an established MTN with members who, in most cases, live in daughter communities in the United States. This creates the MTN effect, which offers an avenue through which it is possible for migration to take place among migrants from urban places of origin. Once urban-origin migrants are absorbed by an MTN, more urban migrants from the same place of origin may be absorbed by the same MTN.

The MTNs also depend on the trust and direct or indirect participation of many other individuals who are not international migrants. Without the direct and indirect participation of those individuals as described earlier, the MTN would not be able to function properly. If the MTN malfunctions, its participants may be transplanted to other geographic locations if at least one of their members can make the connection with another MTN working effectively in another location. The MTNs can absorb outsiders as long as they can trust at least one member of the faltering MTN (see figure 6.2 in chapter 6).

Expanding MTNs occur not only at the place of destination, but also at the place of origin, as MTN participants begin to bring their own contacts once they have been absorbed. For example, this can happen by absorbing the residents of nearby towns via exogenous ties (see chapter 5). Therefore, expanding MTNs can occur in a variety of circumstances as long as trust can be shared by the individuals involved. Once relationships of trust take effect, other social dynamics, such as social homogeneity, the commonality of the immigrant experience, religiosity, and other factors help solidify relationships among new and existing members. This was the case of Martin in the quote at the beginning of chapter 3, and for Pancho and José, who were discussed in the introduction.

The main purpose of this section has been to show that network structure is important in understanding the exchange of social capital among migrants, especially among undocumented migrants. Among undocumented migrants from Mexico, either rural or urban, or even for outsiders, the exchange of social capital through MTNs is effective because they are composed of homogeneous individuals connected by strong ties that generate relations of social trust and social control. When it comes to the exchange of social capital, strong ties that do not belong to clique-like networks are not as effective as those that do. The MTNs can develop in both urban and rural settings, but social norms are what make the relationships of trust and social support perpetuate. The existence of social trust is a necessary condition for MTNs to be transplanted, expanded, and perpetuated in the transnational context.

CHAPTER FIVE

Migration-Trust Networks at the Macro Level

Macro social forces contribute to the creation, mainte-nance, and perpetuation of Migration-Trust Networks (MTNs). In most cases, such forces take place in a transnational context; that is, the con-nection between the social relations at the place of origin and those at the place of destination. The MTNs perform at multiple levels. First, there is the person-to-person interaction at the micro level. Once the network devel-ops, the MTN becomes its own social entity in which all the members of the network act in the form of collective action, which is referred to as collective efficacy. Additional macro mechanisms take place that allow the process of cumulative causation to expand from only one community to other send-ing communities, and from one place of destination to many. Such macro processes help networks to be transplanted into other networks, or MTNs. One community may also send migrants to different destinations, so trans-national relations become more complex as the networks diversify.

Therefore, I claim that the cumulative causation process is influenced by a series of multilevel social and contextual factors out of which MTNs can multiply, expand, and move from one location to another in the destination country, in this case, the United States. In this chapter, I introduce and provide examples of some of these processes. At the place of destination, it is important to consider the circumstances and resources available to the immigrants by looking closely at the context in which they arrive. In addi-tion, collective remittances and exogenous marriages with people outside the community of origin also affect the social structure, composition, and geographical expansion of the MTNs.

Cumulative Causation

Sending communities are transformed once international migration begins. The theory of cumulative causation refers to the tendency of migration to self-perpetuate, regardless of what causes the original migration in the first place (Myrdal 1957; Massey 1990). According to the social network theory of international migration, migration becomes easier and less risky over time as a result of a growing network of social contacts in the receiving community. These contacts share information and resources with future migrants, whether family, friends, or paisanos, that aid in the process of migration and the acquisition of employment in the host country. These resources and connections are forms of social capital that dramatically increase the likelihood of additional migration among persons who have family or friends already living in the United States (Massey et al. 1987). Once migration begins in a community, not only are there contextual transformations that promote further migration, but also the availability of a well-functioning MTN provides the right conditions for further out-migration. During the cumulative causation process, one of the factors influencing future international migration movement is the relative deprivation experienced by some of the people who stay behind in the community of origin. This is less important in urban environments than in rural areas. I address these differences in the following section.

Relative Deprivation

In the context of cumulative causation, the sending community undergoes cultural, social, and economic transformations that change the conditions in which migration decisions are made. These new economic circumstances tend to propel further migration. For example, the infusion of remittances into the local economy accentuates income inequality between households with migrant family members and those without. This causes a sense of relative deprivation among those who do not receive remittances, which is only exacerbated by the conspicuous spending of those who do. Migration then becomes more attractive for households to improve their standing both absolutely as well as relative to others in the reference community (Taylor 1986; Massey 1990).

I found plenty of evidence regarding the presence of relative deprivation in every community I visited, including those in El Salvador. As I argue in chapter 3, sending households that receive remittances experience a higher social status in the community. Upon returning, communities also bestow greater respect on its international migrants than they did before migrating. Cecilia, from one of the rural villages, migrated fifteen years before we implemented the survey. She stated the following when I asked her about how people treated her when she returned to Mexico.

> Oh, no . . . everyone expects that you would have money when you return. They all expect that you will wear the best clothes and build a nice house, etc. This is the case especially if you have been in the US for a long time. Then when you go back, they treat you differently. It is like you are more important or that you are better than them. For that reason, I get very mad when people treat me like if I was superior just because I am a migrant. They are so wrong, that is one of the reasons why I don't like going back home because people make me feel uncomfortable.

Cecilia implies that the relative deprivation not only happens in economic or material terms, but also in social terms. If people think those who migrate are somehow superior, then they may want to migrate too.

Relative deprivation was also evident in urban areas—socially, financially, and materially. Respondents spoke with great respect of those who were absent because they were in the United States. Several people confessed their own desire to leave because the economic conditions were very difficult at home. Nevertheless, the effect of deprivation seemed deeper in the rural areas since those who had never migrated or who did not have migrants in the family lived in deeper levels of poverty than everyone else.

The MTN, when working well, seemed to award access to anyone who wanted to migrate, so I began to ask those who had never migrated why they did not do so. Specifically, I wanted to understand if they had trouble getting access to social networks (or the MTN). I found that in rural areas there were two main reasons that people had not migrated. One was that prior failed attempts discouraged them. Many were scared to make another attempt after previously having a bad experience. The second reason was that they had dependents at home, such as small children, elderly, or someone who was sick. If they left, no one would be there to care for them. Most people I questioned said someone offered to help them migrate in the past, but they did not want to take the offer because of their unusual circumstances. In rural areas, therefore, the inability to access networks was not a problem. It appeared that those deciding to migrate from urban areas were more desperate about their economic situation. Yet I was not able to determine whether social capital was essential for urban dwellers because they generally possessed more human capital than rural migrants and were able to acquire tourist visas more easily. Future research should look more closely at the relationship between access to networks and decisions to migrate by status of origin.

Culture of Migration

The transformation of the sending communities occurs on many levels as the social and economic value of remittances becomes deeply rooted in the local culture. It creates a pervasive "culture of migration" that is transmitted throughout generations and social networks (Kandel and Massey 2002). For young people, the aspiration to migrate eclipses that of continuing their education. The lack of interest in school is just as integrated into their culture as the expectation to live and work abroad at some point in their lives. This is only reinforced by the absence of their parents and family who have migrated to work in the United States. Those left behind, who are largely supported by remittances — as well as those who are not, due to relative deprivation — are directly and indirectly encouraged by their community and family to continue the cycle of migration. This is because education is not a priority. In most of the communities, in Mexico and in El Salvador, kids began to migrate to the United States as young as fifteen years old, with the intention of finding full-time work.

Throughout my visits in destination areas, I observed in disbelief that fifteen-year-olds also arrived and were hired in the same jobs as their parents without employers' questioning their age. Like the adults, children worked full time, and the MTN participants treated them as adults. Observing the children working full time instead of attending school was the most difficult part of my research experience. I learned that children were treated as adults upon arrival to the United States because they had worked back home to help support their household. Only the youngest children of the household remained at the place of origin and completed college, thanks to the remittances from the older siblings who likely had all migrated abroad.

Throughout my years of fieldwork in one of the rural villages in Guanajuato, I followed the case of Octavio. When I met Octavio, he was sixteen years old and the youngest of six brothers, all of whom migrated to the United States. Octavio remained at the place of origin, however, because he wanted to remain in school. I may have influenced his decision to stay, as I remember speaking with him about the importance of education. He periodically wrote letters to me sharing his progress in college. He explained that his brothers sent him money every month for all his expenses. During one of the interviews after he had received his degree, he stated:

> My brothers never missed a single month sending me money for me to complete an education. I think they felt that if they were not able to do it, at least they could help me to do it. They knew that without their help I was not going to be able to rent an apartment in the city of Leon and then attend college. They paid for my food, utility bills, books, tuition. In other words, they paid for everything! I am very thankful to my brothers for helping me to get ahead. I felt pressured to do good in school because of the huge sacrifice they made for me. I had to do well and finish and get my degree, and I did.

Octavio's story was common. It was interesting to see that families, with the help of social networks, were sending many of the household children to the United States, but the youngest children were being encouraged to remain behind and stay in school. Some of these younger siblings shared that they also wanted to migrate at one point, but they felt obligated to stay home because their older siblings had high educational expectations of them and demonstrated such thorough financial investments. Despite these sacrifices, there was a general lack of interest in education due to the culture of migration. The desire to migrate to the United States greatly outweighed the desire for education.

Additional transformations of the sending communities are manifested through other kinds of social and physical changes. For example, people no longer use land for agricultural purposes. Instead, returning migrants use land for building other structures that serve as new homes, businesses, factories, schools, churches, and so forth. These transformations then change the local labor market; for example, some people leave their agricultural work and use their remittances to open new stores or small restaurants and become small local entrepreneurs. These changes create new labor opportunities to other members of the sending communities and contribute to the local development of the communities.

Context of Reception

International migrants from either rural or urban places of origin do everything possible to settle near their social contacts upon arrival. At first, they live with someone who is helping them migrate; but even after they can move into their own apartment, room, or house, they choose to settle as close as possible to those who helped them migrate or to the rest of the migrants from their hometown. As more people arrive from the same place of origin, a daughter community is formed (Massey et al. 1987). Daughter communities then become the receiving communities, which offer the necessary conditions for the newcomers to settle satisfactorily and find jobs, and so forth. Without specific conditions, the flow in incoming migrants to that daughter community begins to cease. Among the factors that play an important role in the context of reception are the demand for labor, availability of affordable housing and transportation, and access to educational facilities, medical facilities, and other resources to begin a satisfactory new life at the place of destination.

Affordable housing: The place of destination must meet certain conditions in order for recent migrants to cluster together. For example, there must be cheap housing available so that newcomers can find homes or apartments to settle near each other. Immigrant enclaves form as new arrivals settle in entire apartment complexes and/or homes on the same block or around the corner from the other settlers from their same community of origin. In many instances, white-flight takes place during the process of settlement to a new migrant destination. That is, non-Hispanic whites tend to leave the neighborhood and move out of the area (in most cases to a suburban area) when they see that the minority population has risen, whether of immigrants or other racial or ethnic groups. Once they leave the area, the vacant houses and apartments left behind are then occupied by the new arrivals. During my first visits in 1998, for example, I saw many non-Hispanic whites living in the apartment complexes where I conducted interviews. Over the years, I observed the outflow of non-Hispanic whites as the new arrivals began renting the units. Non-Hispanic whites who decided to stay were either in charge of the buildings, working as maintenance persons in the buildings, or had become friends with the migrants and were even trying to learn Spanish to know their new neighbors better. Some really took the opportunity to know the newcomers by joining their soccer teams, learning and even adopting some of their cultural practices, and attending their social gatherings. One could argue that these non-Hispanic white neighbors also became part of the MTN in some ways. I claim that the social conditions that develop at the place of permanent settlement (the immigrant enclave), allow for collective efficacy to take place given the geographic proximity of network participants, their frequent interactions, and their dependence on relations of trust among other values.

Labor demand: Another necessary condition for the context of reception is the availability of labor for the newcomers. Labor demand is crucial for an immigrant enclave to form at the place of destination. Sources of employment can vary. Some immigrants may work in restaurants, others in factories, others in fisheries, but without the availability of jobs, other prospective migrants would not be able to survive if they arrived and could not find a job. In most cases, once the employer notices the good work ethic of a worker, he or she asks the employee if he has any friends or family members who would also like to work there. This is because the employer believes that the immigrants' friends and family will also share the same ethic and be hardworking, responsible, and efficient on the job. Therefore, employers' recruiting practices utilize the employee's referrals; in most cases, workers refer their fellow migrants, new arrivals, or others who are prospective migrants. In order to secure employment, migrants must find sources of labor that can hire and/or offer jobs to those without legal documents. Such conditions certainly limit the kind of job opportunities available to the newcomers, but if existent, there is a large probability that the MTN will continue to bring more migrants and perpetuate itself.

In general, I observed that the members of the MTN prearranged employment positions for new migrants. Some new arrivals were even able to choose which job they wanted to try first. Once the new arrival had a set working schedule in that first job, he or she would, if possible, look for a second job. Several of the migrants held multiple jobs, given their low salaries. They wanted to have enough money to provide for themselves in the United States and to send personal and collective remittances. Having two jobs also allowed them to participate in the MTN by helping new arrivals.

Throughout the years, I never learned of an instance in which there were no jobs available. In 2000, however, there was a case in Dallas in which all of the migrant employees at a particular factory were forced to switch jobs and go to work in another factory. Managers at the first factory were notified, through no-match letters by the Internal Revenue Service (IRS), that some of the employers' names did not match the Social Security numbers they provided when the new employees were hired. Such no-match letters were a red flag, indicating that many of those workers lacked legal documents. The employers were likely aware of this but only became concerned when the government began questioning the status of the workers. The factory took action by firing the workers to avoid penalties. The Immigration Reform and Control Act of 1986 issued employer sanction laws, but from 1986 until 2000 they were hardly enforced (Massey, Durand, and Malone 2002).

Transportation to job sites: Some form of transportation from the housing units to the labor sites is crucial. It can either be public transportation, such as a bus or train, a private car, or a collective van. The newcomers must be able to get to their job sites; otherwise, they cannot go to work and will not be able to make ends meet. In many cases, the employers provide the transportation depending on the company, their need for labor, and the availability of transportation possibilities for the migrants.

During my fieldwork, I observed how some migrants learned to overcome the challenge of not having a driver's license. Some migrants managed to live walking distance from their place of work, while others rode bicycles. Most US states, with the exception of New Mexico, Utah, and Washington state, do not allow migrants to obtain a driver's license if they do not have legal residence in the United States (Vock 2010). I observed that as the laws became more restrictive, MTN members devised additional strategies for coping. For example, many began carpooling in larger groups and riding with a driver who had a license. Therefore, they became even more dependent on the support from other MTN members.

Housing amenities: Newcomers must be able to find affordable food and clothes nearby the immigrant enclave. It is preferable if the food stores nearby can supply the type of foods that the immigrants are used to, such as tortillas and other Mexican food items; however, this is not crucial for the immigrant enclave to begin. With time, the new arrivals will either lobby local stores to supply what they need, or they will open their own ethnic stores at some point. Affordable clothes are best if they are available at cheap prices from flea markets or thrift shops. Newcomers, especially those who arrive without clothes or belongings, benefit from the availability of cheap clothes because those who are buying the clothes for them are in a better position to help them out. Other nearby amenities migrants need include laundromats, pharmacies, and cheap furniture stores, among others.

Schools for children: New immigrant enclaves also need to have access to education at all levels, given that families might arrive with children of different ages. The schools nearby would have to be willing to accept the undocumented children and youth in the schools. Some local school systems are able to cater to the needs of the new arrivals by providing bilingual education, but such an amenity is not critical as long as the children can begin attending school upon arrival.

Still, the process of enrolling children into school can be a challenge for those without documents. Most mothers depend on other members of the MTN to find out where to go, what to say to the school authorities, what documents to present, and so forth. While conducting my fieldwork, I witnessed one instance in which a school asked the parents for a state ID in order to enter the school. Members of the MTN asked other members who had legal documentation to go and speak with the teachers on behalf of the parents.

At the time of this writing, many undocumented families left the state of Alabama because a new law passed in which school authorities were given permission to question the legal status of parents with enrolled children, so many parents decided to move to other states where schools did not represent a threat to their status. Those families likely used MTNs to access immigrant enclaves in other states and transplanted their networks, as explained later on in this chapter.

Medical services: New arrivals also need access to medical care when they get sick or when women become pregnant. Most of the new migrants have no access to medical insurance given the nature of the jobs they take on, which often lack safety standards so the employers can save money. As a result of working under very unsafe conditions, they have greater chances of getting either hurt on the job or getting sick and consequently need access to affordable medical care so they can be treated for their injuries and sicknesses. In the absence of affordable medical care, migrants may try to utilize folklore medicine practices, herbal remedies, or bring medications from their place of origin. The absence of affordable medical care may or may not affect the growth of the MTN.

Therefore, the context of reception has to meet certain conditions in order for the chain migration stream to propel and feed itself. Newcomers must be able to find affordable housing near the people from their own social network and have jobs upon arrival, means of transportation to their job, access to food, and access to schooling and medical care.

Entertainment and culture: A form of entertainment is not essential for the settlement of the immigrants into the new place of destination. Instead, transnational cultural practices are transferred and implemented in the receiving community from the place of origin, and these continue to enforce the culture, especially with the subsequent generations. Celebrations such as weddings, *quinceañeras,* baptisms, birthday parties, graduations, and so forth are occasions to celebrate with others and entertain themselves. In fact, such social reunions are the opportunities in which the immigrants can monitor and enforce the behavior of others. They can gossip about whether or not the other people or the new arrivals have been following the values and expectations of the members of the community of origin.

Compadrazgo, culture, and entertainment: The creation of fictitious ties such as compadrazgo also helps the MTN acquire new members and strengthen the trust and social support in the network.

International migrants have few opportunities for recreation given the limited time in their hard-working schedules as well as their low income. Many have to work two jobs or long hours for seven days a week in order to save money to both survive in the United States and send a little back home to their family left behind. The few opportunities they have to entertain themselves within the immigrant enclave are the religious and cultural celebrations for members of the community, such as baptisms, quinceañeras, weddings, first communions, birthdays, graduations, and anniversaries. From these events arises a new manifestation of trust and social support, a custom that is widely practiced at the places of origin and transferred to the places of destination—the compadrazgo gifts. This is an opportunity for others, either at the community of origin or the place of destination, to contribute with gifts in order for the celebration or event to take place.

The person planning the celebration asks community members (not necessarily family members) to contribute something for the celebration, such as the cake, the dress, the jewelry, the mass service, the music (usually a live band), even the limousine, the video, or the photography. Those who help are usually called *padrinos* and they are to be recognized on the invitation as the padrinos. For elaborate events like quinceañeras, when a girl turns fifteen and is thus considered a woman, there are padrinos and madrinas for several additional items, such as the guestbook, the tiara, and the last doll— a symbol that she is no longer a little girl. She also needs flowers, a rosary, shoes, earrings, and a necklace (often made of gold). As the items add up, padrinos and madrinas can also help with something very small, such as the pen with which to sign the guestbook or the glasses to do the toast. In this way, when one of the padrinos is hosting his or her own event on another occasion, he or she can ask around and those being asked will feel obligated to contribute something, especially if that person has supported one of their own events. The tradition of having padrinos and madrinas is more common among the lower-income families, even including those who live in urban areas. The tradition was transmitted from rural to urban places of origin and has now been transmitted to those living in the United States. Therefore, the same expectations enforced at the sending community are also expected at the receiving community when it comes to supporting each other for their celebrations and events. For some occasions, the invitation to the event lists the padrinos and madrinas and how they contributed. At the sending community, the households that receive remittances are more likely to be asked to be padrinos or madrinas for an event. Another common way to help is by being asked to participate in the ceremony as a *chambelan* or a *dama* of a quinceañera. A quinceañera, or birthday girl, usually has seven damas and seven chambelanes who escort her as she enters the mass and who dance the *bals* during the reception. Not just anyone can afford to buy a dress or to rent a tuxedo to be a dama or chambelan. In most cases, only those who receive remittances are able to afford it. I met a boy who had been a chambelan more than thirty times. He was very much in demand not only because of his good looks, but also because he had a few brothers and sisters in the United States who were able to send him money to rent a tuxedo and shoes every time he participated as a chambelan for a quinceañera.

Not everyone could become madrinas and padrinos:

> Some people planned fiestas with the expectation that madrinas and padrinos would sponsor everything; but for some madrinas and padrinos, their economic situation was so bad that at the last minute they didn't come up with what they had promised. Most people who were asked to help sponsor the fiesta were expected to respond. Consequently, those who received remittances from family members abroad had a larger burden because they had to help more often and become padrinos on more occasions. People expected to still have their party and that everyone was going to cooperate for the fiesta.

Therefore, most of the padrinos at the place of origin could no longer engage in the compadrazgo relationships if their economic situation was very bad or they did not receive remittances from the north. Those who lived at the place of destination were better off, as I wrote in the following field notes from a quinceañera in Long Beach, California:

> I went to Lorena's quinceañera. I was verbally invited but I did not know when it was going to be, or where and what time, so I called the mother. She

said that I was cordially invited and that I could go any time after four o'clock. Then I went to the quinciañera and we got there at 8 pm. It was just starting even though they had said it would start at 4 pm. A little after we got there they danced the *bals,* cut the cake, and had the *brindis.* It was a great event because everything was taken care of: the bals, the pictures, the banda, the dj, the food, the beer, the sodas; everything was great. They paid a special choreographer to be in charge of everything, from the bals choreography to the pictures. She danced by herself with all the other chambelans. The main one was her brother. She danced with roses all around and each of the seven chambelans had a flower. They all danced with her and it looked very good.

Celebrations such as these are a very important part of the way the members of the community interact with each other, socialize, and forget their struggles, both in the sending and receiving communities. For this reason, memories of the events are important to send back and forth to both places. During the old days, families would sell or give away video recordings of the events to several members of the community, both in the United States and in their hometown. Today, websites are created and used so that friends and family in both places can see photos and videos from the celebrations. For those who migrate from smaller communities, or even some urban areas (although not as common), a hugely important event for all members of both the sending and receiving communities is called the fiesta patronal, or the patron saint festival. In most cases, those who live abroad are able to collect money and send it back to their community in the form of collective remittances in order for their hometown to finance and celebrate the fiesta patronal.

Collective remittances: Collective remittances are a form of social capital that benefits the community of origin as a whole. Migrants at the place of destination collectively raise money to send back to their hometown in order to finance local infrastructure projects, such as paving streets, installing electricity and sewage systems, or building a church, park, or plaza. In many cases, funds are also used to organize and execute the fiesta patronal, which takes place only once a year and is traditionally when migrants return home, if they can.

When I first began doing my research at the end of the 1990s, collective remittances were still done more informally. A group of migrants collected the money at the immigrant enclaves in different parts of the United States and sent it to their hometown — some of them even took the cash home with them during a returning trip to Mexico. I wrote the following field notes while interviewing a rural-origin migrant in Dallas, Texas:

> Only in the last three or four years has there been an increase in the number of cases in which the whole family migrates. The majority leave behind their wives in Mexico. Once they're in Mexico, crossing the border back to the US is the last thing they worry about; what mattered the most was seeing their families. On January 20, the church has a celebration and on January 11 begins the novena. Everyone gets together from all the nearby ranchos for music, fireworks, a fair, a musical band, and more. There are four people in charge of raising money. They collect funds from all parts of the US where people from the same hometown are living, from Bakersfield to Chicago. Each donation was no less than twenty dollars and the most anyone had donated was seventy dollars. The total for January 1997 was $1,450 from just Long Beach. With everyone's cooperation they also built the church. Inside the church, they displayed trophies from soccer matches they won in the US. The majority of sixteen- and seventeen-year-olds migrate and there is hardly anyone left between the ages of 25 and 40. There are only children and elderly. Very few people study. There are only five to seven professionals in the whole ranch: three teachers and two agricultural engineers. There is a telesecundaria (distance education for secondary and high schools in Mexico) and a high school about two kilometers away from the town.

Once local governments in Mexico began to see money flowing into these communities, they began the 2 × 1 and 3 × 1 programs in which the local governments would match the amount of collective remittances as long as they were invested in local infrastructure. For example, if the collective remittances were designated for a new sewage system, then for every $1,000 invested by the migrants the local government would pay another $2,000 to $3,000. With the involvement of local governments came the formalization of collective remittances and the organizations that managed them. Hometown associations, or HTAs, arose all over the United States. These are organizations formed by migrants in the place of destination that collect and manage remittances for projects that improve their places of origin. Members of HTAs decide how to allocate funds and how to execute the projects, working in collaboration with the local government in the community of origin.

Originally, the practice of remitting collectively formed out of relations of trust and social support among the members of the community. Trust was the basis in which the system of collective remittances operated. International migrants who lived in the immigrant enclave trusted the people collecting the money and trusted that it would be used for the assigned purpose in the community of origin. I interviewed several people who participated in the collection of the money and learned that the migrants would give them the cash without questions, trusting that the money would be well spent. Large amounts of money were collected; in many instances, families donated $100 or more for the cause, and the total amounts collected often reached up to several thousand dollars. For example, one respondent reported having brought with him to Mexico up to $8,000, which had been collected for the town's celebration of the fiesta patronal.

As described in Robert Smith's (2006) book, *Mexican New York*, collective remittances also create transnational political power for the residents abroad, especially for those who actively participate in the collective remittances arena. Those leaders become very influential in the local politics of the hometown community in the sending country. Given that the migrants are investing in the improvement of the infrastructure of the home community, they gain political power through affluence and are able to pressure the local government and the community for things to be done their way. I learned that migrants who sponsored community projects made all of the decisions regarding them. The local government had very little input on the community's list of priorities. Although the decision-making process did involve those in the community of origin, migrants made the final decisions. Collective remittances enhance transnational ties and also enhance the influence of migrants abroad on their home communities via transnational politics.

I observed social organization and commitment to collective remittances in both small and large communities of origin. For example, in the medium-sized town, money from migrants was spent building a mercado or a small market (a mall in which vendors could set up their small businesses). This was an enclosed building where vendors only needed a table to begin selling items such as crafts, fresh produce, and homemade Mexican candy. Community members found the investment worthwhile as it helped some locals generate income. In one urban area, remittances helped the local church maintain a program to reduce street violence and gangs. With the help of donations from migrants, a skate park was built to keep children off the streets. The same program included computer classes and homework assistance.

Exogenous Ties and Social Networks

Fiestas patronales are religious celebrations in which residents from neighboring towns walk in religious processions in order to visit the town and attend masses. During the fiesta patronal there are food stands, a large concert with several bands, folkloric shows, and celebrations. During such an event, people from other towns are encouraged to visit and over the years are able to interact and build relationships. Those looking for boyfriends and girlfriends then have the opportunity to be introduced to each other. Small towns have limitations on who can marry whom, given that they are formed by extended families whose members have kin relations with many town inhabitants. Given the limited supply of prospective spouses within the community, the fiestas patronales allow for the formation of new relationships between people from neighboring towns. Once two people from different towns marry each other, they gain full access to the social networks of migration from their spouse's respective town. He or she is considered a new member of the community and if needed, the new friends, paisanos, or family members would provide all the help necessary for that person, and possibly their family members from their hometown to also migrate. Given that both the new spouse and his or her family members would qualify to receive social capital from the MTN, the migration chain is expanded and perpetuated because people of working age from nearby towns gain access to the MTN through their family member's marriage.

While conducting fieldwork in one of the ranchos, I wrote:

> Most of the people in the nearby ranchos know each other. They also look for boyfriends and girlfriends between the ranchos. I could see how family members were spread out between the ranchos that were nearby; and for that reason, so were the solidarity relations. The people who arrived to the places of destination in many cases included people from the other ranchos. The key was that there had to be some family relationship with someone from the other rancho, or at least a friendship.

Outsiders are not welcomed easily, because the benefits and opportunities are exclusive to those in the community and to those with close ties from nearby towns. During the ethnographic fieldwork, several respondents mentioned that those from nearby towns who were looking for girlfriends were not welcome in their towns.

> The locals were a little rude to those from other ranchos and received them with rocks because they had come to win over the girls from their town. At the end, they told them that there was nothing they could do about it.

The same respondents later admitted that the local community found it challenging to accept the marriage between their girls and outsiders. During the pre-marriage stage, outsiders were antagonized or scared away with violence and threats; males from the local community sometimes threw rocks at the outsiders. Once a couple became engaged, however, people's attitude changed and the outsider was more accepted. If the member of another community married within the MTN of the sending community, then that person would receive all the benefits of belonging to the MTN. With the exception of the fiestas patronales, during which everyone in the town had to show pride and behave as good citizens, community members were openly hostile to outside visitors. However, the larger the town, the less the antagonism shown toward outsiders seeking courtship.

Community Status as a Result of Collective Remittances

Investment in local infrastructure causes relative deprivation for the people in nearby towns. While the sending community competes to look the best and have the best plaza for its fiestas, the best fiesta patronales, and the most amenities possible (such as a nice church, paved streets, street lighting, drinking water, a sewage system, and new schools), the citizens of neighboring towns feel deprived for not having those amenities in their own town. Such relative deprivation might encourage additional migration from neighboring towns and create new migration streams. In addition, it could encourage these new migrants to form their own hometown association, whether formal or informal, in order to improve their town's infrastructure. Therefore, relative deprivation occurs not only at the micro level, but also at the macro level by provoking additional migration from neighboring communities and consequently expanding the social network, creating new social network chains, and broadening and perpetuating the migration streams, but in a geographical scope.

During my fieldwork throughout the years, I became an eyewitness of the competition among communities to build things better than the others. They competed to have a better plaza, a better church, paved roads, and so forth. After one community enhanced their local church, the community nearby made even better improvements to their church. For example, one community (close to the one I studied) made the altar of the church out of *marmol* stone instead of wood (like the neighboring one). A similar thing happened when another nearby town made their plaza more elaborate and modern than others, as shown in figure 5.1. Their plaza had a larger fountain, a playground for children, and a stage for the groups who would play during the fiestas patronales, features that the plaza of the neighboring town lacked.

Another case involved paving streets. One town wanted to have all the streets paved to outdo the neighboring town where only a few streets had been paved. Figure 5.2 shows local workers paving a road of a small rural village in El Salvador using the funds from the collective remittances sent by those from abroad.

Figure 5.1   Main plaza constructed with collective remittances in one of the communities of the study. This photo shows the elaborated amenities of the plaza, which includes a children's playground.

Figure 5.2   Collective remittances were used here for paving the streets of a village in El Salvador. This is a radical transformation that is immediately noticed by those who live in the nearby communities.

Also, the fiestas patronales enjoyed such competition. For example, towns wanted to be known for having the best band during their fiesta patronal compared to nearby towns. To have a higher quality of music required a high contract fee for the band, so such competition required migrants to be more organized and willing to send collective remittances. Those abroad received most of the credit when their towns developed a better reputation than nearby towns.

I also observed the relative deprivation among communities and how those communities that started off with nothing began to organize and send people to the United States, primarily using the MTNs of a nearby community through exogenous marriage. In this way, they were able to fix up their community after a few years through remittances. Transformations within communities occurred rapidly. For example, in just a couple of years a community that did not have a plaza before would have a better one than the other towns nearby. In some cases, the qualities of the plaza, such as having a playground, a fountain, a stage for bands to play music, benches, and so forth, contrasted with the lack of other amenities in most of the town, for example, lack of electricity or nonpaved roads. This is an area available for more research.

The Use of Technology and Transnational Practices

Social surveillance occurs when international migrants monitor each other's social practices and make sure they comply with social values and expectations of the rest of the members of the MTN. This perpetuation of social practices of solidarity is made possible through the use of the Internet and electronics such as video cameras and cell phones. With advances in technology, transnational migrant communication has increased over the years. International migrants can now create websites about their home community and the receiving community in which they post events, blogs, pictures, videos, news, gossip, legal documents, and so forth, that help maintain the two communities connected with each other in a common social space.

The use of cell phones: Given the higher cost of long-distance calls, text messaging has become a common practice among international migrants and their loved ones left behind. Some telephone companies offer low cost or even free international text messaging, allowing migrants to send messages affordably. Families who are separated can more easily communicate, although they are limited to what they can say in text messages. In most cases, texts are also sent as confirmation after money has been wired and after the money has been picked up. In addition, they allow international migrants to keep in more frequent contact with each other than by just using the phone; they are able to share more situations, pictures, and even videos via cell phones. Such communication allows for those in the sending communities to learn more about the daily lives of their loved ones in the United States, or in another place of destination. Unfortunately, the increased use of texting communication, while it costs less, has caused family members to speak to each other on the phone less often. While writing this manuscript in 2010, I called one of the contacts in Long Beach to investigate the use of cell phones and texting. The respondent informed me that before, he used to call his wife every week. Now he only uses texting and only calls his wife and kids every two months or so.

In Mexico, telephone companies have been able to provide home phone service through cell phones. When I began my research in 1997, there was only one phone in each of the rural villages that I visited, usually in a store. When someone wanted to talk on the phone with their family members, they had to call twice. On the first phone call they would tell the store owner to go and find their family member. Then after an hour or so, the person in the United States would call again and his or her family member would be waiting for the phone call.

By the late 2000s, most people in Mexico, even those who lived in rural areas of origin, were able to get their own private home phone service through cell phones that look like home phones. Phone cards were formerly one of the cheapest ways for immigrants to call, but increased costs from phone companies, especially in small towns, have decreased card holders' affordable speaking time. For example, if one dials to a regular home phone using a $5.00 phone card, the call can last over an hour or so, but when dialing to a cell phone or a home-cell phone with the same $5.00 phone card, the call might last about 20 minutes. Text messages, alternatively, cost as little as five cents each. Therefore, communication is more frequent but less personal.

The power of videos and YouTube: In the recent history of international migration, migrants have looked for ways to share their experiences and great moments with their loved ones left behind. Others have looked for ways to send their special moments to their loved ones at the place of destination. As a result, video recording became a very popular practice. Most importantly, one could make copies of the VHS cassettes and share them with more and more people. From the place of origin, special events such as school graduations, weddings, quinceañeras, and the fiesta patronal could be recorded and sent to loved ones abroad so they could take part in the events, the moments, and the culture. Videos were a good way for migrants to keep in touch with their loved ones and see the children grow, the adults get older, and the transformations take place as a result of collective remittances. Video recordings would either encourage or discourage migrants to keep sending collective or individual remittances.

In the same way, migrants abroad would also record family events, children growing, and other memories at the place of destination, so that those left behind could learn a little more about their life in the United States. However, while those in the sending community would perhaps record some of the struggles they were living back home, those in the receiving communities would be more careful not to portray a bad image of their life in the United States. The videos would not usually show any of the harsh living and working conditions that the migrants encountered; instead, most portrayed happy moments, if possible. Showing the struggles would send the wrong message: that those abroad are not successful. For this reason, even though the living conditions of migrants abroad may be questionable, those who are left behind get the wrong stories and the wrong versions about what life is like in the *norte*. The reality is essentially concealed until the newcomers arrive and see it with their own eyes. For this reason, social networks continue to be fueled as more people migrate because the truth is not uncovered to prospective migrants.

Cybercafés: It has become very common for small towns all over Mexico to have a *café internet*, or a cybercafé. Even though only a few people in the town know how to use the computer, the cybercafé is necessary in order for some people to communicate with their loved ones and for the youth to keep up with the times. A typical form of communication for several years was the instant messenger from Hotmail, for example. Later on, Yahoo and other sites developed similar features where people can instantly communicate with others who are simultaneously connected online. With the availability of webcams, people are also able to see the video image and hear the audio of the other person with whom they are chatting. Such means of communication also encourage migration because prospective migrants know that if they leave they would still be able to communicate with their loved ones through the Internet.

Blogs, websites, and networking sites: The growing use of blogs and websites is a relatively recent development of modern communication. Members of transnational communities are able to post pictures and messages to their loved ones at both the place of origin and the place of destination, thus encouraging transnational communication and practices. One of the most important functions of these websites and blogs is to encourage collective remittances from migrants as well as their political participation at the place of origin. Through websites and blogs, issues related to the place of origin are often discussed and challenged. Opinions are shared and suggestions are given on how to fix problems, for example. In addition, recognition to those sponsors of collective remittances is often posted online, awarding a higher status to those who have contributed. Photos of the finished projects or the fiestas patronales are also shared with those abroad. For example, the website http://intipucacity.com contains a number of images of finished projects in a community in El Salvador. On the same website are pictures of community projects of other villages nearby.

Surrounding communities and those abroad are able to judge the success of the celebrations via such website posts. Successes and failures are made known, and political participation is encouraged through commenting and blogging. The opinions of those abroad carry a lot of weight in future decisions and collective remittances projects. Similarly, those abroad are able to show support or disapproval for political candidates at the place of origin, giving them direct political influence in the overall results of the elections at the local level.

Social networking sites such as Facebook are becoming very powerful tools used to connect those at the destination to those at the origin. For example, many respondents showed me their sites through which they shared pictures, videos, and special moments. They also send private messages, which usually involve details about sending monetary remittances. Through this technology, migrants share details about their daily lives such as work and friendships because they can post their status during the day using cell phones. Those who have the same group of friends on Facebook are able to see pictures and posts of other friends. This enables those in Mexico to know friends of their loved ones who are also in the United States, and those in the United States are also able to know the friends of those left behind, thereby strengthening transnational ties.

Skype is also becoming very popular among international migrants, as they are able to have videochats and see one another as they speak. Not only does such technology save immigrants a lot of money on telephone calls, but it also helps them feel better about being so far away from their loved ones. Access to this type of technology is not as widespread as it could be, but more migrants are learning how to use such advances via their MTN. They teach one another how to use a computer and help one another open e-mail and Facebook accounts. Not surprisingly, children largely fill the role of teaching adults the advantages of the new technology.

Social Network Forces at the Macro Level

The successful development, perpetuation, or extinction of social networks of international migration not only depend on the relations of solidarity at the micro level, but also on several conditions and social forces at the macro level.

While there are pull factors at the context of reception that encourage international migration to the place of destination, there are also other sending forces at the place of origin that take part in the process of cumulative causation, such as relative deprivation and the culture of migration. Moreover, transnational forces also play a prominent role in the perpetuation of social networks, such as the flow of collective remittances, transnational political participation, and relations of compadrazgo. These all contribute to the transnational social process that transforms the sending and receiving communities, adapting them to the social, cultural, political, and economic effects of international migration. Furthermore, exogenous forces, such as the expansion of social ties through exogenous marriage, allows for members of other communities to access the social networks of the sending community. In addition, relative deprivation effects of the community as a whole also encourage other communities to adopt and implement similar migratory processes and transnational social processes in order to compete with the sending communities nearby.

Another form of transnationalism that drives social networks of international migration is social interaction. Social interaction through media, such as the Internet and cell phones, enhances relationships and transmits knowledge and human capital in such a way that encourages more migration. It also helps pass along the values, expectations, and customs of the members of the community by which social networks and relations of solidarity are enforced. Media and technology play an important role in the creation, maintenance, and perpetuation of social networks. Through the communication that takes place in those networks, a transnational agenda is more easily executed and social processes such as relative deprivation, the culture of migration, and the status acquisition can be enhanced. So far, the study of social networks of migration has neglected the role of media in the promotion of the social networks among international migrants. It has also failed to take into account the social processes by which social networks of migration are expanded to other communities. Those in other communities either acquire access to the social networks via exogenous marriages, or become victims of relative deprivation because of the higher status of other sending communities.

It is important to also take into account that the elements that cause social networks to develop, perpetuate, or extinguish are interconnected with the context of reception at the place of destination. Without the right conditions, such as housing and job availability, new arrivals cannot acquire employment and the ability to settle. Migrants who are already in the United States must be capable of providing resources to help others migrate internationally, since they feel socially obligated as members of the MTN to do so. The problem migrants run into when providing help for others to migrate is when the context of reception does not provide the newcomers with the necessary resources to sustain themselves in the receiving community, such as a place to stay when they first arrive, affordable housing to settle in after a period of time, labor opportunities, school access for children, or food and medical care. When this is case, the MTN is gradually depleted, despite the willingness of its US members to help others migrate internationally. Without the demand for labor in the receiving community, there would be no supply of labor coming from the sending community. Social networks operate based on the demand for labor at the place of destination. Therefore, the MTN could cease to function if the demand for labor at the place of destination ceases to exist, regardless of all other factors. It is important to state at this point that the MTN has the capability to transplant itself to another location if it is depleted in the original receiving community due to the lack of demand for labor. This is a possibility if the members have access to another MTN in another geographical location that provides all the necessary conditions to sustain them. At this new place of destination, the MTN can revive, transplant itself, and continue to perpetuate through the MTN effect as described in detail in chapter 4.

CHAPTER SIX

Migration-Trust Networks: Expanding Current Theory

Thus far, I have shared ethnographic evidence of how social networks of migration can develop from rural and urban places of origin and how they function. Such networks are Migration-Trust Networks, and they are the focus of this study. I theorize on how such networks function when a large number of the network participants lack legal documentation. The MTNs expand and/or are transplanted to other networks, not only at the place of origin, but also at the places of destination. So far, this research has provided grounds to the claim that the creation, expansion, and perpetuation of social networks of international migration depend on numerous factors.

Social networks do not function magically, as has been suggested in the literature. One reason it has been difficult for scholars to understand how social networks of migration (in this case, MTNs) function, is the difficulty of dissecting and identifying the multiple factors and social processes that appear to be driving these networks. A further challenge is that these different factors and social processes appear to be functioning simultaneously. In addition, many of the social factors that seem to be driving these networks are not necessarily observable or easy to measure. For this reason, my empirical findings and theoretical propositions are a starting point in the area of international migration for understanding how to think about the functionality of the proposed MTNs.

I have suggested that international migrants exchange social capital using preexisting social relationships of trust and social solidarity from their place of origin. They may also form new ties resulting from their international migration experience and/or from the transnational social process in which they have participated. Such new or preexisting ties can then be transformed and adapted within the transnational context. Relations of social trust and social cohesiveness among network participants become the main driving force behind migrant networks, especially if most of the migrants lack legal status to enter, reside, and work at the place of destination.

Through relationships of trust within clique-like social networks at the place of origin, which are transformed and transnationally connected to MTNs for the first time, returning international migrants exchange the necessary social capital in order to depart for, arrive, and settle in the country of destination. The social surveillance and expectations that govern the exchange of social capital help to expand, maintain, and perpetuate the social network. Figure 6.1 exemplifies a Migration-Trust Network and how collective efficacy is created within an MTN in the transnational context between the places of origin and destination. First, preexisting relationships of trust, the common migration experience, and the commonalities of struggle back home may lead to a paisanaje sentiment. Together with religious faith, bounded solidarity is also created. As a result, social cohesion, collective behavior, social bonding, and solidarity behavior are expected from the members of the MTN. Social monitoring then takes place to ensure that the values, norms, and social expectations are being followed. This leads to enforceable trust in which, through social surveillance and a sanctioning capacity among the members of the MTN, the behavioral expectations, values, and norms are enforced. This leads to extremely high levels of trust that are shared by the members of an MTN. The sentiment of social collectiveness is therefore enforced by the sanctioning capacity of the members of the network. This sentiment of social collectiveness (or collective conscience in Durkehim's terms) together with the high labels of social trust result in a form of collective efficacy, which acts as a safe haven for the members of the MTN. These social dynamics within MTNs allow social capital to become accessible to new and returning migrants who provide help and share the benefits of membership in the network to others in the future. The peculiarities regarding the Mexico-US bound international migration flow allow for conditions in which one can observe the mechanisms of well-functioning social networks over time. Such collective efficacy and the monitoring capacity of the members of the MTN take place in the transnational context between the place of origin and destination when migrants travel back and forth, and via regular mail, media communications such as the telephone communications, and the use of the Internet. Figure 6.1 portrays the complexity of this unobserved social system that constitutes an MTN.

Social networks of migration from Mexico to the United States are composed of matured networks, which are a consequence of prior immigration policies and prior agreements between the two countries, such as the Bracero Program that relates to labor, and free trade in the case of NAFTA. In

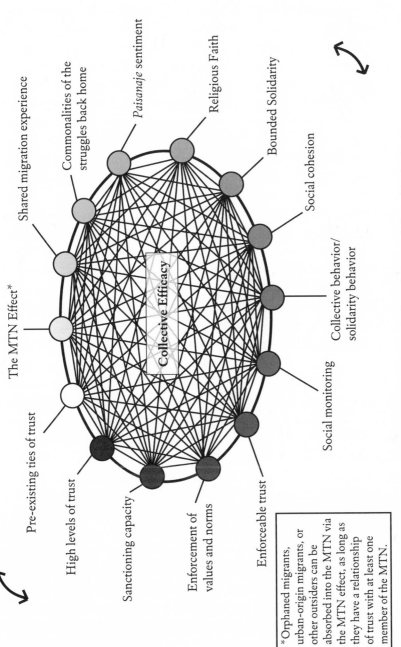

Figure 6.1   Migration-Trust Networks: Transnational relations between place of origin and place of destination.

The MTN Effect*

Shared migration experience

Commonalities of the struggles back home

Paisanaje sentiment

Religious Faith

Bounded Solidarity

Social cohesion

Collective behavior/ solidarity behavior

Social monitoring

Enforceable trust

Enforcement of values and norms

Sanctioning capacity

High levels of trust

Pre-existing ties of trust

Collective Efficacy

*Orphaned migrants, urban-origin migrants, or other outsiders can be absorbed into the MTN via the MTN effect, as long as they have a relationship of trust with at least one member of the MTN.

addition, the lack of legal visas available to Mexican nationals, combined with the huge demand for cheap labor in the United States, has provided the conditions for the increase of the undocumented flow of immigrants from Mexico to the United States. This flow of immigrants has also increased because the US government has not enforced employer sanction laws and because thousands of workers in Mexico have been displaced as a result of NAFTA. Therefore, the concept of Migration-Trust Networks presented in this chapter is based solely on the Mexican case. The same features described in the theory extension following may or may not be observed in international migration flows to and from other countries around the world. In the following pages, I propose an extension of current theories of social networks, such as theories of social capital, but particularly to the current theory of cumulative causation. I describe how social networks of migration form, develop, and how they are perpetuated, expanded, transplanted, or extinguished.

Migration-Trust Networks

One of the most important ideas of this new extension is that these networks are formed in the transnational context and the social processes that take place are functioning at multiple levels simultaneously. At all levels, the most important social behavior to drive these networks is the building of relationships of trust and a sense of cohesiveness among the network members. Of equal importance is the ability of Migration-Trust Networks to expand and adopt new members into the clique-like network based on the empathy members have for each other's harsh realities from the contemporary international migration experience. This empathy is often characterized by high risk due to the lack of legal documents for most international migrants arriving to the United States from Mexico.

Migration-Trust Networks are social relationships of support, trust, and sustenance and function simultaneously between the place of origin and those at the destination. These ties are based on and developed from pre-existing social relationships back home. The members of the network share a collective consciousness, thinking of themselves as part of a group and not as individuals. Social support, cohesion and trust are prized and expected among all network participants. They exchange resources for the international journey, job search, and settlement at the place of destination. Network members carry social expectations for each other and encourage certain behaviors and values for new members. Any act of betrayal places everyone in the social network at risk, especially those who lack legal documentation in the host country. People who do not conform to the expectations of the MTN are usually rejected and/or punished by the other group members. The network can consist of various types of social ties, such as kinship, friendship, paisanaje, compadrazgo, cuatismo, coworkers, neighbors, and others. Outsiders can become members of the MTN as long as they follow the social and behavioral expectations of the network and maintain trust with each other. Examples may include migrants from other hometowns, employers, coyotes, labor recruiters, business and/or salespersons, and city officials, among many others who are able to gain the trust of the members of an MTN. These parties help provide a safe haven for themselves and the immigrants.

On one hand, MTNs develop more readily among rural-origin migrants (from smaller communities) because their society already shares certain commonalities, social homogeneity, cohesiveness, and relationships of trust. In addition, they share a set of social expectations in order to maintain certain values and behaviors. Prospective migrants from rural origins have also developed a collective conscience, and those who do not behave according to the community's expectations are subject to rejection or punishment. On the other hand, urban-origin migrants may or may not already belong to a clique-like network or a peer group of people who expect certain social behavior and values. In some cases, migrants from urban communities may not be able to join an MTN as easily as those who migrate from rural areas. Those who lack connection to a peer group before migration may be absorbed by an MTN via the MTN effect, in which orphan migrants are absorbed into the network due to their vulnerability as undocumented migrants and their ability to project and gain trust from at least one of the members of the MTN.

First, at the MTN level, the set of conditions just described contribute to the creation of a form of collective efficacy in which an MTN acts as a protective social entity for its members, especially for those who lack legal documentation. Then the same relationships of trust embedded within MTNs give rise to broader social processes that will affect the international migration flow at the macro level. Transnational trust relations, such as sending family and collective remittances, for example, transform the place of origin and change the context in which migration decisions are made, thus causing additional migration (Massey et al. 1993, 1998). Furthermore, the residents of other surrounding communities begin to see migration as an attractive option when they experience relative deprivation at the community level. Their communities lag behind economically in comparison to the community that receives collective remittances to improve local infrastructure, and this ultimately encourages further migration from these neighboring towns. The capability of absorbing new members into the MTN (i.e., through exogenous ties in nearby communities) can expand the source of out-migration to a broader geographical area in the country of origin. Trust relationships can further increase the migration flow because the MTNs also expand at the places of destination via "the MTN effect" social mechanisms. In the case of network fragmentation, which can result due to a failure of the context of reception to provide the necessary conditions for incoming migrants to settle (such as demand for cheap labor), the same relationships of trust can lead to the transplantation of the network to another location. This transplantation prevents the MTN from being extinguished.

One of the most important complexities of social networks of migration has to do with the type of ties driving those networks. By the end, all members who belong to an MTN end up developing strong ties with each other, regardless of their social relationships prior to joining the network. In contrast to the assumption that family ties drive social networks of migration the majority of the time, the evidence in this manuscript demonstrates that having family ties may not be the most appropriate way to evaluate a prospective migrant's access to social capital for migrating internationally. Empirical findings suggest that family ties may not usually be available for most migrants when their specific community or clique-like network is at the beginning of its migratory career (Flores-Yeffal and Aysa-Lastra 2011). The first ones to migrate from a specific community are referred to as pioneer migrants (Massey et al. 1987). At first, it is more likely that prospective migrants will receive social capital to migrate from preexisting relationships of trust, in either their community of origin or in their MTN. These preexisting relationships of trust could be with friends, paisanos, coworkers, student buddies, or with other members of their clique-like network who became the pioneer migrants of that specific group. Again, empirical evidence suggests that in urban and rural areas of origin, pioneer migrants are more likely to be paisano ties (see Flores-Yeffal and Aysa-Lastra 2011). It appears that only after the network matures, family members become more available as the ties become diversified within the network over time. As the MTN absorbs outsiders into the clique-like network, weak ties are transformed into strong ties via "the MTN effect" conversion.

Relationships of trust do not necessarily exist all the time within a migrant's family. Any ordinary social ties, including family ties outside of an MTN, lack the social surveillance and social pressure necessary for the enforcement of the behavior, values, and norms by which social solidarity functions. Therefore, those family ties are more easily broken than any other trustful relationships, such as between nonfamily members. Those migrants who lack the preexisting relationships of trust are still able to be absorbed by other rural- or urban-based MTNs through "the MTN effect." These MTNs absorb outsiders due to the commonality they share from the international migration experience or by the outsider's engagement in trustworthy relationships with the network's members. Therefore, MTNs have the capability to expand and absorb new members into the network, regardless of the prior relationship between the new and existing members.

Migration-Trust Networks have the ability to absorb orphaned migrants who lack membership in a network or peer group. Furthermore, they can also absorb entire networks that may be malfunctioning at their location due to the lack of resources or demand for labor. Therefore, this social process can result in the transplantation of entire networks to other or new geographical locations (see figure 6.3). According to Menjívar (2000) and Mahler (1995), this occurs when the conditions at the context of reception are not able to provide future immigrant arrivals with jobs and other amenities necessary for their daily survival. The lack of resources and extreme poverty may also be causes for the rupture of social network relations between international migrants. This process was also observed in the present research. If this is the case, the MTN effect will occur in a different context of reception, which may offer an explanation for why international migrants move to other receiving areas, known as "new destinations," across the United States over time (Zúñiga and Hernandez-León 2006; Singer, Hardwick, and Brettell 2008). Solidarity and relationships of trust mandate how and where the MTN effect would occur for the struggling migrants to be absorbed by another MTN. This means that MTNs are capable of being transplanted to new geographical locations via the relationships of trust between the members of the old malfunctioning network and those of the new MTN. This occurs as long as at least one member is able to gain access to the already existent MTN.

Members of MTNs can become either beneficiaries or victims—the latter if they do not conform to the social expectations of the group. Given that rejection of a Migration-Trust Network is very difficult to remedy, most participants would do everything possible to protect their reputation.

Another important characteristic of MTNs is social homogeneity. It is not necessarily measured by level of education, nor by occupation or socioeconomic status. Instead, social homogeneity among international migrants is measured by the migrants' social situation in the United States, or at the place of destination. In other words, their immigrant status and social experiences as immigrants are the basis through which social homogeneity is measured. International migrants often experience downward mobility economically, as they cannot transfer their human capital skills when they arrive to the new society. In most cases, the immigrant's social status is measured by their legal status, or by their international migration experience while arriving to the place of destination (the type of crossing and their experience while crossing the border, even if it was with a tourist visa). While it may appear that those who cross or enter the place of destination with a tourist visa are better off than undocumented immigrants, the reality is that they too, feel socially and psychologically vulnerable and disadvantaged, as they are also prohibited from working in the United States. They are also subject to persecution and possible deportation by immigration authorities. Given their similar social situation and disadvantage, the international migrants identify with each other and create that perception of homogeneity to each other. For example, two people who do not possess an authorization to work would still identify with each other even if one crossed with a tourist visa and the other did not. Their common vulnerable state of being undocumented increases their mutual trust and social cohesiveness, and they become supportive of each other. Still, as mentioned before, the urban origin migrant who possesses higher levels of human capital would have access to greater opportunities than the rural dweller, with lower levels of education, despite his or her position of disadvantage due to the lack of legal documentation.

The social network structure I observed in the MTNs of the Mexican migrants in this study was complex and not necessarily stable. It was governed by social status within the network in the transnational context. In Bashi's work, exploring the network structure of West Indians from the Caribbean, many of those who provide help to others are called "hubs" (Bashi 2007). In my research, however, I did not find evidence that the social network structure of Mexican migrants was the same as that described by Bashi (2007). She only found two types of social network participants: the hubs (veteran migrants who provide help to many newcomers) and the spokes (those who received the help and only help others when requested to do so by the hub, through a sense of obligation). She also found that spokes never became hubs because the hubs were mostly pioneer migrants. I was able to identify that hubs existed, but I also identified spokes becoming hubs, as well as spokes who helped others without any specific request from the hub. Bashi observed this in her study. The hubs in my study, which I call "emerging pioneers" of migration, could be acting out of mere altruistic motivations or as recruiters of labor after being asked to refer other migrants from their hometown who will demonstrate the same good work ethic (Krissman 2002). They also gained greater social status among other members of the community for helping many migrants during different periods. They gained the reputation of being good to others and for helping more people to migrate. Other people at both the sending community and the place of destination (in the transnational context) showed respect for them and saw them as superior. In many instances, they even became more influential and powerful than the local political leaders. This greater social status often became a substitute for the kind of status one can gain by having a greater economic position. Given the difficulty that migrants have trying to increase their socioeconomic status, becoming an emerging pioneer and helping other people migrate serves as a substitute measure of greater social status in the community. Those who do not help as many people do not gain as much respect and social status among the community.

Moreover, Bashi argues that the hubs were the ones who selected which newcomers to help, depending on qualities such as previous work ethic and reputation. Although similar hubs existed in the social networks I observed (actors who helped many others), I also found frequently that spokes could also become hubs, or simply helpers of others. I found no evidence to suggest that hubs were necessarily pioneer migrants, or that the hubs were the only ones who selected which newcomers to help. Instead, I found that those who arrived later could also potentially become hubs and that no one in particular selected who would migrate next as a result of their perceived personal qualities back at home. It was a matter of belonging in the community rather than a selection of who deserved to migrate or could make the journey. For those reasons, I cannot utilize the same terminology as Bashi when describing the social structure of Mexican networks identified in this study. The difference between Bashi's findings and my findings are that I was able to observe the development of social networks of migration over long periods of time. As a result I was able to identify more longitudinal patterns of social networks than Bashi. Given Bashi's descriptions of the hubs and spokes, one should take into account that the social networks of migration that I observed in the Mexican case were more mature networks and many of its members lacked legal documents to be in the United States as well. Given the peculiarities of the Mexican case described in detail in chapter 1, the social network structure may have changed or acquired different characteristics as it matured. Future research should look more deeply into the similarities and differences between young and mature networks of migration, while taking into consideration other factors such as the legal status of its members and the context of the migrant's place of origin.

Ethnographic evidence suggests that migrant solidarity relations within an MTN are manifested and perpetuated without reciprocity. According to the social networks' classic literature (Wasserman and Faust 1994), reciprocity occurs when the favor is returned to the same person who offered the help; simply said, it means returning the favor. However, my evidence suggested that those who provide help to others are usually economically and socially advantaged compared to those who receive the help. It would be very difficult for those who receive the help to return the favor directly to the migrant who helped them, especially not the same kind of help received. For example, if a migrant is helped with a month of lodging in someone's home, it is difficult for the migrant to return the favor by also providing a month of lodging. Those who originally provide help are usually established migrants in a better social and economic position than the newcomers. They have usually been in the United States for a longer period of time, have accumulated more human capital, have better jobs, and most importantly, many have already become legal US residents or naturalized US citizens. For this reason, new or returning migrants are generally in a disadvantaged position compared to the more established migrants.

The social capital exchanged by network participants is not transferred by reciprocal relations (where the favors are returned directly to those who provided the help). Instead, a form of risk-pooling takes place and the favors are returned by helping different newcomers or returning migrants in the future. As a result, new migrants will later help others in the future, and so on and so forth (see figure 6.2). First-time migrants and returning migrants receive the same kinds of social capital to migrate internationally, but those who are coming for the first time probably need more help and need to

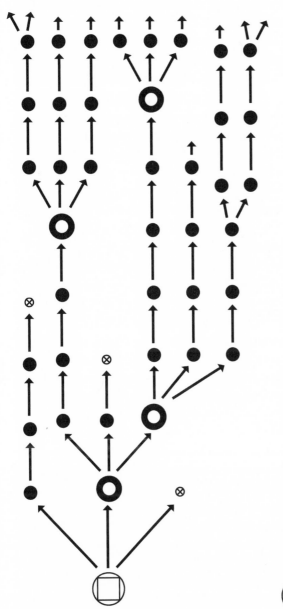

= Pioneer migrant (the first to begin migratory flow)

= Emerging pioneer (helps a significant number of people migrate; emerges as a pioneer for further migration)

= First-time or returning migrant who later helps others migrate (after becoming financially capable of providing help)

= Migrant who does not help anyone else migrate (rare)

= Direction to which help is given

Figure 6.2   Example of risk-pooling: Non-reciprocal exchange of social capital in Migration-Trust Networks.

receive the help for longer periods in comparison to returning migrants. Therefore, MTNs would be essential for those making the international journey for the first time, but returning migrants also depend on the social capital provided by the network because they, too, lack legal documentation. From interviews and having observed the social phenomena over a long period, I have found the following reasons that favors are paid forward to newcomers:

1. *Memories of the experience:* The first migration journey can be so psychologically difficult and overwhelming for migrants that the memory is burned into their subconscious memory. They are inexperienced, terribly afraid, vulnerable, and desperate for assistance. When that assistance arrives, new migrants are never more grateful. While the grim memory of the journey is emblazoned in their minds, so is the memory of the moment their help arrived during such a critical time (as it happened in the case of José and Pancho, described in the introduction). Both memories lead to their desire to help future migrants, whom they know are in need of the same assistance they once received.

2. *Subject to social expectations:* The MTN develops a collective efficacy mechanism in which the social expectations among members include providing social capital to newcomers.

3. *Opportunity to gain status:* Given that some MTN members lack legal status, providing aid to others can become one of the ways in which members can gain respect from others and higher social status within the group.

Unlike the "hubs" presented in Bashi's (2007) study on West Indians from the Caribbean, the pioneer migrants in the Mexican case are not the only ones who help others migrate. As represented in figure 6.2, any first-time or returning migrants who later help others to migrate can become "emerging pioneers" of migration, even though they were not the very first to migrate. Some help few and others help many. There are some newcomers who do not help anyone, though they are rare. This is the process of social capital exchange taking place within MTNs. I found very few instances when those who I interviewed or followed through time during my fieldwork did not help anyone else to migrate. In most instances, there were migrants who helped at least one other prospective migrant in one way or another. At times, migrants collaborated to help one newcomer.

For example, one person provided the lodging, while someone else paid the coyote and a different person provided transportation to work.

Similar to rural-origin migrants, those who migrate from urban places are able to form daughter communities and create, maintain, and perpetuate MTNs. However, this is only possible if they were originally engaged in a clique-like network or peer group in which prior social cohesiveness and relationships of trust were exchanged before migration. In addition to their preexisting relationships, the conditions at the place of destination must be able to sustain their MTNs and new arrivals. The most important factor for MTNs to function effectively is the demand for labor at the place of destination, making employer participation in MTNs crucial. If MTN members trust the employer as a loyal recruiter and not as a threat, then an increasing number of MTN newcomers are referred to that employer for work. Without work for newcomers, the MTN would cease to function.

Network fragmentation may occur when the established migrants are not able to help the new arrivals get jobs, despite their desire to do so. Other resources, such as housing availability, schools for the children, and medical services, are secondary. Without jobs, even if all the other amenities are available, the MTN will not be able to serve the needs of new prospective migrants. One other important resource for MTNs is help at the border. The MTNs cannot function and expand without coyotes and even cooperative border control agents willing to help migrants cross safely and successfully. Without these resources (specifically work), MTNs may begin to fragment or vanish altogether unless they are transplanted to other geographical locations via the MTN effect.

Figure 6.3 presents an example of the transplantation of the MTN, a process that begins with a clique-like network or a peer group at the place of origin. Through migration, it becomes an MTN at the place of destination, now made up of migrant members. If for any reason it becomes fragmented, an orphaned migrant may be able to join another established MTN at the place of destination if he or she has a connection with a member. After the migrant is absorbed into the succeeding network, the remainder of his or her contacts from the failing MTN can also be absorbed into that MTN. Outsiders can become members of expanding MTNs as long as they gain the trust of at least one of the MTN members.

The same is true for urban migrants. If urban migrants borrowed social capital from sources other than an MTN, their social ties may be weak and ultimately disintegrate, leaving them void of support to sustain themselves

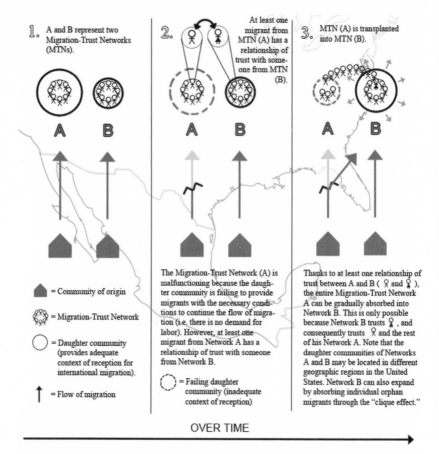

1. A and B represent two Migration-Trust Networks (MTNs).

2. At least one migrant from MTN (A) has a relationship of trust with someone from MTN (B).

3. MTN (A) is transplanted into MTN (B).

A B   A B   A B

= Community of origin

= Migration-Trust Network

= Daughter community (provides adequate context of reception for international migration).

= Flow of migration

The Migration-Trust Network (A) is malfunctioning because the daughter community is failing to provide migrants with the necessary conditions to continue the flow of migration (i.e. there is no demand for labor). However, at least one migrant from Network A has a relationship of trust with someone from Network B.

= Failing daughter community (inadequate context of reception)

Thanks to at least one relationship of trust between A and B (♀ and ♀), the entire Migration-Trust Network A can be gradually absorbed into Network B. This is only possible because Network B trusts ♀ , and consequently trusts ♀ and the rest of his Network A. Note that the daughter communities of Networks A and B may be located in different geographic regions in the United States. Network B can also expand by absorbing individual orphan migrants through the "clique effect."

OVER TIME

Figure 6.3   The Transplantation of a Migration-Trust Network (A) into an Expanding Migration-Trust Network (B).

in the host community. If those orphaned urban-based migrants are able to establish a relationship of trust with a member of a rural-based network or MTN, then that network or MTN would likely absorb them, as shown in figure 6.3. Adopted urban-based migrants would then have access to social capital to sustain them at the destination.

The step-by-step process in which MTNs operate is the following:

1. *International migration begins:* First, pioneer migrants leave their community and settle in the United States. Many belong to preexisting clique-like networks or peer groups and begin to invite their preexisting ties to also join the migration journey. Family members are less available

to provide help, so instead friends and paisanos — especially paisanos — offer prospective migrants the social capital to migrate.

2. *Activation of Migration-Trust Network:* For some communities, only a small number of pioneers are required to migrate internationally in order to activate an MTN. In most cases, the subsequent flow of international migrants would increase only if the conditions at the place of destination allow the MTN to be activated. The demands for cheap labor at the place of destination and, of course, employers who are willing to become part of the MTN, are the most important conditions for the MTN to develop, even if other necessities are scarce. Other conditions at the destination include the availability of housing for new arrivals, transportation back and forth from work, and available stores, schools, and medical services. The prevalence of such amenities provides additional incentives for the MTN to form.

3. *Formation of immigrant enclaves:* In search of social support and the exchange of social capital, recently arriving pioneer migrants begin to live next door to one another upon arrival. Such living arrangements allow for easier enforcement of norms and social monitoring among MTN members.

4. *Preexisting clique-like networks:* Prior membership in a nonmigration clique-like network is necessary for the MTN to form. If the prospective migrant is from a small rural community, it is equivalent to being a member of a clique-like network. For urban migrants, the preexisting nonmigrant clique-like network can be of any other nature, such as work-related, school-related, or sports-related. Prior relationships of trust are essential for the MTN to function properly at the place of destination and in the transnational context. Such preexisting conditions of social trust and social cohesiveness are necessary in order for the MTN to effectively provide social capital to more newcomers and prospective migrants.

5. *Relations of trust:* Trust relations in migrant networks are essential in the decision to migrate internationally, especially if migrants lack legal documentation. The vulnerability of undocumented migrants can only be overcome through reliance on relationships of trust. If a relationship of trust does not exist before migration, then a new relationship of trust may develop at the destination through religious ties and/or the commonalities related to the international migration experience and struggles back home. Religious beliefs encourage migrants to trust and help others in need, thereby linking members to nonmembers with the hope that they

will join the MTN. The MTNs are then governed by relationships of trust due to their vulnerability in the host country.

6. *Creation of new trust ties:* Relationships of trust and social support are enhanced by the international migration experience itself, which creates tighter social bonds among network participants. Through experience, members learn to recognize who they can trust and allow into their network. New members may include prospective or orphan migrants or nonmigrants, such as coyotes and employers. Soon, those strangers also adopt the values and norms of behavior of the MTN.

7. *Nonreciprocal exchange of favors, or risk-pooling:* Favors are not necessarily returned to those who originally assisted migrants. Instead, favors are passed along to the new arrivals or returning migrants, which contributes to the growth of MTNs. In this book I have called this process risk-pooling behavior. While they may help from purely altruistic reasons, migrants do gain social status by helping others.

8. *Sanctioning:* Members may reject or punish in some other way those who do not comply with the social expectations of other members of the transnational community. One of the most common punishments for the person who violates social norms or expectations is to initially be a victim of social gossip. Members then exclude them from social events, refuse to give them access to social capital, and do not allow them to participate in everyday activities with other members of the MTN at the place of origin or destination. Social monitoring not only occurs at the place of destination, but through all the MTN branches at several places of destination.

9. *Collective efficacy:* I claim that once the MTN is able to gain momentum, a form of collective efficacy develops among its members, especially at the destination (but the values and behaviors are also shared at the place of origin). The purpose of such collective efficacy is to protect MTN members from predators. Migrants develop and share strategies for survival that prevent their legal status from being revealed. I consider that collective efficacy is a social behavioral condition in which all network members cooperate so that it operates at a level other than just the personal or micro level. I call this level the MTN level.

10. *Transnational networks:* Expansion of Migration-Trust Networks depends on transnational relations between migrants and those left in the sending community as they exchange social capital and vital information. They maintain transnational relations largely through technology, such as cell phone communication, community websites and blogs, the use of Skype

or Facebook, letters, YouTube videos, movies, and pictures. Through such transnational contact, cultural ideas and practices are exchanged. Migrants are encouraged to carry and maintain their cultural practices at the destination, and they introduce aspects of the host culture to their home communities (Smith 2006).

II. *Transnational exchange:*

a. Communication back home: Another prerequisite for social network activation is the ability of those in the United States and back home to communicate with one another. Maintaining communication enables those back home to learn about the culture of and opportunities in the United States, and in turn influences their decision to migrate. Knowing they can maintain contact with their community also encourages residents to migrate.

b. Technology: The transnational exchange of cultural practices and information is facilitated through technology such as videos, cell phones, websites, network sites, and so forth. The more access MTNs have to technology, the more effectively and rapidly they are activated and perpetuated, as information flows more efficiently between the place of origin and destination. Such technology also assists with social monitoring and the enforcement of norms in the transnational context.

c. Transportation: Effective, secure, and affordable ways of transportation must be available between the origin and destination for the formation of MTNs. This is especially important for undocumented migrants. For example, those who migrate from El Salvador first cross a river to circumvent the Mexico-Guatemala border, ride a freight train to get to the US border, and then cross the border between the United States and Mexico with the help of a smuggler. As long as there is an effective mode of transportation (which may still be dangerous) between the places of origin and destination, MTNs are activated.

d. Smuggling services: Undocumented immigrants must cross the border(s) without legal authorization, avoid inspection upon entry, and arrive safely at the destination so that social networks will continue to grow, making trusted smugglers and coyotes essential. In most cases, because of interior checkpoints, smugglers are hired to deliver the person all the way to the place of destination, not just to the border.

e. Cultural exchange: Migrants need to preserve their culture at the destination in order to feel more comfortable being away from home. They replicate cultural and religious practices such as weddings, quinceañeras, and baptisms at the destination, but sometimes adapt and transform them depending on the resources available. For example, if at the place of origin it is common for the bride and groom to walk around the town before getting married, they may not be able to do so at the destination, as they need to respect the rules and customs of the new society. Therefore, cultural practices are transferred, but also adapted to the conditions of the context of reception (Smith 2006). With time, some aspects of the destination culture are transferred to and adapted at the place of origin, contributing to the culture of migration that develops.

Thus, MTNs are activated and fueled through transnational social relations of trust. In order for those social relations of trust to be maintained, continuous communication between the sending and receiving communities is essential. The same set of norms and expectations are valid in both places. Migrants socially monitor new migrants, and those left behind at the origin monitor those who migrate internationally and vice versa. The MTN members at the origin and destination are involved in each other's affairs, especially through social events such as weddings, baptisms, quinceañeras, and soccer games. Pictures, homemade videos, phone calls, texts, and websites become the media through which members of the transnational community maintain communication with one another. Within the United States, social monitoring also occurs between MTNs in different geographic locations, comprised of members from the same community of origin.

12. *"The MTN effect":* Receiving social capital from family members is possible but easily disintegrates with time, especially if migrants are from urban areas. Once an MTN is functioning, it can absorb such new members and also members of other failing social networks or MTNs. The first person able to gain the trust of at least one MTN member is referred to as the "Initial Trust-Link." This serves as the initial process to gain access to MTNs via the MTN effect. Once a migrant from one MTN gains access to another MTN, all the members of his or her clique-like network would also be given access (see figure 6.3).

13. *Cumulative causation process at the community level:* Transformations of the social context as well as the physical and economic context at the place of origin cause feelings of relative deprivation and thus give rise to a culture of migration. Such conditions create the desire for more people to migrate to the host country, as long as there are jobs available for new arrivals. The cumulative causation effect can have two kinds of limitations

for the flow to continue. First, the demographics of the sending community mean there are fewer working-age migrants to send to the place of destination. Second, there is no longer a demand for cheap labor at the destination. If the latter is the case, the only way the cumulative causation effect can continue is through the transplantation of the social network to another geographical location where the cheap labor demand exists.

14. *Collective remittances:* Not only do those who migrate internationally benefit from MTNs, those who stay behind also gain access to the MTNs' social capital. As a result of social cohesiveness and relationships of trust, migrants send both individual and collective remittances. The role of collective remittances is to improve the infrastructure of sending communities and reinforce cultural and religious practices. Infrastructural changes in the community of origin provoke additional changes in context and perpetuate the culture of migration, which leads to further international movement. Cultural practices are reinforced via the celebration of the Fiestas Patronales and other religious ceremonies financed by the migrants who reside abroad. These celebrations are shared through social media. In addition to improving the infrastructure and promoting religious practices and culture of the sending community, collective remittances also provide an avenue for the sending community to raise its status (and elevate its importance) in comparison to other communities nearby.

15. *Cumulative causation among communities:* Other communities observe the changes and transformations taking place in the nearby sending community as a result of collective remittances, causing feelings of relative deprivation at the community level. The sending community, which makes the largest improvements to its infrastructure, gains a higher community status. Members of other communities feel deprived; therefore, international migration becomes an option for gaining higher status by sending remittances to improve the infrastructure of their communities. This creates competition between the communities, as some communities want to be recognized for better amenities, a better plaza, a larger church, a more successful fiesta patronal, and so forth. In most cases, the community or communities that have more funds for newer amenities gain a higher status compared to the other communities that receive few or no collective remittances. As seen in figure 6.4, exogenous ties can be used to gain access to the social capital of sending communities.

16. *Exogenous ties:* Another way in which social networks are expanded to nearby communities is through the creation of exogenous ties. Those who

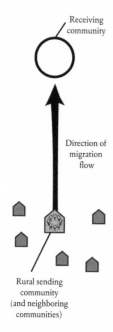

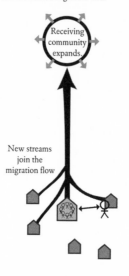

1 | A Migration-Trust Network enabling migration from a rural sending community:

2 | A member of a neighboring community gains access to the Migration-Trust Network of the sending community (often through an exogenous tie). More members from his or her community are then able to migrate as well:

3 | Over time, neighboring communities stop depending on the original sending community and begin developing their own Migration-Trust Networks. They form new daughter communties in the host country:

Receiving community

Receiving community expands.

Direction of migration flow

New streams join the migration flow

Rural sending community (and neighboring communities)

Neighboring communities gain access to the sending community's "Migration-Trust Network" through exogenous ties (marriage, friendship, compadrazgo, cuatismo, etc.). "Relative deprivation" on the community level can also encourage migration from surrounding areas.

New daughter communities and new MTNs are formed.

OVER TIME

Figure 6.4   Geographical expansion of "Migration-Trust Networks" from rural places of origin (over time).

marry residents of nearby communities expand their family relationships to those communities. Such marriages allow for the new spouse and his or her family to also gain access to the MTN. Figure 6.4 illustrates this process. Anyone with family or other social ties to the sending community will gain access to the MTN of that sending community (see step 2 of figure 6.4). This multiplies the number of people with access to the MTN and who share the same destination place or daughter community (as shown in step 2 of figure 6.4). Such connections can serve to intensify the effects of cumulative causation at the community level. Over time, each community develops its own MTN and an independent stream of international migration, eventually leading to the formation of new daughter communities (see step 3 of figure 6.4). Therefore, this process not only leads to the development of new sending communities, but new receiving communities as well.

17. *Flexibility on international migration policy:* As Yu (2008) states, another factor is the openness of immigration policies in the destination countries. The more easily the people from a social network of migration can migrate legally, the more the international migration stream will continue to flow and grow dramatically. In the clandestine international migration from Mexico to the United States, the social networks of Mexican migration remain active due to migrant trust and solidarity. As a result, the lack of legal documents does not become much of an obstacle for Mexican migrants to find and receive help to migrate to the United States.

Migration-Trust Networks are embedded in extremely complex micro and macro social and economic forces that function in the transnational context. Many of these social forces just described act simultaneously. The most important factors that propagate MTNs are the relationships of trust among members, as well as the demand for cheap labor at the place of destination, which serve as magnets for the network to expand.

Migration-Trust Networks are not activated unless certain social and economic conditions are met in both the sending and the receiving communities. In the case of Mexican migration to the United States, MTNs are driven mainly by relationships of social trust and support due to a series of social, behavioral, and cultural conditions. These conditions occur because of the difficulties and dangers associated with the journey from Mexico to the United States. They include paisanaje sentiment, enforceable trust, and bounded solidarity, Risk-Pooling behavior, religion, and collective efficacy. Trust relations and mutual support drive most of these conditions.

The MTN concept is characterized by a complex multilevel supply chain. This means that networks expand not only at the micro level through social relations between individual actors, but also at the macro level by a set of larger transnational processes that exponentially expand the migration flow. Figure 6.5 shows the people of the community of origin gathering after church. It is through those social interactions at the place of origin and at the place of destination that people exchange crucial information

Figure 6.5   Locals gather after church at the place of origin and exchange information. At the places of destination people also gather in the same way after church and talk to each other about their everyday life in the United States and about how to survive as an undocumented migrant.

about their international migration experience and how to migrate internationally. Expansion occurs at an increased rate by means of several MTN effect mechanisms resulting from migrant trust and solidarity, which allow MTNs to draw new migrants from the community of origin or from other MTNs through absorption. The MTNs also expand by absorbing members of nearby communities at the place of origin who gain access via exogenous marriages or other preexisting clique-like networks or peer group relationships. This means that the growth of social networks of migration is not solely dependent on the trust relations of its individual migrant participants; the network is also perpetuated by macro solidarity mechanisms at the places of origin and destination, which are embedded in the functionality of social networks of the international migrants. If an MTN begins to malfunction, it can be transplanted to other geographical locations by gaining access to other existing MTNs that *are* functioning. Therefore, migrant communities may be transplanted in other destinations via the supporting networks, meaning MTNs are unlikely to stop functioning altogether. Instead, they typically expand as a result of MTN social mechanisms such as "the MTN effect" governed by relationships of social trust and support, which are primarily driven by common empathy for the international migration experience.

The aim of this chapter is to explain in detail the concept of Migration-Trust Networks and how they form, expand, and function. This concept expands our knowledge of the existing social network theories, in particular, the theory of cumulative causation (Massey et al. 1993, 1998). Migration-Trust Networks are especially important where the majority of migrants lack legal documentation to enter and to reside in the host country.

CHAPTER SEVEN

Advantages and Disadvantages of Migration-Trust Networks

Migration-Trust Networks, as described in this book, provide both advantages and disadvantages to their members at the places of origin and destination. For those who migrate, especially if it is their first time, membership in an MTN can provide everything they need for their documented or undocumented journey, and to settle and sustain themselves at the place of destination. Most importantly, membership in the MTN will provide a safe haven to protect the undocumented migrants from apprehension, arrest, and deportation. Simultaneously, membership can be a source of disadvantage for migrants because it inhibits advancement and assimilation into the host society (i.e., Nee and Sanders 2001). Other than the disadvantages the membership of the MTN may offer, the greatest disadvantage comes from the lack of legal status of the immigrants at the place of destination. Without legal documents, even if the migrants wanted to incorporate themselves into the host society, their status prevents them from doing so. Given the concerns regarding the disadvantages of belonging to a migration network reflected in the literature, in the next section I discuss the disadvantages of the members of the MTN. Following that section, I present the advantages of membership. One important point for readers to understand is that even though not all the members of an MTN are undocumented, generally at least one undocumented immigrant is in each household of an MTN. The status of even one member jeopardizes all household or MTN members if the undocumented migrant is deported.

Disadvantages at the Place of Destination

First, one should take into account the structure of the MTN, which is clique-like. Social segregation is one of the most important features of this kind of network, as migrants settle near each other in order to have easier access to social capital from other members. This means that the members of the network have frequent contact with each other; their ties are likely to be strong, or at least they become strong once new members become part of the MTN. Membership in an MTN can be considered disadvantageous if the migrants' ability to gain access to other clique-like networks or to other weaker ties outside their own network is hindered. According to the social network literature, the problem with clique-like networks is that they only provide access to a limited amount of information, and it is very difficult for new information to enter them (Granovetter 1973; Wasserman and Faust 1994). Daughter communities of immigrants can be considered clique-like networks because in most instances only the immigrants belonging to that specific network have access to the information being exchanged. The inclusion of outside actors who have the potential to bring new and more accurate information into the MTN may be met with reluctance given that *trust* is essential. Outsiders are not easily trusted compared to those who have membership in the MTN. Trust and confidentiality are especially important for undocumented migrants, who rely on the MTN for protection from apprehension and deportation.

Living in segregated communities as part of an MTN can lead to other significant disadvantages, such as the inability to learn the language of the host country. There can be several reasons why Mexican immigrants, for example, do not learn English in the United States. From the ethnographic work conducted in the United States, respondents suggested that one of the most important reasons was the lack of time to attend night school to learn English. Many work two shifts, long hours, or seven days a week, so their work schedule does not allow them time to attend school. For example, Rafael, who was interviewed in Chicago at his worksite because he insisted that he did not have time to be interviewed at home since he worked long hours, answered the question, "Why don't you go to school to learn English?"

I wish I could go to school to learn English because I really need it. The problem is that I get off very late from work, and when I get home I am already exhausted. I only have time to prepare my lunch for the next day and take a shower, and then I have to go to bed so I can wake up early the next day and go to work. I turn on the TV for a little while, but I am so tired that I usually fall asleep very fast. I have Sundays off, but that day I go to church, and then I use the rest of the day to do laundry and go to the supermarket to buy everything for the rest of the week. I wish I could go to school to learn English, but I don't have the time.

Another common problem is unreliable transportation, even if there is time to attend night school. The most important obstacle, however, is the lack of necessity to learn the host language, given that almost everyone they interact with speaks their native language. Everyone in their community (daughter community) speaks Spanish. Most of their coworkers, who are often from the same MTN, also speak Spanish, including their supervisors. Grocery stores and all other stores where they shop display only Spanish signs and product labels. Store owners learn to speak Spanish to cater to their customers. At church, mass is administered in Spanish. Doctors hire bilingual staff in order to provide medical services to the immigrant population. Overall, there is little need for the members of the immigrant community to learn the English language. Also, even when many of them attempt to learn and practice English, they lack opportunities for further improving their English skills.

Another social disadvantage of living in an immigrant enclave and of membership in an MTN is that the migrants are prevented from learning the new rules and laws of the host society. Long working hours as described by Rafael were very common among respondents; many also worked seven days a week. In fact, the only time they spent outside the home was at work, where they were solely interacting with other members of their own community. Otherwise, they only went to local stores, still interacting with a limited number of individuals who shared the same cultural norms and practices. Such circumstances can prevent the new immigrants from learning the laws and cultural practices of the host society, and this can place them in trouble with the law. For example, many immigrants are not aware that becoming violent with their wives could send them straight to jail, because such behavior is not against the law at their place of origin. Another example is for an older man to get married to a young girl (under the age of eighteen). This practice may be common at the place of origin, but it is against the law in the United States, even with her parents' consent. When possible, the members of the MTN will advise them of the laws of the host society, but in other cases, for one reason or another, migrants are not informed and their lack of knowledge about the new laws can send them to jail. Furthermore, in most instances, immigrants either lack the knowledge about their civil or labor rights, or if they know about it, they just ignore their rights; they are afraid that if they speak up they may become victims of retaliation or be reported to the immigration authorities.

Migrants in MTNs tend to experience a limited labor market because the information received by the MTN regarding jobs is limited. The MTN members are only exposed to specific markets in which they are more likely to be exploited, have very little chance of promotion, are vulnerable to non-existent safety standards, lack benefits, and even receive pay below minimum wage standards. Those from the immigrant enclave become trapped into these jobs for many reasons. Fellow migrants recommend them to the jobs, so if they quit or protest for any reason, employers may be upset with those who recommended them or stop hiring other members from that community of origin. Migrants are aware their actions may hurt other members of their MTN, and they run the risk of rejection by failing to protect the status of the group. Consequently, most of them stay in their jobs and remain silent to any unfairness. Besides protecting the reputation of other members of the MTN, they fear losing their jobs or being reported to immigration authorities by their employers.

The socioeconomic status of migrants is also linked to their MTN membership and residence in immigrant enclaves. Members often live in neighborhoods with very high levels of poverty and underperforming schools with limited educational resources. Children may not have access to "other" kinds of friends from whom they may be able to learn and gain social and cultural capital and economic advantages. Instead, they interact solely with children who are also part of the MTN. Therefore, the future educational and job opportunities for those children may be limited. US-born children may have more prospects for future upward mobility, but for undocumented children, even if they receive a college education in United States, their lack of legal status will prevent them from acquiring a professional job after graduation.

One of the major social disadvantages from the perspective of the host society is the preservation of immigrants' cultural practices and language, making it difficult for them to assimilate. Assimilation is defined as the adoption of language, cultural practices, and behavior of the host society. If the members of the immigrant community fail to adopt the cultural practices and language of the host society, then they are considered to be disadvantaged in that society. Yet immigrants are portrayed as wanting to live in immigrant enclaves for that very reason—to avoid assimilation. In reality, it is not that they wish to avoid adopting the behavior and cultural practices of the host society; instead, the social conditions of immigrant enclaves prevent them from being exposed to those behavioral norms and cultural practices of the host society. Also, their lack of opportunities to become legal in the United States forces them to remain living in the immigrant enclaves since they need protection both from immigration authorities and being discovered and deported.

Living in segregated immigrant enclaves may also lead to social isolation, social exclusion, and racial discrimination by members of the host society. Natives see immigrants as intentionally separating themselves from the host society so that they can preserve their customs and culture, rather than as a strategy for seeking social adaptation and survival—a strategy to share social support and to avoid exposure and arrest by immigration authorities. As discussed at the beginning of the book, Europeans at the turn of the twentieth century also formed immigrant enclaves in order to receive social support, to adapt to the new society, to practice their cultural norms, and to protect themselves from racial discrimination, among other things. Still, as described by Gans (1962), many were eventually able to leave and integrate into the larger society. Such incorporation was viable because most Europeans were able to gain legal status once they passed the inspection through Ellis Island. Immigrants today are not as fortunate, as most are not able to qualify for legal residency even though they have been living in the United States for decades. Therefore, it is more difficult for them to merge into the host society.

The best examples of this are the "Dreamers." They are the students who arrived in the United States as children before the age of fifteen and either completed two years of college, attended the military for two years, or ultimately acquired a college degree. The Dream Act (the Development, Relief, and Education for Alien Minors Act) has been proposed as new legislation at the federal government level since 2001. It would provide legal documents to these children of undocumented immigrants, arguing that it was their parents who made the decision (to immigrate) for them. Unfortunately, the bill has not been passed due to strong conservative opposition against a bill that may look like a form of amnesty. Due to the continuous failure of the Dream Act to provide legal documents to the Dreamers, these kids continue to be members of MTNs across the United States and continue living in immigrant enclaves despite their academic accomplishments because they do not have the legal documentation to work in the United States. Universities in as many as ten US states allow undocumented students to attend their colleges and allow them to pay in-state tuition, but after graduation, they are unable to find positions consistent with their educational status. This prevents them from becoming part of the middle class, moving into more integrated neighborhoods, sending their children to better schools, and of equal importance, contributing equitably to the tax base. For this reason, given the denial and lack of opportunities for the Dreamers to gain legalization, they end up working menial jobs just like their parents, despite holding university degrees. As a result, many children within MTNs, feeling discouraged and uncertain, are reluctant to pursue a higher education, which may be contributing to the high rate of immigrant children who are dropping out of high schools around the country. Just before this book went to press, President Obama created a new law that awards the Dreamers a temporary immigration status, but the work permits would only last for two years and these children would not be able to apply for a green card. The political opposition claims that this is only a political maneuver to gain the Hispanic vote and guarantee reelection as president in November 2012. As for the Dreamers, they will continue to have an uncertain future since this is not a permanent solution.[1]

In general, members of MTNs have limited prospects for assimilation without gaining legal residency. Even for those who have family members with legal residency or citizenship, having at least one undocumented member of the household, especially if it is the head of the household, hinders the entire family, requiring the continued protection of the MTN.

Advantages at the Place of Destination

International migrants who are members of an MTN also have several advantages. The most important advantage is the access to social capital, even if they initially lack social ties (such as family members with migration experience). Access to social capital is possible because any member of the MTN will provide help even if they are not family members. Paisanos, friends, coworkers, old neighbors, compadres, cuates and so forth will provide them with the necessary social capital to make the journey, arrive, settle, and sustain themselves at the place of destination.

One important advantage is that of acquiring *trustworthy* information from members of the group. For undocumented migrants, trustworthy information is essential throughout their journey to the United States. Important information includes how to find a coyote or smuggler whom they can trust to cross safely to the United States. If the information is not trustworthy and reliable, the smuggler may abandon them or take them along a very dangerous route, placing their lives at higher risk. The worst case scenario would be that the smuggler may kidnap the migrants or even kill them if the family does not give the money they demand for the service.

Upon arriving to the United States, undocumented newcomers need information about finding jobs that do not require legal documents and how to acquire an ID or fake green cards for employment. Also, international migrants need basic information for everyday living, such as how to rent an apartment, how to enroll their children in school, and even information as simple as crossing the street at a traffic light (since many do not have traffic lights back home).

Among the advantages of belonging to an MTN is the social support provided by the other members of the daughter community once the migrants arrive. Members of the MTNs tend to live near each other for support, especially during the settlement process. For example, the neighbors can provide transportation to the workplace, grocery store, doctor, laundromat, or other locations, as well as free babysitting so the parents can work.

In addition, those migrants who belong to MTNs have psychosocial support since they have access to friendships and company that enables them to emotionally survive the transition to the new place of destination. Most migrants, when they leave their place of origin to another country, leave behind most of their family and friends. As a result, they may feel very lonely when they arrive to the host destination. Living in the segregated enclave and belonging to the MTN provides newcomers with a sense of comfort, knowing there are people with whom they can interact and who have similar circumstances. Most of these interactions occur during social activities such as soccer games, social gatherings, baptisms, weddings, quinceañeras, and so forth. During such events, newcomers have the opportunity to interact with others and feel as if they were at the place of origin. Moreover, they provide the opportunity for them to learn new information, which they can use to their advantage in their new location.

New information shared in gatherings can be very useful to them, such as information about job opportunities, where to buy used clothing, cheap furniture, or good used cars, and about other things that may help with daily living. To others, this information may not appear useful, but for the newcomers such new information can mean the difference between life and death. Knowing where to go to the doctor, for example, and not pay a lot for the doctor's visit makes a big difference regarding their future health and positions them to receive regular medical treatment in the future.

Sampson (2008) presents empirical evidence of what he calls "collective efficacy." He found that those immigrant communities with a greater number of foreign-born residents experienced less crime than those with a greater number of native-born residents. Sampson argues that this results from collective efficacy—when the members of the community collectively monitor and control one another's behavior in such a way that reduces crime or possibly eliminates it. I also argue that MTNs develop and utilize a form of collective efficacy, which is not only useful for preventing crime, but to protect the undocumented members of the network from exposure to immigration authorities. This is done by sharing crucial information and strategies that are adopted by most of the MTN members who think and act collectively.

Part of remaining a united community involves preserving and practicing cultural and religious customs from back home. Immigrant enclaves allow parents to teach these traditions to their children in the same fashion as they would in the community of origin. Some of the cultural and religious practices passed along are baking, craft-making, prayers, and cooking traditional foods. For example, when I attended a quinceañera, I received a gift of a little basket made out of newspaper. The craftsmanship was very impressive. Later when I visited the hometown again, I saw a similar basket in one of the homes. I was told that making those baskets was a community tradition. Even though it was a quite laborious task to make them, they were inexpensive pieces of art. It was interesting that they continued their tradition in the United States and used the baskets as centerpieces for the tables at the quinceañera.

By living in these communities, newcomers stay informed about their family members back home. Community members who visit the place of origin (the majority of those who have legal documentation) bring back letters, news, personal items, and so forth to give to the families of the newcomers and to keep everyone in the community connected. In many instances, the few minutes that immigrants are able to talk over the phone with their family members using long-distance calling are not sufficient to hear details about their lives back home. Therefore, firsthand information from those who regularly visit the hometown provides more details about situations that affect their loved ones.

The MTNs also help new members to collect and organize collective remittances to send back home, which helps improve the local infrastructure of the sending community. These remittances help their family members back home live in better conditions. For example, if a school is built and new computers are installed, then the children left behind can take advantage of such improvements funded by migrants' donations.

Belonging to an MTN provides advantages not only to newcomers, but also to returning migrants. Because of the social expectations held by the rest of the members in the MTN, everyone is helped regardless of their level of international migration experience. Naturally, newcomers need more support and access to crucial information for their transition and survival in the new setting. However, returning migrants and those with legal documents also benefit from belonging to the network by learning about job opportunities, finding accommodation upon arrival, and so forth.

Empirical evidence from the Mexican Migration Project points out advantages Mexican immigrants have when they use social ties within their network. This includes the ability to increase their wages and gain access to better occupations (Mouw 2002, 2003; Amuedo-Dorantes and Mundra 2007; Aguilera and Massey 2003; Flores 2005; Flores-Yeffal and Zhang 2012). This means that even though there is a limited labor market for undocumented immigrants and even for their legal peers inside the clique-like networks, ultimately, the MTN provides its members with some economic advantages as well. More research is needed in order to understand such economic advantages. In sum, there are several advantages and disadvantages for members of MTNs that are manifested in daughter communities or immigrant enclaves. Most of the disadvantages are measured by comparing members of the immigrant enclave to the expectations of the host society in terms of social assimilation—adopting the language, culture, and behavior of the host society. One indicator of assimilation is to move out of the immigrant enclave and begin living in more integrated areas away from members of the MTN. Another indicator is adopting the language of the host society, in this case, English. In addition, another major disadvantage is the lack of access to information about labor market opportunities that could lead to increased economic advantages or about the host society's laws.

On the other hand, most of the advantages are measured in terms of the benefits acquired by the migrants who participate in the MTN. Such advantages include, but are not limited to, the following: access to social capital, the ability to arrive, settle, and survive, the preservation of their culture, the access to social and emotional support, and the ability to improve the conditions of their community of origin via collective remittances, and therefore benefit those back home.

The assessment of whether immigrants who belong to MTNs and live in immigrant enclaves at the destination are advantaged or disadvantaged may depend on who is making the assessment. If the immigrant is making the assessment, he or she may argue that membership in an MTN carries more advantages than disadvantages to the members of the group. On the other hand, if the assessment is made by a nonmember of the MTN, or by a member of the host society, the conclusion may indicate more disadvantages than advantages. Arguably, neither conclusion fully appreciates the fact that social segregation and living arrangements result from very complex social processes. Moreover, such dependency on the MTN results from complex legal processes. In the United States, without comprehensive immigration reform in which the almost twelve million undocumented immigrants can legalize their status, immigrants will remain dependent on MTNs and isolated from the host society, even if some of the family members are legal residents or US citizens.

The Place of Origin

Advantages and Disadvantages at the Place of Origin

Undocumented international migrants continue to be attached to the place of origin even though they are not able to return due to their undocumented status. Attempting to return may be fatal, especially considering how the undocumented journey has become more and more dangerous as time passes. Still, thanks to the cohesiveness and trust among the members of the MTN, those who cannot leave the United States are still able to contribute to the improvement of their place of origin through individual or collective remittances. No matter how far away they are, they still care for their hometown. When they experience how good things can be in the United States, they begin to dream that the same great things can also happen in their hometown. For this reason, international migrants return home or contribute the collective remittances projects at the place of origin. They want to build homes, buildings, parks, and other structures that resemble the same things they find in the United States—things that are more fancy or have better quality—so they can provide better conditions for those at the place of origin. Figure 7.1 shows houses built by migrants at the place of origin. In most instances one can identify the houses of those abroad as they tend to be generally large structures with very elaborate architecture.

Figure 7.1   The homes of international migrants in one of the sending communities of the study. Places of origin are transformed by the construction of fancy new homes.

The place of origin benefits especially from individual and collective remittances, which promote social and economic advancement. Local individuals at the place of origin who have never migrated and lack job opportunities, economic resources, and access to certain goods and services, are therefore able to receive some money from remittances in order to survive and acquire a better standard of living. Some of that money is used only for household consumption, but other remittances are directly injected into the local economy in the form of savings or investments that end up improving the entire local economy.

This phenomenon of migrant solidarity and the collective remittances that result assist even those who do not have migrants in their families because they are able to take advantage of improvements in the local infrastructure, such as electricity, parks, schools, paved roads, sewage systems, churches, and so forth. In many instances, those who live in the community of origin are able to participate in the construction of the local improvements and may even receive a salary. In other instances, community members donate their time to the local project and do not ask for any payment for their labor. Such participation then helps them feel better about using the new services later on. Non-migrants, as well as the migrants, gain a higher social status in the community from directly participating in the project.

Other advantages for the community of origin include the items they receive from abroad. Immigrants with legal documents who can come and go easily are willing to bring with them letters and material items from their undocumented family members and friends (Hernandez-León 2008). They act as carriers for others who, due to their status, are unable to travel. Such carriers help maintain the transnational context in which information, goods, and the culture of the host society are also transferred and adopted by members at the place of origin. In many cases, as a result of the transnational exchange of information and items, some of the youth or people at the place of origin even begin to learn the language of the host society, which is English in this case. For example, visiting migrants give the English names of some of the items they bring, such as DVD players or Nintendo games. Therefore, the people at the place of origin begin to use English without even realizing they are learning the language.

Finally, another advantage at the place of origin is the participation of the migrants abroad in local hometown politics through transnational relations. Those abroad, who actively participate as leaders in the distribution of collective remittances, are also able to acquire political power, influence public opinion, and advise local authorities in community decisions. The political pressure and power of those abroad can positively influence decision making at the local level and in turn benefit residents of the community of origin.

A number of disadvantages result from MTN membership at the place of origin. Most of the disadvantages relate to the tendency of MTNs to continuously encourage and send people to the United States or another host society through the process of cumulative causation. There comes a time in which too many people have migrated, even those who had no resources at all but were able to leave because the MTN made it possible for them. One example is when all the working-age people leave the community and not enough working-age people are left to do any of the local labor. This kind of situation can hurt the local economy and the local production of items, especially in communities that have historically survived on agricultural production.

Another problem is the adoption of the culture of migration (Kandel and Massey 2002). For example, school children and youth do not place any effort in their education because they plan on dropping out of high school and migrating to the United States instead. The culture of migration comes as a result of collective sentiments of relative deprivation after seeing the benefits associated with migration and remittances for other households or neighboring communities. Households that receive remittances improve their standard of living; therefore, those who have no migrant family members to send them remittances feel deprived and disadvantaged. They aspire to migrate internationally as a result. This culture of migration creates a scarcity of human capital that would otherwise be gained through education. Even though individual and collective remittances may be injecting money into the local economy at the place of origin, the lack of education makes it difficult for those who stay to take advantage of the new resources. In other words, the lack of human capital created by the culture of migration can lead to weaknesses in the local economy because there are no trained local leaders to make informed decisions about making the most of the money flowing in. Those with higher levels of education are the ones leaving for the United States, creating a deficiency of human capital in the local economy.

Finally, other social problems related to MTNs at the place of origin include how to handle those who are deported back to the hometown who have never been there before and only speak English. Migrant relationships of trust can help fellow return-migrants by offering social support to those who are deported, but there are limitations even if those in the sending community want to offer their help. The suffering of family members who are left in the United States and who are separated from their loved ones due to deportations can become a burden to those who want to offer their help. Given that the MTN members are those at the place of origin as well as at the place of destination, this kind of situation presents difficult circumstances that affect those on both sides of the transnational context.

In sum, clique-like networks of migration may provide both advantages and disadvantages for the sending community. Again, in most cases, the advantages trump the disadvantages because the migrant solidarity relations benefit most of the people of the community in the form of individual or collective remittances. The advantages consider the more immediate and direct benefits, while the other more catastrophic social or demographic consequences may not show immediate results or be seen as a major problem by the sending community.

In the transnational context between the sending and receiving communities, the cohesiveness of social relations is what makes it possible for any disadvantages to be dissipated and converted into what the people of the community consider advantageous. At the place of destination, even though the immigrants work very hard, many of them have two jobs and work long hours or seven days a week. They have very limited spare time, uncomfortable living conditions, and little money to spend, but they try to enjoy the little time they have for entertainment with members of the community at the place of destination. The satisfaction that results from having a job, the ability to send money in the form of remittances to their loved ones, communicating with family on the phone or on the Internet, gaining a higher social status by helping others, and living near their fellow community members helps them to ignore the disadvantages they face.

International migrants all around the world initially do not want to leave their place of origin. That is the place where they grew up, and they would leave behind friends and relatives. They feel forced to migrate given the lack of jobs and unemployment benefits in their home country, the extremely high interest rates (above 60 percent APR in Mexico, for example), the lack of credit opportunities to buy homes, the inability to acquire affordable medical benefits, and the lack of high-quality education for their loved ones. Therefore, being able to send money to their loved ones so they can eat, buy shoes, and attend school, for example, makes migrants believe that they have already been successful. They do not see any disadvantages of living in the immigrant enclave. They are meeting their own goals of getting a job and being able to provide for their family members. Many may consider avoiding deportation and holding a secure job a major success. Therefore, one should assess the advantages and disadvantages of MTNs by looking at both the immigrant perspective and the perspective of the members of the host society.

Notes

1. For more information visit http://www.azcentral.com/arizonarepublic/news/articles/2012/06/15/20120615obama-letting-immigrant-dreamers-stay-us.html.

CHAPTER EIGHT

Conclusion and Policy Recommendations

In this book, I have attempted to provide from my own observations a conceptual framework that scholars of international migration can utilize to better understand the functionality of social networks of international migration, especially when network participants are largely undocumented, as in the case of the current Mexican migration flow to the United States. My hope is that this book will help us understand the social forces and behaviors that constitute social capital and drive networks. The conceptual conclusions I have drawn result from thirteen years of observing Mexican migrant networks from the state of Guanajuato. As this is only a case study, I look forward to further research to add new knowledge to these concepts in the future. I also conducted fieldwork in El Salvador on social networks. However, more work is needed to make a sufficient comparison with the Mexican case. Still, based on the two months I was in El Salvador (on two separate occasions) and detailed ethnographic fieldwork in three different communities of different sizes, most of my conclusions described in this manuscript about Mexico hold true for El Salvador as well. This is important given that there is also a very high prevalence of undocumented migration from El Salvador to the United States.

To support my conclusions, I have relied on Tilly's (2007) trust network concept to conceptualize the high reliance of trust among network participants within the proposed concept of Migration-Trust Networks. Even though Tilly claimed that his trust networks took place in transnational migration networks, he was not able to relate his concept to undocumented international migration. His concept is important in the case of undocumented immigrant networks because of the high level of trust required in those networks. I argue that the functionality of regular social networks of migration is different from the functionality of the social networks of undocumented migrants, which I refer to as Migration-Trust Networks. The MTNs rely on higher levels of social trust, and the risk associated with malfeasance is much greater than that of regular networks of migration, where the participants generally possess legal documents at the place of destination.

I have also applied the forms of social capital developed by Portes and Sensenbrenner (1993) to the case of undocumented migration. The concepts of enforceable trust and bounded solidarity are generally applied to migrant enterprises in the current literature. However, these concepts also help to explain the social behaviors I observed among network participants in this case study. Religion is also fundamental in the functionality of MTNs. Faith underscores the importance of trust, mutual support, and collective behavior in these networks.

My observations and empirical data challenge the notion that social capital exchange takes place through the practice of reciprocity. Instead, I have uncovered the nonreciprocal manifestations of social capital exchange that exist among MTN members. Those who assist and provide social capital to first-time or returning migrants do so out of a spirit of altruism and gratitude for the previous assistance they received from others through risk-pooling. Instead of direct reciprocal exchange, migrants return favors by helping other newcomers in the future. This nonreciprocal flow of social capital allows for the international migration stream to continue growing and for more people to acquire the benefit of migrant social capital. Those who receive help will engage in risk-pooling by helping others in the future. Those who help also usually gain a higher "migrant" status as a result of their benevolence. Some international migration scholars have claimed that only those with more resources can begin the international migration journey (see Portes and Rumbaut 1990). However, MTNs can provide the social capital necessary to make the international migration journey in the event that one has very few resources, or none at all, to migrate. Therefore, I argue that membership in an MTN can allow even the poorest migrant to receive the necessary help to migrate internationally.

I have also introduced the notion that social networks of migration function out of relationships of trust at the micro and macro levels of analysis and that both forces operate in conjunction to fuel international migration flows. The MTNs are transnational, requiring specific conditions and actors at both the place of origin and at the place of destination in order to form, mature, and perpetuate over time. One condition in particular is the existence of the preexisting relations of trust among people who later become part of the migrant network. I have identified that through these preexisting clique-like network relationships, MTNs are initially created. While many factors can lead to the development of MTNs, other factors can lead to their disintegration, such as changing employment laws in destination areas.

I argue that the context of the place of origin affects the formation of MTNs. The MTNs can form in both rural and urban places of origin under the right conditions. The major condition for an urban-dweller to migrate is his or her prior membership in a peer group or clique-like network at the place of origin. This clique-like network or peer group — formed at the workplace, school, or on a soccer team, for example — is unrelated to international migration until some of the members begin to migrate internationally. This means that the relationships of trust were established before international migration, and they eventually led to the formation of an MTN. The alternative to those from urban areas who did not belong to peer groups before migration was to eventually gravitate to an MTN as an orphan migrant once in the United States. I call this the MTN effect since orphan migrants are absorbed into MTNs. As clique-like networks expand, they attract orphan migrants and other strangers into the MTN. This happens only after at least one member of the MTN begins to engage in a relationship of trust with an outsider. Once the relation of trust is established, all the other contacts who engage in trust relations with the new member also gain access to the MTN, thereby creating a domino effect.

Paisanaje ties and paisanaje sentiment play crucial roles in the formation and development of MTNs. Paisanaje ties, as argued by Flores-Yeffal and Aysa-Lastra (2011), are the weak ties that serve as substitutes for the lack of available strong ties (especially from family members). They provide social capital to prospective migrants, especially at the beginning stages of the migratory flow. Paisanos then perform a role consistent with the strength of weak ties argument suggested by Granovetter (1973). Once the MTN has been created, those types of ties being absorbed transform into strong ties in which solidarity behavior, social cohesion, collective behavior, and high levels of trust govern their social relations. Finally, I propose a series of other macro social manifestations that drive and help to expand and/or transplant these MTNs to larger geographical areas. The key is gaining access to the MTN, given the high levels of trust relations and collective efficacy characteristic of MTNs. Once a prospective migrant gains access to it, all of his or her contacts, even from other communities, also gain access. As more prospective migrants or returning migrants gain access to an MTN, some begin to create other MTNs, which lead to new migrant destinations.

The case study presented in this book serves as an important contribution to the existing theory of cumulative causation. According to the cumulative causation theory of migration (Massey et al. 1993, 1998), once international migration begins, nonmigrants who are left behind at the place of origin feel deprived in comparison to those who are receiving remittances, building new homes, buying new clothes, and so forth. Relative deprivation makes them also want to migrate internationally. Therefore, a culture of migration develops in which most of the youth lose the desire to continue with their education and instead desire to migrate internationally. Other factors at the destination, such as labor demand, together with social networks, continue to feed the international migratory stream. This theory claims that once migration begins, it creates its own infrastructure to feed and perpetuate itself. In this book, I explain in detail how such an infrastructure operates in the case of migration flows that include undocumented immigrants at the micro and macro levels. More research must be done in order to advance our knowledge about the process of cumulative causation.

The international migrant's endeavor to settle and survive in the host country, especially without legal documents, involves different social processes that cannot be compared to the survival and daily living of other racial and ethnic groups in the United States, such as African Americans. Scholars tend to compare demographic characteristics, such as income, types of occupations, levels of education, levels of segregation, and levels of poverty, when in actuality their social processes differ. Given the particular disadvantages of undocumented immigrants in the United States, I would argue that the social processes of undocumented immigrants differ dramatically from the social processes faced by other immigrant groups who enjoy more access to legal documentation and/or citizenship options. For example, Puerto Rican immigrants enjoy full rights of citizenship in the United States. They do segregate and form immigrant enclaves, but they also have more options for assimilation and incorporation into the broader US society than undocumented immigrants.

International migrants adopt survival strategies that are unique to their situation, given their lack of rights and their need to work without legal authorization. Relationships of trust and solidarity that result in a form of collective efficacy among MTN members are fundamental to their survival and daily existence. Many undocumented immigrants in those enclaves live in fear of being reported to immigration authorities and deported. They fear that immigration authorities will suddenly arrive at their place of work, where they shop, or that they will be stopped by the police while driving. In many states, those immigrants cannot get driver's licenses, open bank accounts, or process an ID to even visit their children at school, among other things. In many places, immigrants without legal documents cannot even rent an apartment under their name because they have no Social Security number or credit history. Therefore, undocumented immigrants have to draw upon migrant trust and solidarity in order to find information to overcome these kinds of obstacles. Besides the fear of deportation and discrimination, they may face other struggles such as exploitation, no unemployment benefits, and existing without health, car, and home insurance. It is through membership to an MTN that they are able to overcome these obstacles and persevere at the place of destination. This is why one cannot compare the social processes, demographic characteristics, upward mobility, or other aspects of this group to those of other racial or ethnic groups and with other recent immigrants who generally enjoy greater chances of gaining citizenship in the United States. Other racial and ethnic groups may also experience structural social and economic disadvantages in the United States, but they still have more options for social upward mobility and incorporation than undocumented immigrants.

As argued in this book, MTNs continue to serve as safe havens for undocumented immigrants. However, these same networks also isolate them in US communities by providing limited access to outsiders they can trust. Tilly (2007) argued that such trust network processes affect younger generations, since the children of undocumented immigrants are also isolated from the larger society even though they may enjoy the full right to US citizenship. Without the creation of new policies that can grant legalization to the current undocumented immigrant population, the younger generation may also grow to become socially dependent on MTNs for their survival in the United States, and continue to live on the periphery of society.

Public Policy Recommendations

In order to develop public policy addressing social network issues, it is important that policymakers first understand the point of view of the immigrant—why did he or she emigrate in the first place? Most emigrate in order to survive through hard work. Others are trying to progress. Why would it be worth it to place their lives and often their family's lives at risk by trying to get across the US-Mexico border clandestinely? Most have no choice because things back home are very difficult. For example, NAFTA between Mexico, Canada, and the United States has displaced thousands of workers in Mexico because many growers, for instance, are not able to compete with the cheaper prices of American imports (Massey, Durand, and Malone 2002). It is important to note here that most of the migrants interviewed for this study claimed that they migrated to the United States because there was nothing back home to move them forward—no jobs or opportunities whatsoever. For example, several respondents expressed their frustration when describing that after NAFTA, they were not able to compete with the prices of imported US corn, which moreover, was better quality than domestically grown corn. Buyers of corn were more willing to pay the lower prices offered by the US growers. For this reason, it became useless to try to continue to grow more corn (which they had dedicated their land to, as well as their whole lives, throughout generations). Consequently, many had to look for other ways to survive, and often the solution was to migrate to the United States.

For Mexicans applying to migrate legally from Mexico to the United States, only those with higher levels of education, professional occupations, or extraordinary abilities are able to get visas (of which there are only a limited number), but there are no other options for those who do not meet these conditions. There are no visas available for the unskilled (Massey, Durand, and Malone 2002). The temporary visas for unskilled workers that exist (H2A and H2B) are very limited and very difficult to obtain. If undocumented immigrants are eligible to get legalized through the family reunification program, the process takes many, many years—in most instances about twelve years or more, given the large backlog of applications for the limited number of visas available per year. This process is also very expensive and complicated for applicants, especially for those with the least money and education. Given that options for obtaining legal documentation to migrate from Mexico into the United States are very limited, especially for unskilled workers, policymakers have to consider options that will legalize more migrants.

Policymakers should question if the current immigration laws are correctly addressing the actual labor needs in the United States. Given that the United States has a very large demand for cheap labor, plus a free trade agreement with Mexico, it seems logical to offer more legal visas to countries like Mexico (Massey, Durand, and Malone 2002). Therefore, given such a large demand for cheap labor, and very little opportunities for legal visas, policymakers should also ask themselves to what extent heightened border enforcement and a border fence would help stop the immigration flow from Mexico. In addition, it is important for policymakers to consider other questions such as: To what extent do current laws like the one in Arizona stop, prevent, or slow down the current immigration flow from Mexico and other places in Latin America? Can international migration be prevented? How? What is the role of MTNs in the process of international migration? What are the social, economic, and demographic consequences of massive emigration at the places of origin and what are the consequences at the place of destination? What must be done in order to effectively curb the migration flows?

Many policymakers are influenced by the anti-immigrant rhetoric, which propagates stereotypes about international migrants, such as the idea that Mexican immigrants come to the United States to take advantage of public services and the American system, and that they bring diseases, violence, and become a burden to society. Think tanks such as the Center for Immigration Studies (CIS) and the Federation for American Immigration Reform (FAIR) have an active anti-immigrant agenda when testifying in front of policymakers. They enforce anti-immigrant stereotypes without taking into account the social and economic consequences for both the sending and receiving country (Flores-Yeffal, Vidales, and Plemons 2011). The anti-immigrant rhetoric is so strong that policymakers tend to overlook evidence showing that immigrants do not pose a threat to society but instead come to work diligently to provide for their families back home and in the United States. Along with other political pressures, policymakers continue to believe that spending money on border control, a fence, raids, and massive deportations (and perhaps magic) will cause the flow to stop (see Massey and Pren 2012).

One of the best examples that immigration in the United States is not taken seriously by legislators but is instead used as a tool to gain political power and votes is the latest attempt to pass the Dream Act. This legislation would provide legal status to the children of unauthorized immigrants who arrived to the United States before the age of fifteen and who have attended at least two years of college or have served in the military. At the time of this writing, the Dream Act had again failed in the Senate by only five votes. The bill has been on the books already for the past ten years. If passed, it would have provided legalization to the youth who arrived with their family members as children without any legal documentation. Immigration policies in the United States do not examine the social reality or explore the immense consequences of neglecting to pass such acts. The Dream Act would enable hundreds of thousands of youth to complete their college education and fully integrate into US society. In the long run, they would contribute to the tax pool and the country's overall progress. Instead, other political pressures having more to do with winning the next election are what drive the voting decisions on immigration policy. President Obama said in the last State of the Union address given before completion of this book that we should not waste the talent of these youth, who in the end have already invested in their education. Why send them away and not let them be part of the United States or contribute to the country's growth? He stated:

> And I am prepared to work with Republicans and Democrats to protect our borders, enforce our laws, and address the millions of undocumented workers who are now living in the shadows. (*Applause*) I know that debate will be difficult. I know it will take time. But tonight, let's agree to make that effort. And let's stop expelling talented, responsible young people who could be staffing our research labs or starting a new business, who could be further enriching this nation. (*Applause*) (Sweet 2011)

As mentioned in chapter 7, President Obama, in his attempt to gain political support from Latinos in the United States, has created a new law that will only allow these Dreamers to gain temporary status. It is not a permanent solution since these kids will not be able to gain legal residency in the United States. In addition, if President Obama is not reelected, the Republican candidate can get rid of the law as soon as he becomes president. Opposition in Congress prevents finding a more permanent solution.

The social processes of international migration create social, economic, and demographic effects at both the sending and receiving places. Immigration polices and anti-immigrant laws created by host countries do not take into account such processes or the consequences of interrupting them. For example, businesses and people who reside or work near new immigrant enclaves unknowingly become active participants of the new MTN as they begin to cater to the needs of new arrivals by providing them services (e.g., selling them food, cars, clothes, cell phones, medicines, gasoline; cutting their hair; and by renting them apartment units). The MTN members become local consumers, and local businesses recognize the new demand for services by expanding to meet their needs. Any local anti-immigrant law that would force the newcomers to leave the area would be a burden for those local businesses that began to depend on the daily consumption of the immigrants, as has already happened in Arizona and other parts of the United States where massive raids have taken place (see Bonello 2009).

While businesses suffer financially, local citizens who establish relationships with migrants suffer personally. Movements of people have social ramifications in which attachments are interrupted and the development of strong communities is disrupted. International migration, on the ground level, is a social phenomenon performed by real people with real lives. Those lives are uprooted from the community of origin and reestablished at the place of destination in many forms and with serious social and economic implications. Newcomers continue their lives at the place of destination and, in one way or another, the members of the host society begin social relationships with them or form social and economic dependencies on them. The relationships of trust and social cohesiveness embedded in MTNs then take many forms and are also shared among outside individuals, depending on the situation and circumstances at the place of destination.

The MTNs do not solely function in order to provide social capital at the time of international migration or throughout the settlement process. The relationships of trust and social support are also transformed into other social manifestations according to the circumstances. For example, in the case of someone dying at the place of destination, the members of the community get together and try to cover the expenses of the funeral, and even send the body back to the place of origin. The desire for repatriation shows the extent to which the members of the immigrant enclave are attached to their place of origin, as most of them were originally planning to return home. Most wanted to migrate temporarily in order to meet their financial difficulties. Instead, because of harsher border enforcement measures implemented by the United States during the 1990s, immigrants were forced to stay permanently in the United States instead of continuing their circulatory migration flow (see Massey, Durand, and Malone 2002). At the time of this writing, the Pew Hispanic Center published a report in which they found evidence that the migration flow from Mexico had been reduced to historical levels in which the net flow of international migration in Mexico was zero (see Passel, Cohn, and Gonzalez Barrera 2012;Cave 2011). This means that even though the migration flow from Mexico may have ceased temporarily, still, those twelve million undocumented immigrants trapped in the United States are more likely to permanently rely on the collective efficacy provided by the MTNs proposed by this study. Such a permanent social condition deserves attention from politicians who are working on public policy to better US society. The MTNs allow for social or economic difficulties to be resolved by its members. They feel protected and secure by sharing trust and social capital. Therefore, policymakers must find a way to take advantage of the social dynamics that occur within MTNs in order to improve the social and economic conditions of those living at the place of origin and at the place of destination.

Policymakers need to reevaluate the social realities of the international migration flows into their country. International migration is a normal social phenomenon in which humans look for alternative ways of survival for themselves and their family members. Given the high demand for cheap labor in the United States, the neoclassical model of supply and demand functions predictably — a supply (of workers) arrives to meet the demand (for cheap labor). In this case, as long as employers in the United States continue to hire workers (mostly undocumented), immigrants will find a way to get across the Mexico-US border in order to provide the supply of labor. Even though employer sanctions were implemented in the United States as a result of the Immigration Reform and Control Act of 1986, no interior enforcement of this law has taken place since then; therefore, employers do not feel the need to stop hiring undocumented workers (see Massey, Durand, and Malone 2002). This means that the large demand for labor continues to attract immigration; it is, in fact, the primary condition in the functionality of social networks of migration. The MTNs then provide the necessary social capital to prospective and returning migrants in order to bring in the supply of labor and meet the demand.

Given that no legal options exist for unskilled migrants from Latin America (especially from Mexico) to gain legal entry into the United States, most of them migrate with undocumented status. Immigration laws do not match the reality of US labor demand. Most of the legal visas are only given to those with professional degrees or extraordinary abilities. However, since the educational systems between most Latin American countries and the United States do not match, the educational and professional degrees cannot be automatically accepted and validated for those educated migrants from Latin America. One exception is the Business Administration degree for those who migrate from Mexico, which was included in the NAFTA agreement.

While I do emphasize that MTNs serve as shields to undocumented migrants so they can protect themselves from the drawbacks of lacking legal documents, my research also informs how increased border and interior enforcement practices also increase the dependency of network members on MTNs. Also, given that residential and labor niches govern these networks, the probability for MTNs to experience some kind of failure increases. This means that dependency in trust relations gradually becomes greater and the protection of MTN members more difficult to accomplish. As this happens, the probability of MTN members to become dependent in more complex forms of social organization also increases. For example, as shown in this study, as the level of security between the Mexico-US border has increased, MTN members increasingly became more dependent on more organized groups, such as drug cartels, for crossing to the United States. Therefore, closer attention should be paid by policymakers to the social and economic consequences of the current policies that are in place and an effort should be made to correct such policies before they lead to outcomes that could end up hurting US society in the long run.

Also, as suggested by Massey, Durand, and Malone (2002), one of the most important goals for the United States should be to help develop the Mexican economy so that it is on par with the US economy. Consequently, Mexican citizens would have little incentive to migrate to escape high unemployment rates, high levels of violence, inflation, lack of credit markets, and so forth. One way in which the United States could provide economic incentives in the Mexican economy would be to take advantage of the MTN relations and perhaps provide mentorship or economic support to collective remittances projects. For example, this could improve the local infrastructure of the sending communities and — most importantly — help create jobs so that people can sustain their families by staying in their hometown.

Public Policy Recommendations at the Place of Destination

The social relations taking place within MTNs at the destination should be considered when thinking about local public policy development. One important characteristic of membership in an MTN is that the migrants think of themselves as a group instead of as individuals. This mind-set helps them develop a form of collective efficacy in which the well-being of MTN members is secured. Social surveillance becomes important in order to ensure group members meet certain values and social expectations, which enforces collective efficacy. This means that public policymakers should think of how such behavioral norms, relations of trust, and mutual support could be used to promote and disseminate essential or new information into the MTN. One example of how policymakers can take advantage of MTN behavior is to implement programs through which essential information is injected into the MTN. Group members disseminate such information, and MTN members trust the new information that comes from them. Social expectations among MTN members, fear of rejection, and notions of ethical responsibility and the collective efficacy of the group would not allow those distributing the information to make false claims or distort the information. Indeed, the functionality of the MTN depends on the prevention of malfeasance. The key for local policymakers is to first gain the trust of some of the members of the MTN and then provide them with information about safety, nutrition, the education of their children, health issues, and other issues regarding the law. Policymakers can also provide guidance for distributing vital information about health, education, and legal rights (among other issues) throughout the rest of the MTN.

One example of taking advantage of migrant trust relationships in the development of public policy is the program called *Maestros de la Comunidad*, which was once implemented at the University of Texas, Arlington, by Manuel García y Griego and others.[1] The objective of the program was to train the parents of children from local high schools on how to maintain communication with the schools in order to demand the best education and resources for their children and help to resolve any problems the teachers or schools have with their children. Given the limited number of people who could enroll in the training, Dr. García y Griego, who designed the program, decided to apply the concept of Migrant Solidarity so that the participating parents would be encouraged to return to their respective clique-like networks and teach the rest of the community or immigrant enclave what they learned. García y Griego was then able to witness how the information was shared effectively by participating parents and the other members of their MTN. They were encouraged to tell those who they shared the information with to also share the information with others, and so on and so forth. Thus, the information was broadly disseminated. In the same fashion, policymakers could find ways to take advantage of the cohesiveness and relationships of trust shared among the members of the immigrant enclaves in order to effectively spread new information, perhaps encouraging them to learn English or be aware of local laws, for example. The key is to understand that social relationships among international migrants in the transnational context are governed by trust. For this reason, in the definition of MTNs, I have included local authorities as possible members of an MTN. This is possible if at least one member of the MTN is able to trust that person in authority, and the person shows loyalty and follows the behavioral and social expectations demanded by the members of the MTN. Once the local authority becomes part of this MTN, that person can inject new and valuable information into the network that can help all the members of the immigrant enclave.

Using this same concept of taking advantage of the relationships of trust and solidarity among the members of the MTN, I have created a column that is published monthly in a local newspaper (printed in Spanish) in the Bryan and College Station area. I am currently coauthoring the column, called "*Pasala*," with Dr. José Villalobos. In this column, we publish essential information for immigrants, and we encourage the readers to pass along the information to others in their community and to tell them to also spread the information. We warn them in the column not to change the information when they pass it along. Up to now, we have published on health issues, fraud prevention, local law, and education. We have found this to be an effective means of communication and hope to continue by addressing a number of other topics. Our goal is to utilize the newspaper affiliates to publish the information in other languages, including English, in order to reach a broader audience, such as the African American population, who may also benefit from the information.

Public Policy Recommendations at the Place of Origin

The social dynamics that drive MTNs should also be considered in the development of public policy decisions concerning the place of origin. The MTNs could also serve the role of providing social capital in ways that encourage local residents to stay home. Instead of sharing social capital to bring migrants to the United States, MTNs could encourage them to stay home by providing them with economic alternatives to migration. The tragic demographic consequences that result when most working-age people leave the community of origin could be avoided if the youth were more encouraged to stay and take part in local projects or work to stimulate the local economy. Therefore, projects that help in the creation of local jobs and engage the members of the MTN at the place of origin could encourage prospective migrants to stay.

The dramatic consequences that result from the culture of migration, such as the lack of interest for continuing education, could be also disseminated by relying more heavily on the social relationships of the MTN at the place of origin. Local public policy could be implemented in order to encourage more people to get educated instead of migrating to the United States, such as granting incentives to those who continue with their education. The MTN relations could also create norms and expectations that encourage furthering the education at the place of origin, discouraging international migration for those who do not finish their education in the local community, for example.

Policymakers need to understand how the social relations of MTNs function in order to think of ways in which the members of the sending and receiving communities could actively participate in creating collective advantages to staying at the place of origin. They must understand how to utilize the same social surveillance, social expectations of the community, and trust in order to distribute information and encourage education at the community of origin, and consequently, discourage international migration to the host country.

The Biggest Problem

Policymakers need to understand that denying access to legal visas to the more than eleven million undocumented immigrants currently in the United States creates a segment of the population that is socially and economically dependent on the functionality of MTNs. Undocumented immigrants depend heavily on MTNs, as they find themselves trapped in a more permanent arrangement in the United States because of current border enforcement policies. They are no longer able to migrate back and forth as in the past (Massey, Durand, and Malone 2002). A new report from the Pew Hispanic Center reveals that as many as two-thirds of current undocumented immigrants have been in the United States for more than ten years and that as many as 46 percent currently have minor children living in their households (Taylor et al. 2011). A different report estimated that there are as many as two million mixed families (i.e., families composed of both legal and undocumented migrants) in the United States (*New York Daily*

News 2008). Family members who are legal residents and citizens are also exposed to becoming isolated as part of the MTN. There is little vision of upward mobility for undocumented migrants, and the possibility of integration and assimilation nearly does not exist. The obstacles that the Dreamers (or undocumented immigrant youth) face, such as the inability to acquire jobs after graduating from college, are a perfect example of the limitations for social incorporation and assimilation that this population currently faces in the United States. Moreover, the population of Mexican migrants in the United States is no longer concentrated in the global cities, but is widely distributed due to the settlement of new destinations (Massey, Durand, and Malone 2002; Zúñiga and Hernandez-León 2006). Policymakers should consider solutions to address the creation and perpetuation of second-class citizen communities that exist across the United States. Even with President Obama's temporary solution, these children won't be able to fully incorporate themselves into the overall society until a more permanent solution is put forward. They are being placed in a "legal limbo" or in a "liminal legality" status that can lead to serious consequences for their future (see Menjívar 2006).

I am an example of someone who came to the United States without legal documents. While I was living in the shadows, I was lucky enough to be absorbed into an MTN via "the MTN effect" described in this book. I lived and depended on the safe haven provided by a Migration-Trust Network. Later on I was lucky enough to acquire my legal status through the amnesty of 1986 (IRCA). Once I became legal, many social and economic opportunities appeared for me. Unlike the Dreamers, I was able to graduate not only with a Bachelor's degree, but with a PhD from University of Pennsylvania (an Ivy League university). As a result, I have had the opportunity to work as a professor in a tier-one research university and study the behavior of the members of my own MTN and that of many others. The Dreamers, on the other hand, cannot get a job even if they graduate from college, so many of them are even discouraged to get an education. Policymakers have to think of what the social and economic prospects of the US population will be if the Dreamers are not allowed to become fully integrated into US society, as I did. Moreover, how will the United States be affected in the future by the creation and perpetuation of permanent immigrant enclaves populated by undocumented immigrants and their families and protected by MTNs? If the Dreamers have no prospects for full integration into US society, the rest of the members of MTNs are less likely to do so. A path for citizenship is needed in order for these immigrants to be integrated fully into society, as most European immigrants did in the past.

Notes

1. "Local community outreach has been conducted principally through public lecture series and through two programs: a series of youth conferences that have brought Metroplex high school students to the UT Arlington campus for a day of activities and a 27-hour seminar for Spanish-speaking immigrant parents who have children in public schools (Maestros de la Comunidad), usually conducted in nine sessions over sixteen weeks." Available from http://www.uta.edu/cmas/outreach, retrieved on December 30, 2010.

References

Aguilera, Michael B., and Douglas Massey. 2003. "Social Capital and the Wages of Mexican Migrants: New Hypothesis and Tests." *Social Forces* 82 (2): 671–701. http://dx.doi.org/10.1353/sof.2004.0001.

Amuedo-Dorantes, Catalina, and Kusum Mundra. 2007. "Social Networks and Their Impact on the Earnings of Mexican Migrants." *Demography* 44 (4): 849–63. http://dx.doi.org/10.1353/dem.2007.0039. Medline:18232215.

Bashi, Vilna F. 2007. *Survival of the Knitted: Immigrant Social Networks in a Stratified World.* Stanford, CA: Stanford University Press.

Bellah, R. N., R. Madsen, W. M. Sullivan, A. Swindler, and S. M. Tipton. 1985. *Habits of the Heart: Individualism and Commitment in American Life.* Berkeley: University of California Press.

Bonello, Deborah. 2009. "Filmmakers Document Consequences of US Immigration Raid." *Los Angeles Times.* September 25. Available from http://latimesblogs.latimes.com/laplaza/2009/09/filmmakers-document-consequences-of-us-immigration-raid.html.

Borjas, George J. 1989. "Economic Theory and International Migration." *International Migration Review* 23 (3): 457–85. http://dx.doi.org/10.2307/2546424. Medline:12282789

Bourdieu, Pierre. 1986. "The Forms of Capital." In *Handbook of Theory and Research for the Sociology of Education,* edited by John G. Richardson, 241–58. New York: Greenwood Press.

Boyd, Monica. 1989. "Family and Personal Networks in International Migration: Recent Developments and New Agendas." *International Migration Review* 23 (3): 638–70. http://dx.doi.org/10.2307/2546433. Medline:12282798.

Burt, Ronald S. 1984. "Network Items and the General Social Survey." *Social Networks* 6:293–339.

———. 2001. "Structural Holes versus Network Closure as Social Capital. Pre-Print for a Chapter." In *Social Capital: Theory and Research,* edited by Nan Lin, Karen S. Cook, and R. S. Burt. New York: Aldine de Gruyter.

Cave, Damien. 2011. "Better Lives for Mexicans Cut Allure of Going North." *New York Times.* July 6. Available from http://www.nytimes.com/interactive/2011/07/06/world/americas/immigration.html.

Chomsky, Aviva. 2007. *"They Take Our Jobs!" And 20 Other Myths About Immigration.* Boston: Bacon Press.

Coleman, James S. 1988. "Social Capital in the Creation of Human Capital." *American Journal of Sociology* 94 (s1): S95–120. http://dx.doi.org/10.1086/228943.

Cook, Karen Schweers. 2005. "Networks, Norms, and Trust: The Social Psychology of Social Capital, 2004 Cooley Mead Award Address." *Social Psychology Quarterly* 68 (1): 4–14. http://dx.doi.org/10.1177/019027250506800102.

Durand, Jorge, and Douglas Massey. 1995. *Miracles on the Border: Retablos of Mexican Migrants to the US*. Tucson: University of Arizona Press.

Durand, Jorge, D. S. Massey, and R. M. Zenteno. 2001. "Mexican Immigration to the United States: Continuities and Changes." *Latin American Research Review* 36 (1): 107–27. Medline:17595734

Durkheim, Emile. (1933) 1997. *The Division of Labor in Society*. New York: The Free Press.

Fischer, Claude S. 1972. "Urbanism as a Way of Life: A Review and an Agenda." *Sociological Methods & Research* 1 (2): 187–242. http://dx.doi.org/10.1177/004912417200100203.

——— 1975. "Toward a Subcultural Theory of Urbanism." *American Journal of Sociology* 80 (6): 1319–41. http://dx.doi.org/10.1086/225993.

——— 1982. *To Dwell among Friends: Personal Networks in Town and City*. Chicago: University of Chicago Press.

——— 1995. "The Subcultural Theory of Urbanism: A Twentieh-Year Reassessment." *American Journal of Sociology* 101 (3): 543–77. http://dx.doi.org/10.1086/230753.

Fitzgerald, David. 2008. "Colonies of the Little Motherland: Membership, Space, and Time in Mexican Migrant Hometown Associations." *Comparative Studies in Society and History* 50 (1): 145–69. http://dx.doi.org/10.1017/S001041750800008X.

Flores, Nadia Y. 1999. "Reciprocity, Solidarity and Gender in Mexican Migration to the US: A case study." Undergraduate Honor's Thesis in Social Science. University of California, Irvine.

——— 2000. "Place of Origin and Social Networks of Migration from Mexico to the US" Presented at the American Sociological Association meetings. Washington, DC. August 2000.

Flores, Nadia Y. 2005. "The Clique Effect: The Dynamics of Urban Undocumented Migration Networks from Mexico to the US." In *Scientific Series: International Migration of Population: Russia and Contemporary World*, vol. 15, edited by Vladimir Iontsev, 62–74. Moscow: MAX Press.

Flores, Nadia Y. 2010. "Human Capital Transferability into the US Labor Market among Latino Immigrants to the United States." *Annals of the American Academy of Political and Social Science* 630 (1): 196–204. http://dx.doi.org/10.1177/0002716210368110.

Flores, Nadia Y., Ruben Hernandez-León, and Douglas Massey. 2004. "A Comparison of Urban and Rural Origin Migration from Mexico to the U.S." In *Crossing the Border: Research from the Mexican Migration Project*, edited by Douglas Massey and Jorge Durand, 184–200. New York: The Russell Sage Foundation.

Flores-Yeffal, Nadia Y., and Maria Aysa-Lastra. 2011. "Place of Origin, Types of Ties, and Support Networks in Mexico-US Migration." *Rural Sociology* 25 (3): 1–30.

Flores-Yeffal, Nadia Y., and Paulina Martinez. 2010. "The Effects of Extreme International Migration in Origin Communities: A Comparative Study between Mexico and El Salvador." Paper presented at the IV Congress of the Asociación Latinoamericana de Población (ALAP) or (Latin-American Association of Population). Havana, Cuba. November 16–19.

Flores-Yeffal, Nadia Y., Guadalupe Vidales, and April Plemons. 2011. "The Latino Cyber-Moral Panic Process in the US" *Information Communication and Society* 14 (4): 568–89. http://dx.doi.org/10.1080/1369118X.2011.562222.

Flores-Yeffal, Nadia Y., and Li Zhang. 2012. "The Role of Social Networks in Determining Earnings: A Comparison Analysis of Four Racial and Ethnic Groups." *Sociology Mind* 2 (2): 235–46.

Foner, Nancy. 2000. *From Ellis Island to JFK: New York's Two Great Waves of Immigration.* New Haven, CT: Yale University Press.

Frank, Robert H. 1988. *Passions within Reason.* New York: Norton.

——— 1993. "The Strategic Role of the Emotions: Reconciling Over- and Undersocialized Accounts of Behavior." *Rationality and Society* 5 (2): 160–84. http://dx.doi.org/10.1177/1043463193005002003.

Fussell, Elizabeth. 2004. "Sources of Mexico's Migration Stream: Rural, Urban, and Border Migrants to the United States." *Social Forces* 82 (3): 937–67. http://dx.doi.org/10.1353/sof.2004.0039.

Fussell, Elizabeth, and Douglas S. Massey. 2004. "The Limits to Cumulative Causation: International Migration from Mexican Urban Areas." *Demography* 41 (1): 151–71. http://dx.doi.org/10.1353/dem.2004.0003. Medline:15074129

Gans, Herbert J. 1962. *The Urban Villagers.* New York: The Free Press of Glencoe.

García, Carlos. 2005. "Buscando Trabajo: Social Networking among Immigrants from México to the United States." *Hispanic Journal of Behavioral Sciences* 27 (1): 3–22. http://dx.doi.org/10.1177/0739986304272353.

Granovetter, Mark. 1973. "The Strength of Weak Ties." *American Journal of Sociology* 78 (6): 1360–80. http://dx.doi.org/10.1086/225469.

———. 1983. "The Strength of Weak Ties: A Theory Revisited." In *Social Structure and Network Analysis*, edited by Peter V. Marsden and Nan Lin, 201–33. London: Sage. http://dx.doi.org/10.2307/202051

———. 1985. "Economic Action and Social Structure: The Problem of Embeddedness." *American Journal of Sociology* 91 (3): 481–510. http://dx.doi.org/10.1086/228311.

Hagan, Jaqueline. 1998. "Social Networks, Gender, and Immigrant Incorporation: Resources and Constraints." *American Sociological Review* 63 (1): 55–67. http://dx.doi.org/10.2307/2657477.

——— 2008. *Migration Miracle: Faith, Hope, and Meaning on the Undocumented Journey.* Cambridge, MA: Harvard University Press.

Hatton, Timothy J., and Jeffrey G. Williamson. 1994. "What Drove the Mass Migrations from Europe in the Late Nineteenth Century?" *Population and Development Review* 20 (3): 533–59. http://dx.doi.org/10.2307/2137600.

Hernandez-León, Ruben. 1999. "A La Aventura!: Jovenes, Pandillas y Migracion en La Conexion Monterrey-Huston" [To the Adventure!: Youth, Gangs and Migration between Monterrey and Houston]. In *Fronteras Fragmentadas* [Fragmented Borders], edited by Gail Mummer, 115–43. Zamora: El Colegio de Michoacan/Centro de Investigaciones y Desarrollo del Estado de Michoacan.

———. 2008. *Metropolitan Migrants: The Migration of Urban Mexicans to the US.* Berkeley: University of California Press.

Kandel, William, and Douglas Massey. 2002. "The Culture of Mexican Migration: A Theoretical and Empirical Analysis." *Social Forces* 80 (3): 981–1004. http://dx.doi.org/10.1353/sof.2002.0009.

King, Amanda. 2006. "Ten Years with NAFTA: A Review of the Literature and an Analysis of Farmer Responses in Sonora and Veracruz, Mexico." *Congressional Hunger Center/CIMMYT*. Available from http://apps.cimmyt.org/english/docs/special_publ/special Report06-01.pdf.

Korinek, Kim, Barbara Entwisle, and Aree Jampaklay. 2005. "Through Thick and Thin: Layers of Social Ties and Urban Settlement among Thai Migrants." *American Sociological Review* 70 (5): 779–800. http://dx.doi.org/10.1177/000312240507000503.

Kramer, Roderick M., and Tom R. Tyler, eds. 1996. *Trust in Organizations: Frontiers of Theory and Research*. Thousand Oaks, CA: Sage Publications.

Krissman, Fred. 2002. "Apples and Oranges?: Recruiting Indigenous Mexicans to Divide Farm Labor Markets in the Western US." Paper presented at the Conference Indigenous Mexican Migrants in the US: Building Bridges between Researchers and Community Leaders. UCSC. October 11–12.Available from http://www.lals.ucsc.edu/conference.

———. 2005. "Sin coyote ni patron: Why the 'Migrant Network' Fails to Explain International Migration." *International Migration Review* 39 (1): 4–44. http://dx.doi.org/10.1111/j.1747-7379.2005.tb00254.x.

Levitt, Peggy. 2001. "Transnational Migration: Taking Stock and Future Directions." *Global Networks* 1 (3): 195–216. http://dx.doi.org/10.1111/1471-0374.00013.

———. 2007. *God Needs No Passport: How Immigrants Are Changing the American Religious Landscape*. New York: The New Press.

Lindstrom, David P., and Adriana Lopez-Ramirez. 2010. "Leaders and Followers: Migrant Selectivity and Development of US Destined Migration Flows in Latin America." *Annals of the American Academy of Political and Social Science* 630 (July): 53–77. http://dx.doi.org/10.1177/0002716210368103.

Lomnitz, Larissa. 1977. *Networks and Marginality*. New York: NewYork Academic Press.

Loury, Glenn C. 1977. "A Dynamic Theory of Racial Income Differences." In *Women, Minorities, and Employment Discrimination*, edited by Phyllis A. Wallace and Anette M. LaMond, 153–86. Lexington, MA: D.C. Health & Co.

Lozano-Ascencio, F., B. Roberts, and F. Bean. 1999. "The Interconnections of Internal and Inter-national Migration: The Case of the US and Mexico." In *Migration and Transnational Social Spaces*, edited by L. Pries, 59–76. Brookfield, VT: Ashgate.

MacDonald, John S., and Leatrice D. MacDonald. 1974. "Chain Migration, Ethnic Neighborhood Formation, and Social Networks." In *An Urban World*, edited by Charles Tilly, 226–36. Boston: Little, Brown & Co.

Macy, M.W., and J. Skvoretz. 1998. "The Evolution of Trust and Cooperation between Strangers: A Computational Model." *American Sociological Review* 63 (5): 638–60. http://dx.doi.org/10.2307/2657332.

Mahler, Susan. 1995. *American Dreaming: Immigrant Life on the Margins*. Princeton, NJ: Princeton University Press.

Marcelli, E. A., and W. A. Cornelius. 2001. "The Changing Profile of Mexican Migrants to the United States: New Evidence from California and Mexico." *Latin American Research Review* 36 (3): 105–31.

Massey, Douglas S. 1986. "The Social Organization of Mexican Migration to the United States." *Annals of the American Academy of Political and Social Science* 487 (1): 102–13. http://dx.doi.org/10.1177/0002716286487001006.

——— 1987. "The Ethnosurvey in Theory and Practice." *International Migration Review* 21 (4): 1498–522. http://dx.doi.org/10.2307/2546522. Medline:12280921.

——— 1990. "Social Structure, Household Strategies, and the Cumulative Causation of Migration." *Population Index* 56 (1): 3–26. http://dx.doi.org/10.2307/3644186. Medline:12316385.

——— 1995. "The New Immigration and Ethnicity in the United States." *Population and Development Review* 21 (3): 631–52. http://dx.doi.org/10.2307/2137753.

Massey, Douglas S., Rafael Alarcon, Jorge Durand, and Humberto Gonzalez. 1987. *Return to Aztlan: The Social Process of International Migration from Western Mexico*. Berkeley: University of California Press.

Massey, Douglas S., Joaquín Arango, Graeme Hugo, Ali Kouaouci, Adela Pellegrino, J. Edward Taylor. 1993. "Theories of International Migration: A Review and Appraisal." *Population and Development Review*, 19 (3):431–466.

Massey, Douglas S., Joaquín Arango, Graeme Hugo, Ali Kouaouci, Adela Pellegrino, and J. Edward Taylor. 1998. *Worlds in Motion: International Migration at the End of the Millennium*. Oxford: Oxford University Press.

Massey, Douglas S., and Maria Aysa. 2011. "Social Capital and International Migration from Latin America." *International Journal of Population Research*, Article ID 834145, 18 pp.

Massey, Douglas S., and Jorge Durand. 2004. *Crossing the Border: Research from the Mexican Migration Project*. New York: Russell Sage Foundation.

Massey, Douglas S., Jorge Durand, and Nolan J. Malone. 2002. *Beyond Smoke and Mirrors: Mexican Immigration in an Era of Economic Integration*. New York: Russell Sage Foundation.

Massey, Douglas S., and Kristin E. Espinosa. 1997. "What's Driving Mexico-US Migration? A Theoretical, Empirical and Policy Analysis." *American Journal of Sociology* 102 (4): 939–99. http://dx.doi.org/10.1086/231037.

Massey, Douglas S., and Karen Pren. 2012. "Unintended Consequences of US Immigration Policy: Explaining the Post-1965 Surge from Latin America." *Population and Development Review* 38 (1): 1–29. http://dx.doi.org/10.1111/j.1728-4457.2012.00470.x.

———. 2000. "A Validation of the Ethnosurvey: The Case of Mexico-US Migration." *International Migration Review* 34 (3): 766–93. http://dx.doi.org/10.2307/2675944.

Menjívar, Cecilia. 2000. *Fragmented Ties: Salvadoran Immigrant Networks in America*. Berkeley: University of California Press.

———. 2006. "Liminal Legality: Salvadoran and Guatemalan Immigrants Lives in the United States." *American Journal of Sociology* 111(4): 999–1037.

Mouw, Ted. 2002. "Racial Differences in the Effects of Job Contacts: Conflicting Evidence from Cross-Sectional and Longitudinal Data." *Social Science Research* 31 (4): 511–38. [Online] Available from http://www.unc.edu/~tedmouw/papers/mouw%20cv.htm.

———. 2003. "Social Capital and Finding a Job: Do Contacts Matter?" *American Sociological Review* 68 (6): 868–98. http://dx.doi.org/10.2307/1519749.

Myrdal, Gunnar. 1957. *Rich Lands and Poor*. New York: Harper and Row.

Nee, Victor, and Jimmy Sanders. 2001. "Trust in Ethnic Ties: Social Capital and Immigrants." In *Trust in Society*, edited by Karen S. Cook, 374–92. New York: Russell Sage Foundation.

New York Daily News. 2008. "Toughened Immigration Laws Affecting Mixed Families." March 7. http://www.nydailynews.com/latino/toughened-immigration-laws-affecting-mixed-families-article-1.287327.

Passel, Jeffrey S. 2005. *Estimates of the Size and Characteristics of the Undocumented Population*. Washington, DC: Pew Hispanic Center.

Passel, Jeffrey S., and D'Vera Cohn. 2010. "US Unauthorized Immigration Flows Are Down Sharply Since Mid-Decade." Washington, DC: Pew Hispanic Center. Available from http://www.pewhispanic.org/files/reports/126.pdf .

Passel, Jeffrey S., D'Vera Cohn, and Ana Gonzalez Barrera. 2012. "Net Migration from Mexico Falls to Zero: And Perhaps Less," Washington, DC: Pew Hispanic Center. Available from http://www.pewhispanic.org/files/2012/04/PHC-04-24-Mexican-Migration.pdf.

Portes, Alejandro, and R. Rumbaut. 1990. *Immigrant America, a Portrait*. Berkeley: University of California.

Portes, Alejandro, and Julia Sensenbrenner. 1993. "Embeddedness and Immigration: Notes on the Social Determinants of Economic Action." *American Journal of Sociology* 98 (6): 1320–50. http://dx.doi.org/10.1086/230191.

Roberts, Bryan, Reanne Frank, and Fernando Lozano-Ascencio. 1999. "Transnational Migrant Communities and Mexican Migration to the US." *Ethnic and Racial Studies* 22 (2): 238–66. http://dx.doi.org/10.1080/014198799329477.

Saenz, Rogelio. 2005. "The Changing Demographics of Roman Catholics." Population Research Bureau. Available from http://www.prb.org/Articles/2005/TheChanging DemographicsofRomanCatholics.aspx.

Sampson, Robert J. 2006. "Collective Efficacy Theory: Lessons Learned and Directions for Future Inquiry." In *Taking Stock: The Status of Criminological Theory*, Advances in Criminological Theory, vol. 15, edited by Francis T. Cullen, John Paul Wright, and Kristie Blevins, 149–67. Piscataway, NJ: Transaction Publishers.

——— 2008. "Rethinking Crime and Immigration." *Contexts* 7 (1): 28–33. http://dx.doi.org/10.1525/ctx.2008.7.1.28.

Schlenker, B. R., B. Helm, and J. T. Tedeschi. 1973. "The Effects of Personality and Situational Variables on Behavioral Trust." *Journal of Personality and Social Psychology* 25 (3): 419–27. http://dx.doi.org/10.1037/h0034088. Medline:4705673.

Selznick, P. 1992. *The Moral Commonwealth: Social Theory and the Promise of Community*. Berkeley: University of California Press.

Singer, Audrey, Susan W. Hardwick, and Caroline Brettell. 2008. *Twenty-First Century Suburban Gateways: Immigrant Incorporation in Suburban America*. Washington, DC: Brookings Institution Press.

Smith, Robert. 2006. *Mexican New York. Berkeley and Los Angeles Ca*. Berkeley: University of California Press.

Spener, David. 2009. *Clandestine Crossings: Migrants and Coyotes on the Texas-Mexico Border*. Ithaca, NY: Cornell University Press.

Stark, O., and J. E. Taylor. 1989. "Relative Deprivation and International Migration." *Demography* 26 (1): 1–14. http://dx.doi.org/10.2307/2061490. Medline:2737350.

Sweet, Lynn. 2011. "The Scoop from Washington: Obama 2011 State of the Union Address. Transcript as delivered." *The Chicago Sun-Times*. Available from http://blogs.suntimes.com/sweet/2011/01/obama_2011_state_of_the_union.html.

Taylor, J. E. 1986. "Differential Migration, Networks, Information and Risk." In *Research in Human Capital and Development*, vol. 4: *Migration, Human Capital, and Development*, edited by O. Stark, 147–71. Greenwich, CT: JAI Press.

Taylor, Paul, Mark Hugo Lopez, Jeffrey S. Passel, and Seth Motel. 2011. "Unauthorized Immigrants: Length of Residency, Patterns of Parenthood." Washington, DC: Pew Hispanic Center. Available from http://www.pewhispanic.org/files/2011/12/Unauthorized-Characteristics.pdf.

Thomas, William I., and Florian Znaniechki. 1918. *The Polish Peasant in Europe and America*. Boston: William Badger.

Tilly, Charles. 2005. *Trust and Rule*. Cambridge: Cambridge University Press. Also see http://understandingsociety.blogspot.com/2010/04/trust-networks.html

———. 2007. "Trust Networks in Transnational Migration." *Sociological Forum* 22 (1): 3–24. http://dx.doi.org/10.1111/j.1573-7861.2006.00002.x.

Valdez, Zulema. 2011. *New Entrepreneurs: How Race, Class and Gender Shape American Enterprise*. Stanford: Stanford University Press.

Vock, Daniel. 2010. "Driver's Licenses for Immigrants Becoming Rarer." The Pew Charitable Trusts. Available from http://www.pewstates.org/projects/stateline/headlines/drivers-licenses-for-immigrants-becoming-rarer-85899374794.

Wasserman, Stanley, and Katherine Faust. 1994. *Social Network Analysis: Methods and Applications (Structural Analysis in the Social Sciences)*, 1st ed. New York: Cambridge University Press.

Weber, Max. (1922) 1963. *The Sociology of Religion*. Boston: Beacon.

Wellman, Barry, and Scot Wortley. 1990. "Different Strokes from Different Folks: Community Ties and Social Support." *American Journal of Sociology* 96 (3): 558–88. http://dx.doi.org/10.1086/229572.

Wierzbicki, Susan. 2004. *Beyond the Immigrant Enclave: Network Change and Assimilation*. New York: LFB Scholarly Publishing.

Wilson, Tamar D. 1998. "Weak Ties, Strong Ties: Network Principles in Mexican Migration." *Human Organization* 57 (4): 394–403.

Wirth, Luis. 1938. "Urbanism as a Way of Life." *American Journal of Sociology* 44 (1): 1–24. http://dx.doi.org/10.1086/217913.

Yu, Bin. 2008. *Chain Migration Explained:The Power of the Immigration Multiplier*. New York: LFB Scholarly Publishing LLC.

Zahniser, Steven. 1999. *Mexican Migration to the US; The Role of Migration Networks and Human Capital Accumulation*. New York, London: Garland.

Zepeda, Eduardo, Timothy A. Wise, and Kevin P. Gallagher. 2009. "Rethinking Trade Policy for Development: Lessons from Mexico under NAFTA, 1–22: Carnegie Endowment for International Peace." Available from http://www.carnegieendowment.org/files /nafta_trade_development.pdf.

Zúñiga, Victor, and Rubén Hernandez-León, eds. 2006. *New Destinations: Mexican Immigration in the US*. New York: Russell Sage Foundation.

Index